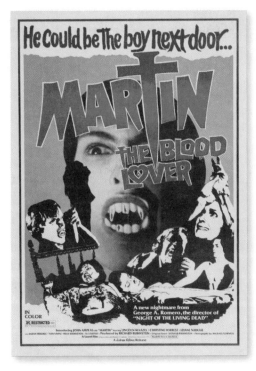

MONSTERS
IN THE MOVIES

100 YEARS OF CINEMATIC NIGHTMARES

John Landis

▲ *Glenn Strange, Béla Lugosi,*
Lon Chaney, Jr. in Abbott and
Costello Meet Frankenstein
[Charles Barton, 1948].

For Deborah,
The Love of my Life,
who lives with the Monster
that is sometimes me.

**LONDON, NEW YORK, MELBOURNE,
MUNICH, AND DELHI**

SENIOR EDITOR: Alastair Dougall
SENIOR ART EDITOR: Guy Harvey
EDITOR: Jo Casey
DESIGNERS: Rhys Thomas, Laura Brim, Yumiko Tahata,
Nick Avery, Mark Richards, Sophia Tampakopoulos
MANAGING ART EDITOR: Ron Stobbart
PUBLISHING MANAGER: Catherine Saunders
ART DIRECTOR: Lisa Lanzarini
PUBLISHER: Simon Beecroft
PUBLISHING DIRECTOR: Alex Allan
PRODUCTION EDITOR: Clare McLean
PRODUCTION CONTROLLER: Nick Seston

First American Edition, 2011

Published in the United States by
DK Publishing,
375 Hudson Street,
New York, New York 10014
11 12 13 14 15   10 9 8 7 6 5 4 3 2 1
001—181224—10/2011

Picture research by The Kobal Collection

Published in Great Britain by Dorling Kindersley Limited.

A catalog record for this book is available from the Library of Congress.

ISBN 978-0-7566-8370-2

DK books are available at special discounts when purchased in bulk for sales
promotions, premiums, fundraising, or educational use. For details, contact:
DK Publishing Special Markets, 375 Hudson Street, New York, NY 10014
SpecialSales@dk.com

Color reproduction by Media Development Printing, UK
Printed and bound by Star Standard Industries Pte Ltd, Singapore

Discover more at
www.dk.com

▲ **Boris Karloff** in *Abbott & Costello Meet Dr. Jekyll and Mr. Hyde* [Charles Lamont, 1953].

▶ **Margaret Hamilton** as the Wicked Witch of the West in *The Wizard of Oz* [Victor Fleming, 1939].

MONSTERS
IN THE MOVIES

100 YEARS OF CINEMATIC NIGHTMARES

JOHN LANDIS

"From ghoulies and ghosties and long-legged beasties, and things that go bump in the night, good Lord deliver us."

Traditional Scottish prayer

IMAGES FROM THE KOBAL COLLECTION

Contents

s, Inc.
Lee Unkrich,
han, 2001]
ey.

Foreword

I busied myself to think of a story, which would speak to the mysterious fears of our nature and awaken thrilling horror. One to make the reader dread to look around, to curdle the blood, and quicken the beatings of the heart.

Mary Shelley, author of *Frankenstein*

Film as dream, film as music. No art passes our conscience in the way film does, and goes directly to our feelings, deep down into the dark rooms of our souls.

Ingmar Bergman, film director

Fantasy, horror, and science-fiction films are where most of the monsters in this volume are to be found. These three genres have among the most ardent and faithful fans. Just Google "horror film websites" and see how many people are deeply passionate about this stuff.

There are many books about the movies, and like the movies, most of them are not that good. So I feel the need to clarify that this has been a labor of love and not a class assignment. This book is meant to be fun. It is not some heavy tome on the meaning of violence in the cinema, or a ponderous examination of film theory. This is a book with a lot of photographs of monsters in the movies. The films represented here are included not because they are necessarily good or bad films, but only because of the monsters that appear in them.

As for any movie monsters that are omitted, my only excuse is the finite number of photos my publisher would allow in the book.

▲ *Michael Jackson's Thriller* **[John Landis, 1983]** Michael as a zombie in this all-talking, all-singing, all-dancing horror film.

Even though this book is mostly illustrations, included are some conversations with a few of my friends that will be of interest. I spoke with people who have made enormous contributions to the cinema, and in particular the cinema of monsters! Let me express my deep thanks and appreciation to Ray Harryhausen, Sir Christopher Lee, David Cronenberg, Rick Baker, Joe Dante, John Carpenter, and Sam Raimi for participating. You will be impressed by what these guys have to say.

Most of what is written here is from my memories of the films, with additional research at the Beverly Hills and Los Angeles Public Libraries, as well as the Internet for fact-checking names and dates. The Internet is an amazing source of information. It is an equally amazing source of misinformation, and often disinformation. The Internet allows literally anyone to say anything, which is a very sharp double-edged sword. Reading the Internet postings of some people, it is clear that the writers have issues far beyond whatever ignorant or hateful bile they are spewing forth. On the other hand, there are often thoughtful and fascinating insights to be found on the web (said the spider to the fly!).

I apologize for any factual errors (blame my editors for not catching them). However, I do take full responsibility for any opinions expressed. Just remember that the quality of anything is entirely subjective.

Have a good time. I know I did.

Opposite page: A one-sheet poster advertising a triple feature showing of *Frankenstein* [1931], *Dracula* [1931], and *The Wolf Man* [1941]. In the late '40s and early '50s, actor and cowboy Glenn Strange (who played the Frankenstein monster in both *House of Frankenstein* [1944] and *Abbott and Costello Meet Frankenstein* [1948] would put on the costume and a rubber mask and, with other performers dressed as Dracula and the Wolf Man, rampage through the theater as the kids screamed with delight.

Introduction

This book is not meant to be an encyclopedia of every monster that has ever appeared in a movie. Nor is it my intention to write an exhaustive history of horror, fantasy, and science-fiction cinema. It is a pictorial overview of monsters from the movies that I have chosen. Most of the images come from The Kobal Collection; others come from friends who make monster movies.

My criteria for inclusion of a particular monster is simple: the illustrations in this volume are there because I think they are cool. Some have cultural and historic importance, some are terrifying, some are beautiful, some are repulsive, and many are just silly. Please remember my ambition is that of an entertainer, not of a scholar. You may learn quite a bit of useful and fairly esoteric information, but that is entirely up to you.

What is it about the movies that holds such power over the popular imagination? Although the medium itself is a relatively new one, pictures projected from strips of film to create moving images have had a massive impact on world culture. Hollywood movies and the international cinema have become the basis of what can only be described as our global mythology.

Montage is the juxtaposition of images to create a narrative. Even children, the first time they watch a film, instantly understand the concept of montage. When one is shown the outside of a building and then the characters inside it, the viewer understands this radical shifting of time and place at once. When we are presented with a close-up of a man looking out a window and then "Cut To" a car driving down the street, we do not have to be told that the car is what the man on screen is seeing (his "point of view"), we just know it. Human beings from around the world automatically accept and comprehend this film language.

▲ **The Author** as the Schlockthropus in *Schlock* [John Landis, 1971]. I was 21; the make-up artist Rick Baker was 20. The movie was shot in 12 days for $60,000.

Even more magically, when two characters are on screen and one says, "You drive the car, and I will take a bus. We will go to the airport and fly to Paris. There you will rent another car and I will take a taxi and we will meet at the Eiffel Tower in two days." Then the screen CUTS TO: EXTERIOR EIFFEL TOWER—DAY and our two characters approach one another and shake hands. All we've been shown is the Eiffel Tower and our two characters, and we instantly know that it is two days later, that one drove a car to the airport and the other took a bus. We know they checked in, went through airport security, boarded the plane, flew to Paris, got off the plane, went through Passport Control, and that one rented a car while the other took a taxi, both driving to the Eiffel Tower.

I believe that people instinctively understand film language because it is exactly the way we dream. I am sure you have heard someone say that the dream they had last night, "was so vivid, so real, it was like a movie." Exactly. Our dreams are "cinematic." And when we dream, we often have nightmares. Since the cinema is the perfect medium to depict our dreams, the movies have always been an ideal way to show our nightmares. Our nightmares are often populated with monsters. And that is the subject of this book: monsters in the movies.

The word "monster" comes from the Latin *monstrum*. "Monstrous" means a perversion of the natural order, usually biological. The word monster is associated with something that is wrong or sinister. A monster is either physically or mentally detestable, often an aberration in appearance and behavior. The word monster is generally

Previous pages: Boris Karloff and Mae Clarke in *Frankenstein* [James Whale, 1931].
Opposite page: Doug Jones as the mysterious Faun in Guillermo Del Toro's poetic *Pan's Labyrinth* [2006].

associated with the concept of evil, both in thought and action. Normal-looking people who behave in reprehensible ways are also referred to as monsters.

Monsters are found in the legends and folklore of all nations. Monsters appear in the world's religions and philosophies, and have always been well represented in works of art. From the earliest primitive cave paintings to today's most sophisticated digital technology, humans continue to feel the need to create images of monsters.

Monsters are not always frightening or evil. The monsters of Pixar's *Monsters, Inc.* [Pete Docter, Lee Unkrich, David Silverman, 2001] and certainly the title character in *Harry and the Hendersons* [William Dear, 1987] were charming and sweet. Even the most famous monster of them all, the Frankenstein Monster, as portrayed by Boris Karloff in *Frankenstein* [James Whale, 1931] is vulnerable and sympathetic. The one thing that most monsters have in common is their abnormal appearance; monsters are usually not considered conventionally beautiful. Monsters are often grotesque, and sometimes downright ugly.

Monsters are the physical embodiment of our fears. Humanity's fears can be summed up in three words: injury, pain, and death.

People need an explanation, a reason, for why things happen. Not knowing the cause of an event is unacceptable to us. So humans have invented philosophies and religions to cope with and to try to explain the unknowable. No one truly knows what there is before we are alive, and what happens to us after we've died. Different cultures have created different answers. Most of these answers involve monsters. From the winged angels in the clouds above to the demons down below, the religious view is chock-a-block with fantastical beings.

Are we afraid of the dark? Or are we afraid of what is out there in the dark?

In the early days of the European exploration of our planet, men went to sea in ships to discover just what was out there beyond the horizon. Their

maps and charts showed where they had been and what they knew of so far. The places people had not yet been were labeled on their maps and charts "Here Be Dragons." This phrase meant that these places were unexplored and therefore unknown. And people consider the unknown dangerous. In medieval times, the blank areas of the map were filled with illustrations of sea serpents and dragons. These monsters are meant to warn us off, to scare us. However, what really scares us are not the sea serpents or dragons, but what they represent. The Unknown.

Dinosaurs

Young boys tend to love the giant beasts of prehistoric times. Almost every boy goes through his "fascination with dinosaurs stage." Movies have exploited this fascination from the very earliest days of cinema to the present. And when we look at the stories and paintings of giant serpents and dragons throughout recorded history, it makes us wonder if there is a connection between the dragons of legend and the dinosaurs of the fossil record. No paleontologist has ever found evidence of a dinosaur that could blow flames from his mouth and nostrils, at least not yet. So where did that concept come from? Why did humans come up with these gigantic Thunder Lizards?

Countless sculptures and paintings show us Saint George slaying the dragon. In reality, very large alligators and crocodiles and Komodo dragons exist on land, and huge whales and giant squid inhabit the oceans. Could these be the animals that inspired the Hydra, the dragon guarding the Golden Fleece, or the monstrous Kraken who dragged ships down into the depths of the sea?

There is a theory that mastodon skulls, with their large holes in the center, were believed to be the skulls of giant Cyclops. If you came across the skull of a Tyrannosaurus Rex what conclusion would *you* come to?

In *One Million B.C.* [Hal Roach, Hal Roach Jr,. 1940], and Hammer's *One Million Years B.C.* [Don Chaffey, 1966] humans are shown living during the same time as the dinosaurs. The fossil record tells us that this cannot be true. But some believe that there is a dinosaur alive now in Scotland—the Loch Ness Monster. People are convinced there are Lake Monsters living in Africa and China. We

Opposite page: Three ways to make dinosaurs in the movies. **(1)** Tumak (Victor Mature) protects Loana (Carole Landis) from a superimposed iguana [*One Million B.C.*, Hal Roach, Hal Roach, Jr,. 1940]. **(2)** In the remake, Tumak (John Richardson) protects a little cave-girl from Ray Harryhausen's stop-motion allosaurus [*One Million Years B.C.*, Don Chaffey, 1966]. **(3)** Effects artist Stan Winston's full size audio-animatronic T. Rex in *Jurassic Park* [Steven Spielberg, 1993]. *Jurassic Park* also made extensive use of CG dinosaurs. (CGI or CG is the abbreviation used for Computer Generated Images, or computer animation.)

desperately want to coexist with dinosaurs—a desire exploited by Michael Crichton, who wrote the novel and then the screenplay *Jurassic Park* [Steven Spielberg, 1993], in which scientists clone living dinosaurs from DNA samples of dinosaur blood taken from mosquitoes trapped in amber millions of years ago! In much the same way as Sir Arthur Conan Doyle's Professor Challenger made the treacherous journey to *The Lost World* to prove that dinosaurs still lived on a plateau in the Amazon, we all seem to be prepared to go to great lengths to be with dinosaurs.

Man is Not Meant to Know

The fear of science is behind many of our greatest monsters. "There are some things man is not meant to know," is a line from many movies in which someone pays the price for tampering with "God's work." The classic "mad scientist" is Mary Shelley's Frankenstein. Her revolutionary novel is titled *Frankenstein; or, The Modern Prometheus* [1818].

In Greek mythology, Prometheus the Titan stole fire from the Gods of Mount Olympus and gave it to us mortals. To punish Prometheus, Zeus had him chained to a rock where a giant eagle would come every day, rip out his liver, and eat it in front of him. According to Zeus's curse, Prometheus's liver grew back every night so that the eagle could tear it out again the next day, and the next, for all eternity. With Prometheus's gift, the human race could now cook their food and warm their homes and fend off wild beasts of prey. But ask Prometheus; was it worth it? Ask Dr. Frankenstein, or Dr. Jekyll, or Dr. Moreau, or Dr. Morbius and all the other doctors, professors, and scientists who have dared to explore the unknown in the movies.

Vampires

Vampires have never gone out of style. Bram Stoker's 1897 novel *Dracula* created one of the most popular monsters in literary and film history. There are more movies in which the character Dracula appears than any other real or fictional person. Actors diverse as Béla Lugosi, Carlos Villarías, Christopher Lee, John Carradine, Louis Jourdan, Frank Langella, Leslie Nielsen, George Hamilton, Udo Kier, Jack Palance, John Forbes-Robertson, Francis Lederer, Charles Macaulay, Klaus Kinski, and Gary Oldman have all portrayed Dracula. And Dracula's bitter foe Dr. Van Helsing

has been played by actors as varied as Edward Van Sloan, Laurence Olivier, Peter Cushing, Anthony Hopkins, Hugh Jackman, and Mel Brooks!

Vampires drink human blood. They sleep in their coffins during the day. Like so much of what we believe is ancient folklore, authors and screenwriters invented most of what is now accepted to be vampire behavior. The rules change from book to book, movie to movie. Stake through the heart? Check. Afraid of a crucifix? Sure. Can't stand garlic? Okay. Cannot enter a room unless invited in? Really? Cannot be in direct sunlight? Have no reflection in a mirror? Well, the rules all depend on which movie you're watching.

What is well known is that male vampires are often sexy. From Lugosi's matinée-idol Dracula, to Brad Pitt and Tom Cruise's bloodsucking heartthrobs in *Interview With the Vampire* [Neil Jordan, 1994] to Robert Pattinson's pale teenage idol in *Twilight* [Catherine Hardwicke, 2008], male vampires continue to make the hearts of women beat faster.

The movies have shown us that female vampires can also be very sexy. Actress Theda Bara was one of Hollywood's first sex symbols and the *femme fatale* roles she played earned her the nickname of "The Vamp." Elsa Martinelli and Annette Vadim were the gorgeous vampires of *Blood and Roses* [Roger Vadim,1960], which was based on the scandalous "lesbian novel" *Carmilla* by J. Sheridan Le Fanu. *Carmilla* was also the inspiration for *The Vampire Lovers* [Roy Ward Baker, 1970] with the voluptuous Ingrid Pitt. Beautiful actresses continue to portray vampires—Sadie Frost in *Bram Stoker's Dracula* [Francis Ford Coppola, 1992], Anne Parillaud in *Innocent Blood* [John Landis, 1992], and no doubt will continue to do so far into the future. We all know the effect beautiful women have on men that also involves blood flow.

Perhaps the most interesting aspect of vampires in film is their bisexuality. When Christopher Lee bites down on the neck of his female victims, they always "swoon." What happens when he sinks his fangs into a man? In *The Fearless Vampire Killers* [Roman Polanski, 1967] a very camp, blond, gay vampire has his eyes on

Opposite page: Theda Bara poses as a "vamp" in a publicity shot for *A Fool There Was* [Frank Powell, 1915].

Professor Abronsius' assistant Alfred (Roman Polanski). Lesbian vampires are a genre unto themselves. In *Bram Stoker's Dracula,* when Mina says, "Come kiss me, Lucy," she is not just being affectionate. Since the early 1980s, the AIDS crisis has helped bring about a vampire revival in the movies, there being an obvious parallel between vampirism and an illness spread by the exchange of bodily fluids.

Werewolves

The rules of werewolf movies are just as elastic as those of vampire films and often change movie to movie. In Stoker's book, Dracula can change himself into a wolf at will, but Larry Talbot in Universal's *The Wolf Man* [George Waggner, 1941] cannot control his transformation and unwillingly turns into a werewolf on the night of a full moon. Lon Chaney, Jr. played the unfortunate Mr. Talbot in five movies for Universal and always walks upright on two legs as the Wolf Man. In *An American Werewolf in London* [John Landis,1981] David Naughton's werewolf rampages through Piccadilly Circus on all fours. In *I Was a Teenage Werewolf* [Gene Fowler Jr., 1957] troubled teen Tony Rivers (Michael Landon) is given "hypnotherapy" and "Scopolamine" injections by mad Dr. Alfred Brandon (Whit Bissell) to bring him back to a "pre-evolution state." How this would be helpful, or why a "pre-evolution state" would be a werewolf is never explained. Anyway, Rivers becomes a werewolf at the sound of a bell! Wait a minute; Rivers turns into a werewolf when he hears a bell? Once again, how one becomes a werewolf depends on which picture you happen to be watching. A gypsy's curse, a werewolf's bite, being born on a certain date, or being the offspring of a rape may make you a werewolf. For all these reasons, the ancient poem rings true:

Even a man who is pure in heart
And says his prayers by night
May become a wolf when the wolfbane blooms
and the autumn moon is bright.

This "ancient poem" was actually written in 1941 in Hollywood by Curt Siodmak for his screenplay *The Wolf Man* for Universal Studios. This is how ancient legends are born.

Opposite page: The Wolf Man (Lon Chaney, Jr.) about to pounce on unsuspecting Gwen Conliffe (Evelyn Ankers) [George Waggner, 1941].

Ghosts and Zombies

A ghost is the spirit or soul of someone who has died that manifests itself to the living. A zombie is one of the "living dead," meaning that a zombie is a reanimated corpse, someone who has died but whose cadaver is still walking around. I've often wondered if a zombie has a soul? Or once you have killed a zombie (often by shooting him or her in the head), does the re-dead zombie beget a ghost zombie?

The entire concept of ghosts develops from our natural longing to remain in contact with a loved one once they have died. Death is the ultimate unknown, and that means man needs to create all kinds of reasons that the dead are not really dead. When a person has passed away, people want to believe they have "gone to a better place." Or at the very least, someplace. The idea that once you die you no longer exist is just too disturbing for most of us. Hence we find tales of ghosts and zombies returning from the dead in every culture around the world.

Ghosts can be malevolent or vengeful, but sometimes they are lonely and sad. Ghosts are perhaps the most difficult of fantastic beings to show on screen and retain their reality. In two of the most frightening ghost movies ever made, *The Innocents* [Jack Clayton, 1961] and *The Haunting* [Robert Wise, 1963], no ghosts are ever seen!

The director George A. Romero is rightly crowned as the King of the Zombie Movies for his remarkable series of zombie pictures that began with the classic *Night of the Living Dead* [1968]. George's "blue collar" zombies have become the standard for the living dead ever since. They stagger around in the clothing they were wearing when they died, as opposed to the funeral suits they were buried in. With glazed eyes, torn flesh, and bloody faces, Romero's zombies are in nightgowns, dresses, jeans, T-shirts, shorts, and uniforms—the costumes of the real world. Romero has used his zombies for scathing political commentary all through his series of zombie pictures.

Voodoo used to be the main resource for zombies in movies, from *White Zombie* [Victor Halperin, 1932], to *The Serpent and the Rainbow* [Wes Craven, 1988]. In more recent films, atomic radiation or bizarre diseases create zombies. When unforeseen consequences to scientific research in radiation or germ warfare results in an outburst of the living dead, you can bet the government is doing the dastardly experimentation. The zombie has grown to be one of the most popular types of monster. All of us are going to die one day. Ghosts and zombies somehow reassure us that even death can be overcome.

Giant Monsters

The word monster can also mean big. As in REALLY BIG. Monstrous apes, lizards, insects, robots, aliens, men, women, and even children have stomped their way down the streets of our cities. Creatures of every description come in Large, Extra Large, even King-Sized.

King Kong [Merian C. Cooper, Ernest B. Schoedsack, 1933] is the prototype of the big monster creating havoc in an urban setting. And even before Kong was abducted from Skull Island and brought in chains to the island of Manhattan, the silent film version of *The Lost World* [Harry O. Hoyt, 1925] ended with a brontosaurus causing mayhem in London before swimming away down the Thames. Thirty-six years later another great dinosaur-like beast was brought to London, *Gorgo* [Eugène Lourié, 1961], only to have his mother come to rescue him and show us what BIG really means. The whole movie, Gorgo is a pretty large beast, but he is dwarfed by the enormous size of his mom. She towers over him as they make their way back down the River Thames together to go back to the sea. The truly colossal monster alien that comes from outer space to trash New York in *Cloverfield* [Matt Reeves, 2008] is so large that it strides through the city, taller than the tallest skyscrapers.

The advertising campaign for the American remake of *Godzilla* [Roland Emmerich, 1998] proclaimed "SIZE MATTERS." The iconic poster for *Attack of the 50 Ft. Woman* [Nathan H. Juran, 1958] is a clear demonstration of why this statement is true.

Human Monsters

History has given us too many examples of political leaders who can easily be classed as monsters. Hitler and Stalin are two of the more obvious examples of men whose actions led directly to destruction and murder on a vast scale.

This book deals with human monsters that operate on a more intimate scale of death: the serial killers, cannibals, and pathologically insane, whose exploits have inspired so many truly disquieting movies. We will meet and discuss Norman Bates, Hannibal Lecter, and many other fiends that have populated the Hollywood sound stages.

Criminals have always held a fascination for the public. But these criminals' actions are so perverse that the films about them are no longer mere crime movies—they are horror films.

A number of the cinema's human monsters are actually physically disfigured, either maliciously or by accident of birth. Others are profoundly damaged in the way they view the world. And some may appear completely normal. As Norman Bates says in Alfred Hitchcock's extraordinary *Psycho* [1960], "We all go a little mad sometimes."

Filmmakers Tobe Hooper and John Carpenter have made some of the most visceral and scariest movies in history. I asked them what monsters scared them. Both replied, "There are no such things as monsters. Monsters don't scare me, *people* scare me."

My wife, Deborah, is not bothered by most of the monsters in the following pages, but she refuses to see *Psycho*, *The Texas Chainsaw Massacre* [Tobe Hooper, 1974], or *The Silence of the Lambs* [Jonathan Demme, 1991], because these monsters, she says, "are real."

Vampires, werewolves, dragons, ghosts, zombies, mummies, aliens, psychopaths, and more await you inside. Have fun. And, oh yes, tonight when you're in bed and the lights are off and you hear an odd noise just outside your window... or was it just outside your door... or even *inside* the room..? Please do not even think about the monsters you've seen in this book. And whatever you do... DO NOT OPEN YOUR CLOSET!

Opposite page: One of the most iconic movie posters of the 1950s—Allison Hayes on the rampage in *Attack of the 50 Ft. Woman* [Nathan H. Juran, 1958].

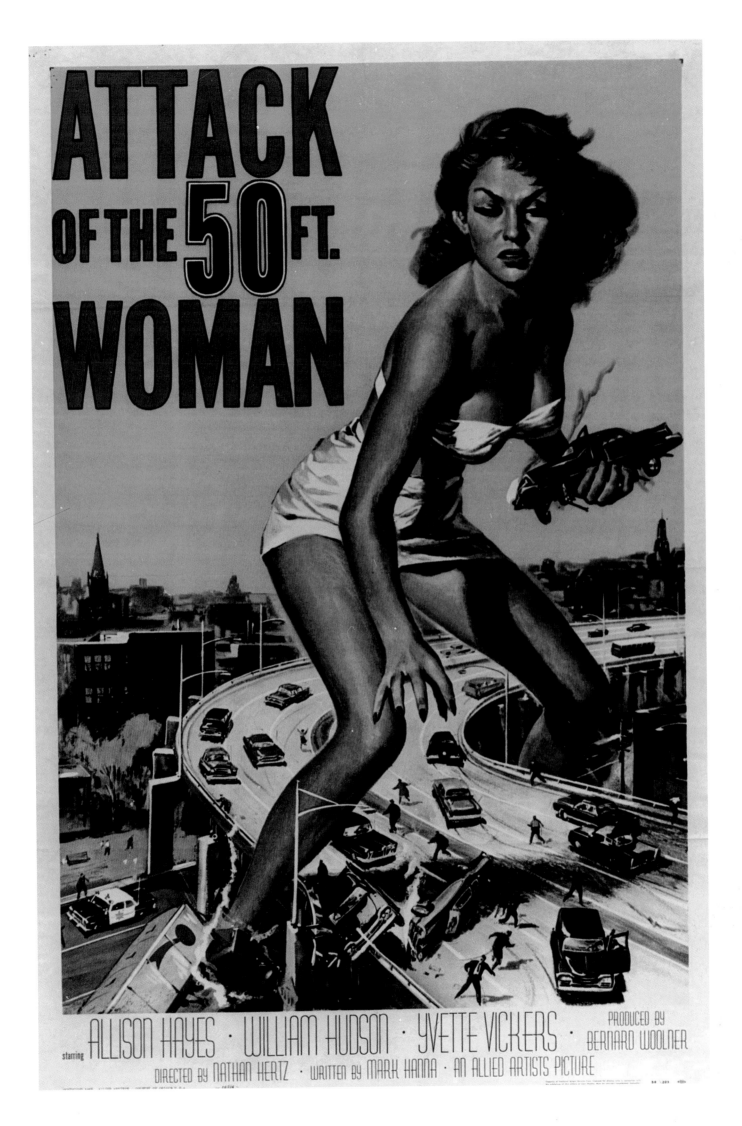

ATTACK OF THE 50 FT. WOMAN

starring ALLISON HAYES · WILLIAM HUDSON · YVETTE VICKERS

PRODUCED BY BERNARD WOOLNER

DIRECTED BY NATHAN HERTZ · WRITTEN BY MARK HANNA · AN ALLIED ARTISTS PICTURE

Vampires

More films have been made featuring Dracula than almost any other fictional character. Tarzan is (forgive me) neck and neck.

Bram Stoker's novel *Dracula* appeared in 1897 and was an instant success. It was influenced by J. Sheridan Le Fanu's 1872 novel *Carmilla*, about a lesbian vampire who preys on young women— later the inspiration for the trilogy of Hammer films, *The Vampire Lovers* [Roy Ward Baker, 1970], *Twins of Evil* [John Hough, 1970], and *Lust for a Vampire* [Jimmy Sangster, 1971].

Varney the Vampire, a penny-dreadful serial by James Malcolm Rymer, preceded Le Fanu's *Carmilla*. And the first notion of the vampire as an aristocrat appeared in *The Vampyre* [1819], written by John Polidori on a holiday with Lord Byron and the poet Percy Bysshe Shelley. On that same holiday, Shelley's wife, Mary Shelley, wrote *Frankenstein*!

The first cinematic version of Stoker's *Dracula* was the German silent *Nosferatu* [F. W. Murnau, 1922] with the unforgettable Max Schreck as "Count Orlock." This beautiful film was, in fact, entirely ripped off from Stoker's book and Stoker's widow suppressed its release in the courts.

Bram Stoker's novel was adapted into a play by Hamilton Deane that toured England for three years before it opened in London's West End to tremendous acclaim. The play was heavily revised by John L. Balderston in 1927 for its debut on Broadway, where it was a sensation. Hungarian matinée idol Béla Lugosi played

▲ *Varney the Vampire or The Feast of Blood* An illustration from the 1847 "penny dreadful" pamphlet edition of James Malcolm Rymer's gothic vampire story. Many persistent vampire behaviors originated here.

Dracula and veteran stage actor Edward Van Sloan portrayed Van Helsing. They reprised their roles in *Dracula* [Tod Browning, 1931], Universal Studios' follow-up to their smash hit *Frankenstein* [James Whale, 1931]. Lugosi was actually offered the role of the Monster in *Frankenstein* on the strength of his success in the play *Dracula*, but he felt the role of a non-speaking brute beneath an actor of his talent. The lead in a Hollywood adaptation of *Dracula* was another matter, however. The movie version followed the plot of the Balderston/Deane play rather than the novel.

Sadly, Lugosi's distinctive performance as the elegant Count typecast him for the rest of his career. Whenever movie work was scarce, Béla would go out on another theatrical tour of the play, eventually performing the role thousands of times.

Dracula is an early "talkie." Before sound dubbing, studios would often shoot different language versions of their movies on the same sets. Tod Browning shot during the day and a Spanish-language *Dracula* [George Melford, 1931], with Carlos Villarías as the vampire Count, shot on the same sound stages at night. Many believe this Spanish-language version to be superior to the English one.

Just as Universal capitalized on box-office powerhouse *Frankenstein* with *The Bride of Frankenstein* [James Whale, 1935] and *Son of Frankenstein* [Rowland V. Lee, 1939], so they soon followed *Dracula* with *Dracula's Daughter* [Lambert Hillyer, 1936]. Gloria Holden starred in the title role of a movie that is much better than it sounds. Keeping it in the family, the studio continued with *Son of Dracula* [Robert Siodmak, 1943], featuring a debonair Lon Chaney, Jr. as Count Alucard (Dracula spelled backwards).

Previous pages: Helen Chandler as Mina and Béla Lugosi as Count Dracula in *Dracula* [Tod Browning, 1931].
Opposite page: Christopher Lee as the Count in *Dracula Has Risen From the Grave* [Freddie Francis, 1968].

Lugosi played a Count Dracula lookalike named Count Mora in *Mark of the Vampire* [1935], Tod Browning's remake of his own *London After Midnight* [1927], the lost Lon Chaney silent. There is a nice twist at the end of *Mark of the Vampire*, which I will not spoil here.

Abbott and Costello Meet Frankenstein was Lugosi's last hurrah as Count Dracula for Universal. He is excellent in this well-mounted comedy. The fact that Béla ended up starring in Ed Wood movies does not dull his monumental contribution to Dracula lore.

Hammer's first Technicolor horror film introduced the world to a new, dynamic, sexy, and powerful Count Dracula: Christopher Lee. *Dracula* [*Horror of Dracula* in the US, Terence Fisher, 1958] also brought Lee's Dracula a worthy foe in Peter Cushing's driven Van Helsing. Both Lee and Cushing would go on to play these roles for decades although, unlike Lugosi, their wide range of character roles continued (and for Christopher Lee, continues) for the rest of their careers.

Hundreds of *Dracula* movies have been produced since then, including an excellent BBC adaptation starring Louis Jourdan as the Count and Frank Finlay as Van Helsing, and two big-budget feature productions: *Dracula* [John Badham, 1979], with Frank Langella as the Count and Laurence Olivier as Van Helsing, and *Bram Stoker's Dracula* [Francis Ford Coppola, 1992], starring Gary Oldman, with Anthony Hopkins as Van Helsing. Universal tried to milk this bat once again with the monster rally *Van Helsing* [Stephen Sommers, 2004], starring Hugh Jackman as an action-man Van Helsing, in an attempt to create a new franchise.

The folkloric rules of vampirism have been reinvented in almost every vampire film. Kathryn Bigelow's terrific *Near Dark* [1987] brought us a motley group of vampires trying to survive in the modern American west. Anne Rice's bestseller *Interview With the Vampire* was made into a lavish film [Neil Jordan, 1994] starring Tom Cruise and Brad Pitt, with the young Kirsten Dunst playing an older woman still in the body of the child she was when bitten. Her anger and frustration with her plight is identical to the vampire boy-child Homer in *Near Dark*, who is played by Joshua Miller with a raging intensity. The wonderful, Swedish, *Let the Right One In* [Tomas Alfredson, 2008] deals with a child vampire in a stark and poetic way.

Innocent Blood [John Landis, 1992] stars Anne Parillaud as Marie, a vampire who finds herself stranded in Pittsburgh alone and hungry. She refuses to take what she calls "innocent blood," and so must feed on criminals. Although she is careful not to create more bloodsuckers, by mistake she creates a vampire out of Sal "The Shark" Macelli (Robert Loggia), a vicious mafioso. She joins undercover cop Joe Gennaro (Anthony LaPaglia) to try and deal with a developing plague of monster mobsters. He falls in love with her, but isn't quite sure if he can trust a vampire, let alone make love to one.

In *30 Days of Night* [David Slade, 2007], a gang of vampires led by Danny Huston besiege an Alaskan town. *Daybreakers* [Michael and Peter Spierig, 2009] takes place in 2019, after a plague has turned the majority of the world's population into vampires.

Vampires continue to intrigue, scare, attract, repel, and entertain us. I'd like to end with a strange request in a book about movies: I urge you to read Stoker's original book. The story is told through letters and diaries and it's not only postmodern, it's really scary!

▲ *Nosferatu* [F. W. Murnau, 1922] Max Schreck as Nosferatu in this, the first (and unauthorized) screen version of Bram Stoker's novel *Dracula*. This German expressionistic silent was remade as *Nosferatu the Vampyre* by Werner Herzog in 1979.

◀ *Nosferatu*
[F. W. Murnau, 1922]
Max Schreck in the title role arrives in Wisborg; everyone else on board the ship is dead, apparently killed by a plague that leaves strange marks on the necks of victims.

▲ *Nosferatu the Vampyre*
[Werner Herzog, 1979] Klaus Kinski, in make-up based on Schreck's in Murnau's silent original, realizes too late that the sun is coming up. The beautiful Isabelle Adjani is Lucy Harker.

◀ *London After Midnight*
[Tod Browning, 1927]
In this movie mystery, the "vampires" are a red herring used to trap the real culprits. One of the most sought-after "lost films," mainly because of Lon Chaney's extraordinary make-up. Remade as *Mark of the Vampire* [Tod Browning, 1935] with Béla Lugosi as the "vampire."

"You're not in London now, Dr. Garth, with your police. You're in Transylvania, in my castle!"

Countess Marya Zaleska (Gloria Holden), *Dracula's Daughter*

▼ *Dracula's Daughter* [Lambert Hillyer, **1936]** Universal Studios' first sequel to *Dracula* [Tod Browning, 1931] begins with Edward Van Sloan as Professor Abraham Van Helsing being taken to Scotland Yard and accused of Count Dracula's murder!

▲ *Vampyr* [Carl Theodor Dreyer, 1932] Allan Gray (Nicolas de Gunzberg) dreams that he sees himself in a coffin. Dreyer's haunting, dreamlike vampire film was disliked upon release, but its reputation has grown with time. Based on *In a Glass Darkly* [1872], J. Sheridan Le Fanu's collection of supernatural stories.

▲ *Mark of the Vampire*
[Tod Browning, 1935]
Carroll Borland as Luna and Béla Lugosi as Count Mora, her father, in this remake of *London After Midnight* [1927]. In the original, Lon Chaney played both the "vampire" and the Inspector from Scotland Yard. Lionel Atwill portrays the Inspector in this remake.

▲ *Son of Dracula*
[Robert Siodmak, 1943]
Lon Chaney, Jr. as Count Alucard holds Louise Allbritton as Katherine Caldwell in his power in this story, which brings the Transylvanian Count to New Orleans long before author Anne Rice had a similar idea.

▶ *Dracula* [Tod Browning, 1931] Béla Lugosi as Count Dracula about to bite Helen Chandler as Mina in the film that forever typecast the Hungarian actor as the vampire. Lugosi never wore fangs as Dracula.

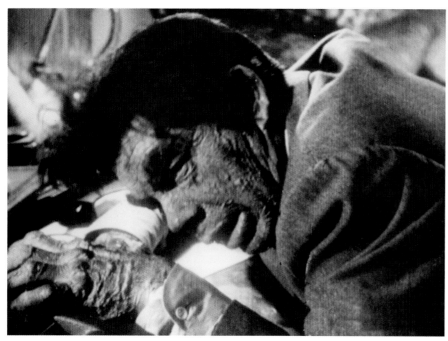

▲ *The Vampire* [Paul Landres, 1957] John Beal as Dr. Paul Beecher, a small town doctor who becomes addicted to the pills from another doctor's research with vampire bats. This could be a morality tale about drug addiction, but maybe it's just a B monster movie.

▲ *Dracula* [aka *Horror of Dracula*, Terence Fisher, 1958] The first time Christopher Lee played the Count in this international Hammer sensation. With a steadfast Peter Cushing as Van Helsing and in vivid Technicolor. Lee's powerful presence and sensual performance made a remarkable impact on movie audiences around the world. Here, the Count is about to indulge in a snack in this typical Hammer publicity shot.

▲ *House of Dracula* [Erle C. Kenton, 1945] The direct sequel to *House of Frankenstein* [Erle C. Kenton, 1944], this Universal "monster rally" features Wolf Man Larry Talbot (Lon Chaney, Jr.), and Dracula (John Carradine) asking Dr. Edlemann (Onslow Stevens) to cure their monstrous afflictions.

◀ *The Return of Dracula* [Paul Landres, 1958] Count Dracula (Francis Lederer) rises from his coffin in a small town where he tries to convince an all-American family that he is their cousin!

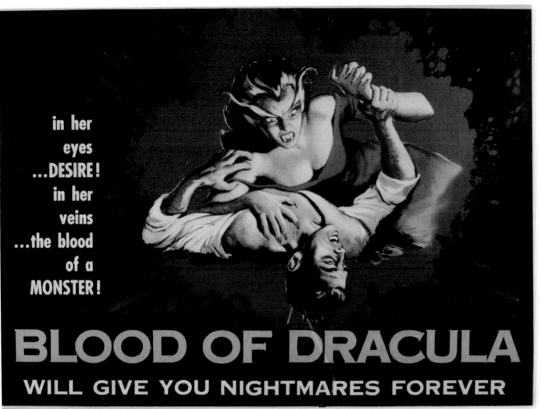

in her eyes ...DESIRE! in her veins ...the blood of a MONSTER!

BLOOD OF DRACULA
WILL GIVE YOU NIGHTMARES FOREVER

▲ **Blood of Dracula** [Herbert L. Strock, 1957] A thrilling poster for a decidedly boring movie.

▲ *Plan 9 From Outer Space* [Ed Wood, 1959] A famously inept movie from Ed Wood, here is the exotic Vampira (Maila Nurmi) as a Vampire Girl from outer space!

"Greetings, my friend. We are all interested in the future, for that is where you and I are going to spend the rest of our lives."

Criswell, *Plan 9 from Outer Space*

▲ **Blood and Roses** [Roger Vadim, 1960] One more movie based on Le Fanu's *Carmilla*. Vadim's film features the gorgeous Annette Vadim as Carmilla and the equally gorgeous Elsa Martinelli as her victim.

▶ **Atom Age Vampire** [aka *Seddok, l'erede di Satana*, Anton Giulio Majano, 1963] Alberto Lupo as the mutated Professor Alberto Levin needs blood!

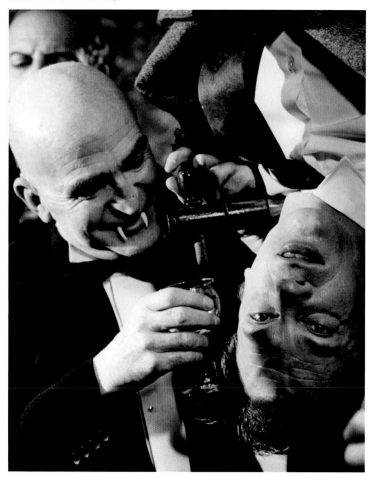

▲ *Kuroneko* [Kaneto Shindō, 1968] An amazing samurai vampire story set in the Sengoku period in Japan. This is Nobuko Otowa as Yone, the samurai's mother, who just wants her arm back. I first saw this at the Los Angeles County Museum of Art in a theater full of screaming people. Great!

▲ *The Vault of Horror* [Roy Ward Baker, 1973] In another Amicus portmanteau movie, Daniel Massey discovers that he is on the menu when he enters a restaurant for vampires. Based on the EC comic book.

▲ *The Fearless Vampire Killers* [aka *Dance of the Vampires*, Roman Polanski, 1967] Count von Krolock (Ferdy Mayne) abducts Sarah Shagal (Sharon Tate) from her bath in Polanski's vampire romp.

▲ *Goliath and the Vampires* [aka *Goliath and the Island of the Vampires*, Sergio Corbucci, Giacomo Gentilomo, 1961] Goliath faces a zombie who kidnaps women so his soldiers can drink their blood. As the poster says: "See: the virgin-harem of the vampire god!"

Dr. Van Helsing

◀ **Edward Van Sloan** [*Dracula*, 1931] Van Sloan also appeared in Universal's *Frankenstein* [1931] and *The Mummy* [1932] which makes him one of the classic Universal Monsters Players.

▼ **Peter Cushing** [*The Brides of Dracula*, 1960] Cushing was not only one of the Hammer stock company, but always an outstanding presence in countless British and American films.

▲ **Black Sabbath** [Mario Bava, 1963]
Bava's virtuoso direction makes this Italian anthology film a treat. Boris Karloff not only introduces the three stories, but stars in "The Wurdalak," based on a story by Tolstoy. As the loving grandfather who may be a Wurdalak, a vampire who feasts only on those he loves, Karloff is deeply frightening. The other two stories are equally scary. A Bava classic.

▲ **The Vampire and the Ballerina** [Renato Polselli, 1960] Black and white Italian horror schlock about a troupe of ballerinas who seek shelter in a spooky castle filled with vampires. The US prints have all of the nudity cut out, and since the nudity was the point of the whole exercise you can imagine the American audience's disappointment.

▲ **Mel Brooks** [*Dracula: Dead and Loving It*, 1995] Brooks makes an excellent and believable Van Helsing.

▶ **Anthony Hopkins** [*Bram Stoker's Dracula*, 1992] Van Helsing has killed Dracula's concubines, one of those heads was on a young Monica Bellucci.

▶ **Hugh Jackman** [*Van Helsing*, 2004] Indiana Jones he is not.

▶ *Innocent Blood* [John Landis, 1992] Anne Parillaud as the beautiful and lonely vampire Marie, who will only take "innocent blood" to survive. She accidentally lets violent mob boss Sal "The Shark" Macelli survive her attack, creating an even more monstrous mobster who envisions creating an army of mafia vampires. Marie joins forces with undercover cop Joe Gennaro (Anthony LaPaglia) to destroy Macelli. Robert Loggia is brilliant in a brave and very funny performance. With Don Rickles as Manny Bergman, Macelli's lawyer. From an original screenplay by Michael Wolk.

▲▼ *The Vampire Lovers* [Roy Ward Baker, 1970] Ingrid Pitt as Marcilla Karnstein, a character based on the J. Sheridan Le Fanu novella *Carmilla*. One of the so-called Karnstein Trilogy of lesbian-themed vampire films from Hammer. Above: Marcilla seduces Emma Morton (Madeline Smith). Below: General von Spielsdorf (Peter Cushing), having driven a stake through Marcilla's heart, cuts off her head, just to make sure she's really dead this time.

▲ *Countess Dracula* [Peter Sasdy, 1971] Ingrid Pitt as Countess Elisabeth Bathory Nadasdy, about to regain her youthful beauty by bathing in the blood of the virgin she has just murdered. A Hammer film.

▲ *Fright Night* [Tom Holland, 1985] Sweet and wholesome Amanda Bearse falls under the spell of vampire Chris Sarandon. A distinctly unsettling make-up in a scary scene from this entertaining movie.

▲ *Vampire Circus* [Robert Young, 1972] A woman brings a little girl to give to a vampire to eat in the genuinely shocking prolog to this film. The woman then makes love to the vampire. The villagers have had enough. They attack the castle, and stake the vampire through the heart. The vampire curses all of them and a plague falls upon the village. Fifteen years go by and a traveling circus arrives miraculously through the quarantine that has been set up by the outside world. Good news for the village? No, it turns out this is a circus of vampires.

"You must die! Everybody must die!"

Marcilla Karnstein (Ingrid Pitt),
The Vampire Lovers

▲ *Twins of Evil* [John Hough, 1971] Mary and Madeleine Collinson, identical-twin Playboy Playmates, are the stars of this, the third in the Karnstein trilogy from Hammer. Peter Cushing shines as a fanatical Puritan eager to burn witches and stake vampires.

▶ *Lust for a Vampire* [Jimmy Sangster, 1971] Yutte Stensgaard as Mircalla Karnstein in the second of the Karnstein trilogy from Hammer, which found that blood and topless lesbians were a profitable combination.

33

▼▶ **The Hunger** [Tony Scott, 1983] Catherine Deneuve is Miriam Blaylock and David Bowie is John, her lover. Blaylock is an immortal vampire, but John has begun to decompose. Bowie aging and dying while sitting in a waiting room is a beautiful and moving sequence. Based on Whitley Strieber's 1981 novel. Dick Smith did the aging make-up on Bowie (see page 306).

"Don't worry. A naked girl is not going to get out of this complex."

Dr. Hans Fallada (Frank Finlay), *Lifeforce*

▶ **Near Dark** [Kathryn Bigelow, 1987] A rushed happy ending is the only flaw in Bigelow's Western vampire masterpiece. Lance Henriksen and Bill Paxton (pictured) give fantastic performances as outlaw vampires trying to survive in the contemporary American West. Joshua John Miller as Homer, an aged vampire trapped forever in a child's body, is both repulsive and heartbreaking. A very good movie.

◀◀ **Lifeforce** [aka *Space Vampires*, Tobe Hooper, 1984] A delightfully insane science-fiction extravaganza from Tobe Hooper with a great score by Henry Mancini. The lovely Mathilda May (far left) as a female vampire from outer space is nude the entire film. Pictured is a doctor about to have his soul sucked out of him by a dead astronaut. Patrick Stewart, Frank Finlay, Peter Firth, and Steve Railsback all manage to keep from giggling as John Dykstra's very fine special effects cause all hell to break loose in London. Based on the novel *The Space Vampires* by Colin Wilson.

▲▶ The Lost Boys
[Joel Schumacher, 1987]
An entertaining comedy/horror picture with extremely chic teenage vampires in a small California town.

▶ Transylvania 6-5000
[Rudy De Luca, 1985]
Jeff Goldblum, Ed Begley, Jr., and other talented actors do their best Joe DeRita imitations in this comedy. At least Geena Davis plays a sexy vampire. There is a 1963 *Merrie Melodies* Bugs Bunny cartoon with the same title directed by Chuck Jones, which I advise you to watch instead.

◀ Zoltan, Hound of Dracula [aka *Dracula's Dog*, Albert Band, 1978]
Michael Pataki is Count Dracula in a flashback and José Ferrer is in it briefly. Hard to believe that Albert Band thought this was a good idea. Maybe it could be a fun movie, but this isn't it.

▶ The Lair of the White Worm
[Ken Russell, 1988]
Very loosely based on the novel by Bram Stoker [1897] and the English folklore legend of the very large Lambton Worm. Ken Russell crafted a quirky and very British, camp monster movie, with Amanda Donohoe as a sexy vampire you do *not* want to take a bath with!

▲Vampires [aka *John Carpenter's Vampires*, John Carpenter, 1998] Sheryl Lee seems unaware of that guy on the ceiling behind her in Carpenter's vampire Western. James Woods is the head of a Vatican vampire hit squad who roams the West killing bloodsuckers.

▲ *Cronos* [Guillermo Del Toro, 1993] Jesus Gris (Federico Luppi) examines the Cronos device which can give you youth and strength, but at a great price. The film that introduced the great Del Toro to an international audience. An original and haunting vampire story from Mexico.

▶ *Buffy the Vampire Slayer*
[Fran Rubel Kuzui, 1992]
Paul Reubens as Amilyn, one of the vampires Buffy (Kristy Swanson) slays in this teenage comedy/ horror film that spawned a much more successful, long-running television series, starring Sarah Michelle Geller as Buffy.

◀ *The Little Vampire*
[Uli Edel, 2000]
Jonathan Lipnicki in the title role in this film based on the German children's book *Der kleine Vampir* by Angela Sommer-Bodenburg. With Richard E. Grant and Alice Krige.

▲▲ *From Dusk Till Dawn* [Robert Rodriguez, 1996] Salma Hayek as stripper Santanico Pandemonium before and just after she reveals her true vampiric nature. A fun grindhouse movie filled with famous actors having a good time.

▲ **Blade II** [Guillermo Del Toro, 2002] A sequel that is superior to the film it follows, as Del Toro continues the story of the half-human vampire killer played by Wesley Snipes and based on the Marvel Comics character.

▼▶ *Interview With the Vampire*
[Neil Jordan, 1994] Brad Pitt, Kirsten Dunst, and Tom Cruise are all vampires in this big-budget movie version of the Anne Rice novel.

▶ *Vampire in Brooklyn*
[Wes Craven, 1995]
Eddie Murphy as Maximillian, who is a vampire in Brooklyn. Murphy also co-wrote and plays two other roles in the film.

"Lucy is not a random victim... She is the Devil's concubine!"

Van Helsing (Anthony Hopkins), *Bram Stoker's Dracula*

▶ *Bram Stoker's Dracula* [Francis Ford Coppola, 1992] Sadie Frost as Lucy is not too pleased to see that cross, in Coppola's imaginative retelling of *Dracula*.

▶ **The Horde** [aka *La Horde*, Yannick Dahan, Benjamin Rocher, 2009] French cops go after drug dealers in the Parisian hood and are captured by the bad guys—just then a zombie Apocalypse breaks out! Proof that the French make silly movies, too, as the gangstas and the flic join forces to fight the zombie horde.

▶ **Daybreakers** [Michael & Peter Spierig, 2009] A variation on Richard Matheson's novel *I Am Legend* (which has been made into three films already). A pandemic has turned most of the world's people into vampires and they want a cure. Good actors and cool special effects.

▲ **Blood: The Last Vampire** [Chris Nahon, 2009] A live-action remake of the anime film with the same title, this Hong Kong/French/British co-production is notable only for its star Gianna Jun, who makes a very credible, half-human vampire slayer.

▶ **The Fearless Vampire Killers** [aka *Dance of the Vampires*, Roman Polanski, 1967] Alfred (Roman Polanski) notices that Herbert von Krolock (Iain Quarrier) has no reflection! Polanski's love letter to Hammer.

◀▲ **Van Helsing** [Stephen Sommers, 2004] Above: Josie Maran as the flying vampire Marishka. Left: Richard Roxburgh as Count Vladislaus Dracula, holding Kate Beckinsale as Anna Valerious, looking into a mirror. Mel Brooks repeated this gag in *Dracula: Dead and Loving It* [1995].

▲▲ *Underworld* [Len Wiseman, 2003] The first in Wiseman's vampires vs. werewolves franchise. Kate Beckinsale as Selene and the wonderful Bill Nighy as Viktor. Stylish and dumb.

"I live off blood... I'm twelve. But I've been twelve for a long time."

Eli (Lina Leandersson), *Let the Right One In*

◀ *Let the Right One In*
[Tomas Alfredson, 2008]
Lina Leandersson as Eli in this marvelous Swedish vampire film based on the novel and screenplay by John Ajvide Lindqvist. A young boy named Oskar (Kåre Hedebrant) is bullied by the other boys in his small town. He slowly builds a friendship with the strange girl who moves into his apartment block with her uncle. A quietly great horror film.

▲ *Night Watch* [Timur Bekmambetov, 2004]
Loosely based on the novel *The Night Watch* by Sergei Lukyanenko, this Russian fantasy/horror film was quickly followed by *Day Watch* [2006] from the same director. A complicated plot concerning the forces of Light and Dark, full of special effects and brooding Russians.

▲ *30 Days of Night* [David Slade, 2007]
Danny Huston as Marlow, the leader of the vampires who besiege a small Alaskan town in the dead of winter. Huston is terrific as a vicious vampire out for blood.

DRACULA

▲▼ **Béla Lugosi** [*Dracula*, Tod Browning, 1931] Lugosi's entrance: "I am Dracula. I bid you welcome." Below: some publicity person painted blood coming from the wounds on Helen Chandler's neck from Lugosi's bite on this photo. The movie itself is entirely bloodless.

Bram Stoker's character Count Dracula has proven consistently popular since the novel was first published in 1897. He has been portrayed as handsome and suave, hideous and loathsome, and oftentimes all four. Here are just some of the actors who have donned the cape and fangs.

▲ **Christopher Lee** [*Dracula*, aka *Horror of Dracula*, Terence Fisher, 1958] Lee introduced both blood and fangs in his compelling and indelible portrayal of the vampire Count.

▲ **Robert Quarry** [*Count Yorga, Vampire*, Bob Kelljan, 1970] Count Yorga is Count Dracula with another name. The same director and star brought us *The Return of Count Yorga* the following year.

▲ **Louis Jourdan** [*Count Dracula*, Philip Saville, 1977] A BBC production, this film is one of the most faithful to the novel. Jourdan makes a fine, aristocratic Dracula with the stench of decay about him.

"My, what a big bat!"

John Harker (David Manners), *Dracula* [1931]

▲ **Lon Chaney, Jr.** [*Son of Dracula*, Robert Siodmak, 1943] Chaney, Jr. makes a strong physical presence work in his favor as the European bloodsucker in the American South.

Paul Naschy [*El Gran Amor de Conde Dracula*, aka *Count Dracula's Great Love*, Javier Aguirre, 1974] Paul Naschy (Jacinto Molina) not only played Dracula, but a Wolf Man character named Waldemar Daninsky in 12 movies! Known as the "Spanish Lon Chaney," Naschy also played the Mummy, the Hunchback, Dr. Jekyll and Mr. Hyde, and any other horror icon that was laying around.

▶ **Shin Kishida** [*Lake of Dracula*, Michio Yamamoto, 1971] Perhaps the name Dracula was added for the Western release of this Japanese vampire movie, but he sure looks and acts like Dracula!

◀ **Jack Palance** [*Dracula*, aka *Dan Curtis' Dracula*, Dan Curtis, 1974] Seen here with Fiona Lewis as Lucy, Palance's Dracula was a ferocious and physically imposing figure of lust and power.

▲ **Udo Kier** [*Blood for Dracula*, aka *Andy Warhol's Dracula*, Paul Morrissey, 1974] Kier is funny and sad as a sickly Count Dracula who needs to travel from Transylvania for young virgin blood. He finds four lovely young girls in the house of their father (played by Italian film director Vittorio De Sica), but the estate's handyman (Joe Dallesandro) deflowers each one before Dracula can drink their blood. Very funny and rather elegant for such an outrageous plot. Roman Polanski shows up for a cameo.

▲ **William Marshall** [*Scream, Blacula, Scream*, Bob Kelijan, 1973] AIP schlockmeister Sam Arkoff wanted a blaxploitation Dracula and somehow William Marshall gave the role dignity with his regal bearing and beautiful voice. A fun, crap movie, with Marshall rising above the fray.

▲ **Leslie Nielsen** [*Dracula: Dead and Loving It*, Mel Brooks, 1995] Nielsen, doing his best Lugosi, is actually quite dignified in this blood-soaked farce from Mel Brooks.

▶ **Gary Oldman** [*Bram Stoker's Dracula*, Francis Ford Coppola, 1992] Dracula licks Jonathan Harker's straight razor after Harker (Keanu Reeves) has cut himself shaving! Oldman is excellent in Coppola's florid retelling of the tale.

▲ **Richard Roxburgh** [*Van Helsing*, Stephen Sommers, 2004] Roxburgh tries to remain as menacing as he can under the circumstances.

A Stake Through the Heart!

Methods for killing a vampire remain fairly consistent in the movies. A wooden stake driven into the vampire's heart with a mallet is always effective, although you must make sure your aim is true. Garlic and crosses, even running fresh water, are all well and good for fending off an attack but, to make sure, keep a hammer and a wooden stake handy just in case.

▲ *House of Frankenstein* [Erle C. Kenton, 1944] Dr. Gustav Niemann (Boris Karloff) threatens Count Dracula (John Carradine) in this Universal monster rally.

▲ *Dracula* [aka *Horror of Dracula*, **Terence Fisher, 1958**] Jonathan Harker (John Van Eyssen) manages to stake the vampire woman (Valerie Gaunt) who has bitten him, unaware that Dracula himself (Christopher Lee) is about to show up.

▲ *I Bought a Vampire Motorcycle* **[Dirk Campbell, 1990]** I haven't seen this movie, nor had I even heard of it before I saw this photo of Neil Morrissey staking his vampire motorcycle. I am pretty sure it's a spoof.

◄ *Dr. Terror's House of Horrors* **[Freddie Francis, 1965]** An Amicus portmanteau film. In this story, a young doctor (Donald Sutherland) is convinced by a medical colleague (Max Adrian) that his new French wife (Jennifer Jayne) is a vampire. After Sutherland drives a stake through her heart, Adrian informs him that the town is too small for two vampires and two doctors and reveals his true self!

▲ **The Fearless Vampire Killers** [aka *Dance of the Vampires*, **Roman Polanski, 1967**] Alfred (Roman Polanski) is about to stake Count von Krolock (Ferdy Mayne) in this bloody comedy.

▲ **The Vampire Lovers** [**Roy Ward Baker, 1970**] After staking Ingrid Pitt through the heart, Peter Cushing then cuts off her head (see page 32), just to make sure.

◀▼ **Dracula Has Risen From Th**
Grave [**Freddie Francis, 1968**] The p
has lost his faith and the man his nerv
when they stake Count Dracula. But
aim is not true and Dracula pulls out
stake (with lots of gushing red gore,
unusual at the time)!

> "I am the monster that breathing men would kill. I am Dracula."

Count Dracula (Gary Oldman),
Bram Stoker's Dracula [1992]

▲ **Lost Boys: The Tribe** [**P. J. Pesce, 2008**] In this sequel to *The Lost Boys* [1987], an older Corey Feldman prepares to stake a vampire.

Christopher Lee

Schlock reads *Famous Monsters of Filmland* magazine sitting next to its editor, Forrest J Ackerman. On the cover is Sir Christopher Lee as Dracula.

JL: Chris, you were just about to say why you shy away from the term "horror film."

CL: It's a very simple answer. I did films with Boris Karloff who, like myself, made his name as a monster. He was a wonderful man, a superb actor, far better than the parts he was often given to play. What he had to do, and what I had to do, was to make the unbelievable believable. And that's very difficult, especially with today's audience. The reason I don't like the word "horror," is because it conjures up something really nasty, horrific, horrendous, evil, vile. The word that Boris used to use, and indeed I use, is "fantasy." The French always refer to these films as "films of the fantastic," which I think is a very good description. I never looked upon my films as horror films. I always tried to give the impression that the characters I played were doing things they couldn't help doing. And Boris did the same.

JL: You've played some of the classic monsters. You are the definitive Dracula, and you've played the Mummy, as well as Frankenstein's Monster. Your Dracula is pretty ferocious, whereas your Frankenstein's creature is very sympathetic…

CL: This is what I've always tried to do. Even when playing, not necessarily a monster, but the bad guy, I've always tried to do something, say something, the audience doesn't expect.

JL: Your performance in *The Curse of Frankenstein* [Terence Fisher, 1957] is fabulous.

CL: The Creature is a very pitiful character. He didn't ask to be made; he's a victim. More so than the people he kills.

JL: I think the people he kills are victims, too.

CL: Well, I didn't kill many people, as I remember. And Boris didn't either. In (the Karloff *Frankenstein*), there was that famous scene when he throws the little girl into the lake thinking that she will float like the flowers. The censors cut that out, but I believe it's back in now. That scene is pitiful, pitiful. The audience has to see this other side to the Creature.

JL: What's interesting about *The Curse of Frankenstein*, is that Peter Cushing's role, Dr. Frankenstein, is the real monster.

CL: Oh, absolutely. As you say, I'm the victim.

JL: And in the sequels, Frankenstein's creature becomes less and less important.

CL: I never saw them.

JL: Well, they vary greatly in quality. But Peter's always good!

CL: He was a superb actor.

JL: Marty Scorsese said that your entrance in *Horror of Dracula* [aka *Dracula*, Terence Fisher, 1958] made a huge impression on him. You walk quietly down the stairs and say, "I am Count Dracula. And this is my house." Something elegant and simple like that.

CL: I remember our first night in New York with Peter [Cushing]. I'd never been to America. This was about '57, I think. There was a great big building near the theater that was covered with an enormous painting of me (as Dracula) carrying one of the girls.

JL: How many stories high was it?

CL: At least 10 stories. That made me reel! Then we had to go to the first performance. And I'm not good in public, few actors are. I said to Peter, "I don't think this is a very good idea." And he said, "Oh, my dear fellow, this is what we've come for! We've got to do it!" It was close to midnight, and many in the audience had had a few, to put it mildly. So I said to Peter, "I'm going to sit in the very top row, underneath the projection booth with you, near the exit, so that if anything happens I can leave." Because I didn't like seeing myself on screen, and I didn't know what the audience reaction was going to be. Finally, the lights go down, the curtains part, up come the credits, and I recall there was a coffin with my name and blood splashes onto it. There was a huge roar of applause, and then the moment comes where you see me at the top of the stairs: a silhouette. The place exploded. Everyone shouting and yelling, and laughing, and I thought, "Oh God, this really is the end." And I walk down the stairs in a perfectly normal way, and I say quite calmly, "Mr. Harker," or "Good evening, Mr. Harker" or something, and he says, "Count Dracula," and I say, "Yes, I am Dracula," or something… The audience went completely quiet! Total silence for the rest of the film!

JL: The audience must have reacted to the scares?

CL: A few shudders or squeaks, but every time I appeared on screen—silence. The biggest shock in the film, was when the girl [Valerie Gaunt credited as "Vampire Woman"] tries to seduce Jonathan Harker. And there's a shot of me in the doorway, teeth bared, wearing those contact lenses—couldn't see a thing— and I leap up onto a table, and I leap off— that's no stunt, no fake—shoot across the floor, fling her aside and go straight for him. There were no cuts. I don't think anybody had ever seen an actor playing a vampire do anything like that before.

JL: Your Dracula is terribly physical, and very, very sexual.

CL: Which I did not intend.

JL: Whether you intended it or not, it made a big impression.

CL: I know it did, but I tried to play him as a man with a kind of compulsion. I obviously gave the impression that he enjoyed it.

JL: You played it very sexual, though, Chris. You're saying it was an accident?

CL: I tried to make him attractive to women. That was in the script!

JL: Now, what about all the sequels. They got sillier and sillier.

CL: That gives rise to a true story. The first film came out, and it rocketed around the world.

JL: It was a huge hit.

CL: And it made me world famous. As Dracula, though, not necessarily as Christopher Lee.

JL: But not only was your Dracula so striking and remarkable, it was really the first color Dracula movie. And the blood was so Technicolor red.

CL: Well, that was Hammer's idea. Eight years later, they asked me…

JL: …It was 8 years until the second one? I didn't know that.

CL: Yes, 7 or 8. I did *Rasputin* [full title, *Rasputin, the Mad Monk*, Don Sharp, 1966] and *Dracula: Prince of Darkness* [Terence Fisher, 1966] back to back. Same sets. When I read the script, I said to my agent, "I'm not saying any of this dialog. It's appalling."

JL: You don't say anything in the movie!

CL: Not a word.

JL: But you have a hell of a presence!

CL: When Chekhov went to see one of his plays at a local theater, they asked him at the end what he thought of it, and he came up with this wonderful expression: "Not enough gunpowder." That's the secret. If you have the physical presence, all right: you're lucky. If you have power, well, you're lucky. But, gunpowder, that's the real secret!

JL: Well, your Dracula certainly has fire and brimstone.

CL: I refused to do the second one at first. In the end, I played Dracula five or six times…

JL: I hope they paid you well!

CL: Oh, you're joking. I think they paid me about £750.

JL: Even for the later ones?

CL: I think they paid me a little bit more later, but not much. Certainly not five figures.

JL: But you were the selling point of the movies!

CL: I bought my first car when I was 35. It was a second-hand Merc. I could just about afford it. Anyway, the process went like this: The telephone would ring and my agent would say, "Jimmy Carreras [President of Hammer Films] has been on the phone, they've got another Dracula for you." And I would say, "Forget it! I don't want to do another one."

JL: So how would Hammer get you to agree?

CL: I'd get a call from Jimmy Carreras, in a state of hysteria. "What's all this about?!" "Jim, I don't want to do it." "You've got to do it!" "Jim, I don't want to do it, and I don't have to do it." "No, you have to do it!" And I said, "Why?" He replied, "Because I've already sold it to the American distributor with you playing the part. Think of all the people you know so well, that you will put out of work!" Emotional blackmail. That's the only reason I did them.

JL: "Emotional blackmail" is a tradition in the movie business. Tell me about *The Mummy* [Terence Fisher, 1959].

CL: The Mummy was a real person at one time, a high priest, and he falls in love with a princess.

"I never looked upon my films as horror films."

JL: It's a romantic story.

CL: Oh yes! This love is forbidden, and they find out, cut out his tongue, and ball him up.

JL: Was that terribly uncomfortable?

CL: Yes! Swathed in bandages. Boris [Karloff, star of the original *The Mummy*, Karl Freund, 1932] said it was absolute hell, because he was covered in make-up and wrapped so tightly in bandages. If he took a deep breath, the bandages would crack and you would see there was a real person underneath.

JL: Luckily for him, Karloff is only the bandage-wrapped Mummy in one scene…

CL: The way I played it, I tried to make people feel sorry for me. The problem with the role was a physical one. I had to move like an automaton, but the Mummy also had a mind of its own. Because of the bandages I could only act with my body movements and my eyes. In one of the most effective scenes, I come crashing through the windows and Peter Cushing thrusts a spear into me, which goes right through, and shoots me. And then Yvonne Furneaux comes in. And Peter shouts, "Let down your hair! Let down your hair!" while I'm strangling her with one hand. And she does. And it's Ananka, the princess I fell in love with. I see her and I am riveted. And after quite a long time, I just turn around and walk away. Which I thought was very moving.

JL: And didn't you have to go into a swamp?

CL: Ah, the business in the swamp: I had to carry about three or four girls, sometimes as much as 80 yards, and they were pretending to be unconscious, so they were dead weight. It didn't help my shoulder muscles! In the swamp, Yvonne was saying to me under her breath, "Don't drop me, don't drop me," and I was using the most appalling language, because I was crashing into these pipes which were producing the bubbles in the water and the mud.

JL: Which brings us to Mr. Hyde.

CL: I'd forgotten that one. I think that was one of the best things I've ever done. But it had a ridiculous title: *I, Monster* [Stephen Weeks, 1971]. And they changed Jekyll's name.

JL: He's not called Dr. Jekyll?

CL: Jekyll and Hyde became Marlowe and Blake. But all the other people in the story have the correct names.

JL Why on earth would they do that?

CL: Don't ask me!

JL: Fredric March played Hyde as a bestial, ape-like character.

CL: Yes, and Spencer Tracy was very frightening, too.

JL: Tracy played him more like a psychopath. It was John Barrymore who first made Hyde into a physical monster.

CL: Oh yes, that was extraordinary.

JL: And he did it live on stage on Broadway!

CL: I don't know how he did that.

JL: George Folsey, the camera operator on the silent *Dr. Jekyll and Mr. Hyde* [John S. Robertson, 1920], told me that on stage Barrymore would drink from the flask, then stagger and fall down behind a desk and quickly get right up again transformed into the hideous Mr. Hyde! It happened very fast. All he did was put on a pointed, bald cap and shove crooked teeth into his mouth. He could distort his face so grotesquely.

CL: I played Hyde in stages of degeneration. I became worse and worse and worse. In the name of science. Curiosity. What would happen if I took this drug? All scientists are curious. The make-up man, Harry Frampton, did a wonderful job. There were about five or six stages of degeneration.

JL: Is there any particular monster that you were frightened of as a kid?

CL: Well, I remember after seeing Boris Karloff in *Frankenstein*, aged 11, I used to wake up in the middle of the night and think he was in the room. And I wasn't the only one!

WEREWOLVES

Michael & John "Thriller" 1983

WEREWOLVES

The belief in shape-shifting is universal. In every culture, from the ancient Greeks to the Native Americans, men and women often become animals and vice versa. In stories like the god Zeus turning himself into a swan to seduce the mortal Leda, or the magical Puck giving Bottom the head of an ass in Shakespeare's *A Midsummer Night's Dream* (see page 136), the theme of man-into-animal appears countless times in art and literature. In cinema, by far the most popular shape-shifter is the werewolf.

The shape-shifting "rules" change from film to film. Usually a man becomes a werewolf by being bitten by another werewolf, as in *Werewolf of London* [Stuart Walker, 1935], *The Wolf Man* [George Waggner, 1941 and Joe Johnston, 2010], and *An American Werewolf in London* [John Landis, 1981].

In *The Curse of the Werewolf* [Terence Fisher, 1961] Oliver Reed is born a werewolf because his mother was raped and he is born on Christmas Day! This movie claims that for an unwanted child to share his birthday with Jesus Christ is "an insult to heaven." When the poor bastard baby is to be baptized, the Holy Water in the baptismal font begins to boil. Not a good sign.

In the *Underworld* series of films, an entire race of werewolves battles a race of vampires for supremacy, and in Neil Marshall's *Dog Soldiers* [2002], a troop of British soldiers has the

▲ *Little Red Riding Hood,* German postcard illustration [c. 1900]. Charles Perrault wrote the first account of the French folk tale in the 17th century. In Perrault's telling, Little Red Riding Hood ends up as a tasty meal for the devious Wolf.

misfortune of running into a family of werewolves in the Scottish Highlands. In *How to Make a Monster* [Herbert L. Strock, 1958], an insane make-up artist uses Michael Landon's actual make-up and mask from the earlier film *I Was a Teenage Werewolf* [Gene Fowler, Jr., 1957] to turn an innocent actor into a homicidal wolf man! Val Lewton's production *Cat People* [Jacques Tourneur, 1942], centers on a beautiful woman (Simone Simon) descended from an ancient European race. When her passions (jealousy and lust) are aroused, she turns into a murderous black panther!

The full moon has long been associated with violence and madness—the word "lunatic" shows the power we give the full moon. Against his will, the body of the lycanthrope changes into that of a werewolf whenever a full moon appears in the night sky.

A common term for the natural menstruation cycle of women is "the curse." This idea is explored in the clever Canadian picture *Ginger Snaps* [John Fawcett, 2000]. This film, like *I Was a Teenage Werewolf* and *The Beast Within* [Philippe Mora, 1982], uses lycanthropy as a metaphor for adolescence. In adolescence, youngsters begin to grow hair in unexpected places and parts of their anatomy swell and grow. Everyone experiences these physical transformations in their bodies and new, unfamiliar, sexual thoughts in their minds. No wonder we

---

Previous pages: *The Wolfman* [Joe Johnston, 2010] An atmospheric shot from the very disappointing remake.
Opposite page: (1) *An American Werewolf in London* [John Landis, 1981] Scotland Yard's Inspector Villiers (Don McKillop)

attacked by the werewolf in Piccadilly Circus (see page 183).
(2) **Michael Jackson** as a teenage werecat "strangling" me on the set of *Michael Jackson's Thriller* [John Landis,1983]. Photo by Douglas Kirkland.

(3) *The Werewolf* by Lucas Cranach the Elder [1472-1553]. This woodcut by the German Renaissance painter, engraver, and printmaker shows a lycanthrope attacking a village.

...readily accept the concept of a literal metamorphosis.

In Curt Siodmak's original screenplay for Universal's seminal The Wolf Man, he emphasized the notion of the werewolf as a victim. The Wolf Man of the title, Larry Talbot, (played by Lon Chaney, Jr. in all five Universal Wolf Man movies), is horrified by his plight and spends most of his time trying to find a cure or contemplating suicide.

Every single werewolf film always has a major "transformation" sequence: Larry Talbot's transformation was accomplished by a series of optical dissolves. Chaney sat very still (usually with his head, hands, and feet held in place) while make-up man Jack Pierce gradually applied more and more yak hair and putty to his face. This was a tedious, time-consuming process, and the use of optical dissolves resulted in a rather gentle transformation from man into wolf man.

When I wrote the script for An American Werewolf in London (written in 1969, produced in 1981), I envisioned the metamorphosis from man to beast as a violent and painful one. The character of David Kessler (David Naughton) would transform from a two-legged human into a four-legged "hound from hell." I also specified that the sequence take place without cutaways and in bright light. The gifted make-up artist Rick Baker accomplished this with an elaborate combination of make-up, foam appliances, and what he called "change-o" body parts. These were elaborate puppet reproductions of parts of Naughton's body (including his torso, hands, feet, head, and face) that could actually stretch and transform into the wolf monster in real time on camera. This sequence took five days to shoot. I ended up using one cutaway: of a toy Mickey Mouse silently watching. Rick won the first of his many Academy Awards for his groundbreaking work.

In Joe Dante's terrific The Howling [1981], the character of Eddie Quist (Robert Picardo) positively relishes his lycanthropy and gleefully transforms in front of a terrified Terry Fisher (Belinda Belaski). In this movie, werewolves seem to transform either at will or from sexual arousal. TV anchorwoman Karen White (Dee Wallace-Stone) has a particularly disturbing encounter with Quist in a porno booth at a sex shop while a film of a rape is being projected. Karen White eventually turns into a sort of fluffy, poodle-dog-werewolf during a live television news broadcast!

As in the Underworld pictures, the popular Twilight movies also chronicle the conflict between a race of vampires and werewolves. Also like the Underworld movies, the Twilight series uses computer-generated imagery to accomplish not only the man-into-wolf transformations, but also the monsters themselves. In Eclipse [David Slade, 2010] the werewolves tend to all be very buff, shirtless young men who transform into wolves by leaping into the air.

Hogwarts' unfortunate Defense Against the Dark Arts teacher Professor Lupin (David Thewlis), introduced in Harry Potter and the Prisoner of Azkaban [Alfonso Cuarón, 2004] is another werewolf who uses CGI to "morph," while Jack Nicholson in Wolf [Mike Nichols, 1994] uses a far more subtle, traditional make-up by Rick Baker.

Since the werewolf is here to stay, I suggest taking the excellent advice given by the customers of The Slaughtered Lamb pub in An American Werewolf in London: "Stay on the road. Beware the moon."

▲ **The Wolf Man** [George Waggner, 1941] This ad for Universal Studios' newest monster stresses the transformation "from Man to Beast" as a major marketing strategy.

Opposite page: Cat People [Jacques Tourneur, 1942] French actress Simone Simon stars as Irena Dubrovna in this intelligent thriller from the Val Lewton B Picture Unit at RKO Studios. The sequence where a jealous Irena follows her husband's secretary to her apartment building's swimming pool is still eerie after all these years.

▲ *The Wolf Man* [George Waggner, 1941] Lon Chaney, Jr. as the tragic Wolf Man of the title holding the lovely Evelyn Ankers in his arms. I've never understood why the werewolf that bit him (the Gypsy Bela, played by Béla Lugosi) was a proper, four-footed wolf and Talbot became a two-footed wolf man.

◄ *Werewolf of London* [Stuart Walker, 1935] Henry Hull refused to wear the make-up Jack Pierce designed for the werewolf, as he felt it hid too much of his face. Pierce and Hull settled on the face pictured here in a highly retouched publicity photo from the original release. Pierce ended up using his first *Werewolf of London* design on Lon Chaney, Jr. in *The Wolf Man*.

▲ *House of Frankenstein* [Erle C. Kenton, 1944] Lon Chaney, Jr. as mournful Larry Talbot again, this time with Boris Karloff as the mad Dr. Gustav Neimann and John Carradine as Count Dracula.

> "The werewolf is neither man nor wolf, but a Satanic creature with the worst qualities of both."

Dr. Yogami (Warner Oland), *Werewolf of London*

◀ *The Howling* [Joe Dante, 1981] Serial murderer Eddie Quist (Robert Picardo) is the epitome of the young punk our parents warned us to stay away from. He is also a werewolf. Note the poster design for *The Howling* is essentially the other side of the poster for *I Was a Teenage Werewolf!*

▲ *Abbott and Costello Meet Frankenstein* [Charles Barton, 1948] The last gasp of the classic Universal monsters: The studio threw Dracula (Béla Lugosi), the Frankenstein monster (Glenn Strange), and the Invisible Man (Vincent Price) into the pot. Here, Larry Talbot (Lon Chaney, Jr.) approaches the oblivious Lou Costello. Surprisingly, this was a handsome production that treated the monsters with respect.

▶ *I Was a Teenage Werewolf* [Gene Fowler, Jr.,1957] A troubled teen is exploited by an evil scientist. As we were told in school, this is where masturbation can lead. Not to mention rock'n'roll!

◀ *How to Make a Monster* [Herbert L. Strock, 1958] Actor Gary Clarke in Michael Landon's Teenage Werewolf make-up from the earlier film, poses with Gary Conway, the Teenage Monster from *I Was a Teenage Frankenstein* [Herbert L. Strock, 1957].

▲ *The Werewolf* [Fred F. Sears, 1956] Duncan Marsh (Steven Rich) is injected with serum made of wolf's blood by two scientists trying to restore his memory after he is in a car accident. Naturally this turns him into a vicious werewolf.

▶ *Teen Wolf* [Rod Daniel, 1985] Scott Howard (Michael J. Fox) is the quintessential high-school nerd. But when he discovers he comes from a family of lycanthropes, he uses his lycan abilities to become the big man on campus as a basketball star. A Disney movie in everything but name.

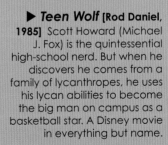

▲ *The Undying Monster* [aka *The Hammond Mystery*, John Brahm, 1942] The Hammond family has been cursed with lycanthropy since the Crusades. A detective tries to discover which Hammond is the werewolf as the bodies pile up.

▶ *Werewolf in a Girls' Dormitory* [Paolo Heusch, 1962] is the title that MGM gave the Italian-Austrian co-production *Lycanthropus* for its US release. A fairly grisly early *giallo* set in an all-girls' school, the murderer this time turns out to be a werewolf.

◀ *Ginger Snaps* [John Fawcett, 2000] A smart take on werewolf mythology and a clever examination of teenage angst and sexuality. Two "goth" sisters, Ginger and Brigitte Fitzgerald (Katharine Isabelle and Emily Perkins) meet the Beast of Bailey Woods and find out that it's a lycanthrope.

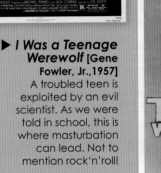

◀ *Legend of the Werewolf* [Freddie Francis, 1975] A boy is raised by wolves and then displayed as a circus freak. But even the presence of such reliable old pros as Peter Cushing, Ron Moody, and Hugh Griffith cannot lift this one above average.

▲ *Return of the Vampire* [Lew Landers, 1944] Pictured here with Nina Foch is Matt Willis as the Werewolf slave to vampire Béla Lugosi in London during the Blitz!

"Their dream of love a nightmare of horror!"

From the trailer for *The Curse of the Werewolf*

◀ *The Curse of the Werewolf* [Terence Fisher, 1961] Oliver Reed makes a splendid werewolf in this handsome Hammer film. Roy Ashton, Hammer's go-to monster maker, did Reed's werewolf make-up.

▲ **Wolf** [Mike Nichols, 1994] Jack Nicholson with Michelle Pfeiffer in a modern werewolf story. James Spader steals the picture as a rival werewolf.

▲ **The Monster Squad** [Fred Dekker 1987] In this enjoyable monster mash-up, Jonathan Gries plays an unnamed character; however, when he turns into the Wolfman, he is played by Carl Thibault.

Female Shapeshifters

Women are also known to become animals when the moon is full, or sometimes just when the mood is right.

▲ **She-Wolf of London** [Jean Yarbrough, 1946] When a series of murder victims is found with their throats ripped out, and a "Wolf Woman" is seen in the park, young June Lockhart believes she may be responsible.

▶ **Cat People** [Paul Schrader, 1982] Nastassja Kinski stars in Schrader's more explicitly erotic remake of the original 1942 classic.

▶ **La Lupa Mannara** [aka **Werewolf Woman**, Rino Di Silvestro, 1976] Annik Borel stars as a woman who dreams she is a werewolf, then seduces men and tears out their throats.

▲ **Deer Woman** [John Landis, 2005] Beautiful Cinthia Moura stars as the deadly Deer Woman of Native American mythology, with disbelieving detective Brian Benben on her trail.

▲ **The Company of Wolves** [Neil Jordan, 1984] Danielle Dax as Wolfgirl in Angela Carter and Neil Jordan's interpretation of "Le Petit Chaperon Rouge." Perrault's moral is read over the beginning credits: "...beware of charming strangers."

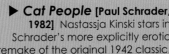

55

AN AMERICAN WEREWOLF IN LONDON

This was my attempt to make a movie dealing with the supernatural in a completely realistic way. Because there is no such thing as men who become monstrous wolves when there is a full moon, I tried to explore how one would react when confronted with this as truth. What do you do when the unreal is real? That was my premise and *An American Werewolf in London* is the result.

▲ *David Kessler* (David Naughton) wakes up to find himself naked inside the wolf cage in The Regent's Park Zoo.

▼ *David Kessler* (David Naughton) halfway through his painful metamorphosis.

▲ *A publicity shot* of David surrounded by the victims of his "carnivorous lunar activities" at a porno theater in Piccadilly Circus. His best friend Jack (Griffin Dunne), now also one of the "Living Dead," is on his right. Jack is not a fresh kill and by now looks a little worse for wear.

> "The wolf's bloodline must be severed. The last remaining werewolf must be destroyed. It's you, David!"
>
> Jack (Griffin Dunne),
> *An American Werewolf in London*

◀ *The transformation* from a man into four-legged "hound from hell" is a painful one. Sinew, muscle, and bone stretch, bend, and crack. New, non-human flesh grows and limbs elongate, teeth become fangs, hair sprouts from all over the body, claws burst from fingers. The jaw unhinges from the skull and actually begins to grow into a snout. I recommend you do not try this at home.

▲ *Santo y Blue Demon vs. Drácula y el Hombre Lobo*
[**Miguel M. Delgado, 1973**] El Santo was the most popular Mexican
Luchador Enmascarado (masked wrestler) and starred in many
movies. This time, he teams up with another popular masked
wrestler, Blue Demon, to take on both Dracula and the Wolf Man!

▲ *The Howling* [**Joe Dante, 1981**] Belinda Belaski watches
in horror as Robert Picardo changes into a werewolf. Dante's
movie is full of sly references to other werewolf films and has a
truly wacky ending, as TV station manager Kevin McCarthy
watches in amazement as anchorwoman Dee Wallace-Stone
turns into a kind of were-poodle on live television. Joe's witty
movie has spawned too many terrible sequels. Sequels in
name only.

▼ *Bram Stoker's Dracula* [**Francis Ford Coppola,1992**]
As in the Stoker novel, Dracula can become a wolf
(or whatever that thing is) at will.

▲ *The Monster Club* [**Roy Ward Baker, 1981**]
An almost unwatchable movie from producer
Milton Subotsky where you can literally see
Vincent Price, John Carradine, Donald
Pleasence, Britt Ekland, and Stuart Whitman
take the money and run.

▲ *The Boy Who Cried Werewolf*
[**Nathan H. Juran, 1973**] The star (Kerwin
Mathews) and the director of *The 7th
Voyage of Sinbad* [1958] reunited to make
this ludicrous movie.

◀ *Silver Bullet*
[**Dan Attias, 1985**]
Based on the novella
Cycle of the Werewolf
by Stephen King, about
a werewolf on the loose
in Maine. This time the
lycanthrope turns out to
be a man of God!

▲ *Dog Soldiers* [Neil Marshall, 2002] A squad of British soldiers on a training mission in the Scottish Highlands has a nasty encounter with a family of werewolves in Neil Marshall's exciting, action-packed horror movie.

▲ *The Chronicles of Narnia: Prince Caspian* [Andrew Adamson, 2008] The sequel to *The Lion, the Witch and the Wardrobe*. Pictured is a good example of Howard Berger's Academy Award-winning make-up work.

"They were always here. I just unlocked the door."

Megan (Emma Cleasby), *Dog Soldiers*

▲ *Underworld: Evolution* [Len Wiseman, 2006] The second movie in the *Underworld* series, the story of the ongoing battle between the Vampires and the Lycans (short for lycanthrope, get it?), chock-full of computer-generated effects. Pictured is an excellent, practical werewolf costume in action.

▲ *The Twilight Saga: New Moon* [Chris Weitz, 2009] The second film in the *Twilight* series. In this picture all of the werewolves have nice bodies and rarely wear shirts in their human form.

▲ *Skinwalkers* [James Isaac, 2006] A half-Skinwalker/half-human boy is protected by his family and friends from another group of Skinwalkers who believe he may end their curse.

▲ *The Wolfman* [Joe Johnston, 2010] Despite production difficulties and an inane departure from the original Curt Siodmak story, Rick Baker won his seventh Academy Award for his make-up, turning Benicio Del Toro's Lawrence Talbot and his stunt doubles into the Wolf Man.

▶ *Underworld* [Len Wiseman, 2003] A great-looking CG Lycan from Len Wiseman's first film in his epic saga of the battle for supremacy between the Vampires and the Lycans.

Lon Chaney, Jr.

Lon Chaney, Jr.'s famous father didn't want his son to become an actor, but Chaney, Jr. nonetheless had a notable career. His breakout role was Lennie in the first film of John Steinbeck's novel *Of Mice and Men* [Lewis Milestone, 1939]. Chaney, Jr.'s powerful performance as the gentle monster tended to typecast him in brutish roles. Although he appeared in other roles, he is forever remembered as Lawrence Talbot, the tragic Wolf Man. Chaney, Jr. is the only actor to play all of the classic Universal monsters: Dracula, the Wolf Man, the Mummy, and the Frankenstein Monster.

▲ *The Wolf Man* [George Waggner, 1941]
The Wolf Man gives make-up maestro Jack Pierce a dirty look. Lon did not enjoy the tedious and uncomfortable make-ups his roles often demanded.

▼ *The Wolf Man* [George Waggner, 1941] Lon menaces his co-star, Evelyn Ankers. Until the unfortunate 2010 remake, Chaney was the only actor to ever play Larry Talbot, starring in all five Universal movies to feature the Wolf Man.

"Don't try to make me believe that I killed a man when I know that I killed a wolf!"

Larry Talbot (Lon Chaney, Jr.), *The Wolf Man*

▲ **The Mummy's Curse** [Leslie Goodwins, 1944] By this time, Kharis was not a particularly challenging part to play and Chaney resented stalking around wrapped in bandages. Universal however, was always keen to exploit his "horror" marquee value.

▶ **Man-Made Monster** [aka **The Atomic Monster**, George Waggner, 1941] Chaney plays a sideshow performer named "Dynamo Dan, the Electric Man" whom a mad scientist (the always reliable Lionel Atwill) turns into a "electrobiologically driven" monster who can kill by touch. A nifty sci-fi thriller from the director of *The Wolf Man*.

▲ **Son of Dracula** [Robert Siodmak, 1943] Chaney is suitably suave as Count Alucard, the son of Count Dracula, who comes to the USA at the invitation of the daughter of a wealthy New Orleans plantation owner. This film boasts the very first onscreen human-into-bat transformation in the movies.

▲ **The Ghost of Frankenstein** [Erle C. Kenton,1942] Chaney as the Frankenstein Monster ends up with Ygor's brain by the end of this movie! Béla Lugosi shines as Ygor; Chaney mostly goes "Grrrrrr!"

Joe Dante

Director Joe Dante checks a shot on the set of *Gremlins* [1984].

JL: So, Joe, here on your office wall you have a poster from *Creature From the Black Lagoon* [Jack Arnold, 1954]…

JD: One of the great monsters of all time.

JL: Why?

JD: It's one of the best-designed monsters. It's a triumph, considering what was available at the time. There has to be something recognizably human about a great monster. And the greatest thing about the Creature is, of course, that he lusts after Julie Adams!

JL: But what's he going to do when he gets Julie Adams? Isn't he a fish?

JD: Well, I think he's certainly part fish.

JL: Okay, we love the Creature. And you also have a large poster of *La Belle et la Bête* [Jean Cocteau, 1946] on the wall.

JD: Yes. That monster is also a great design, by Jean Cocteau. It's kind of a Wolf Man design. The great thing about wolf men characters is that they are sort of dog-like, and so we tend to feel a kinship to them. The Jack Pierce make-up for *The Wolf Man* [George Waggner, 1941] is great, but there is something dog-pet-like about him.

JL: What about your werewolves in *The Howling* [1981]?

JD: The werewolves in *The Howling* were an attempt to get away from that dog-like look. We thought they should be more lupine, like they are in the old woodcuts.

JL: Do you really think the most effective monsters are humanoid?

JD: Well, what is a monster? A monster is something that isn't normal, that doesn't look like regular people. In the Middle Ages, anybody who had any kind of a deformity was considered to be a monster. There are a lot of superstitions about deformity. There are many fantasy creatures that are half man and half something else, like the Minotaur. But the fascination for monsters for my generation was basically that we were powerless kids and monsters were misshapen individuals who didn't fit into society, who didn't have any power, and who had to strike back. So, as a kid, you felt a kind of power watching a monster doing his stuff.

JL: Do you have a theory on why people like monster movies?

JD: It's a difficult question. It's confronting death without having to really die.

JL: What was the first monster movie that genuinely frightened you?

JD: I remember finding Christopher Lee's Frankenstein Monster very scary [*The Curse of Frankenstein*, Terence Fisher, 1957].

JL: How old were you? Five?

JD: I was eleven. I imagined that he was going to be coming upstairs from the cellar in our house! The whole thing about these movies is that you took them home with you. When I saw *Them!* [Gordon Douglas, 1954], the giant ants made a sort of cricket-like, chirping kind of noise, very much like the sounds that would come from the field behind my house. Whenever a tree branch would rap on the window pane, I would think it was a giant ant antenna!

JL: But you really enjoyed seeing these movies, even though they would haunt you when you got home.

JD: I would come home and have nightmares, and my parents would say, "If you're going to have nightmares, then why do you go to see these pictures?"

JL: And how would you answer them?

JD: "I have to." I had to go see them. I couldn't *not* go. I loved those movies. I loved all movies when I was a kid—particularly cartoons—but there was something about those pictures. They weren't like other movies. They took place in worlds that I couldn't even imagine, places that I couldn't go to.

JL: *The Exorcist*, for me, is still probably the most successful horror movie.

JD: Yeah, it's a brilliantly nasty movie. It's very cleverly put together. At the beginning of the movie there are no make-up tricks or revolving heads or green vomit. By the time you get to that stuff, the audience has been pummelled into a state of being unable to resist watching whatever they're going to do. They've got a girl peeing on the floor, they've got her masturbating with a crucifix… The movie breaks down your defenses until you're just numb and ready to take all of the classic horror tropes which, had they been at the beginning, would not have worked.

JL: What was the first monster movie you saw?

JD: *The Mad Monster* [Sam Newfield, 1942]. It's about a mad scientist (George Zucco) who turns this dim-witted handyman (Glenn Strange) into a werewolf. The reason this picture was so fascinating to me was that there was a little girl in it, whom the monster kills off-screen. We just see her ball bouncing back into frame.

JL: Were you scared by it?

JD: Sure I was scared: He killed a little girl! But it was a contained scared, because I saw it on TV. When I saw movies in the theater, that's when I had nightmares. When you're in a big theater and it's dark, it's truly scary! I was small and I didn't want to have any heads to see over, so I would always sit in the front row, looking upwards, which I'm sure is why I have to wear glasses. I really liked movies that were about things that didn't happen in real life—the fantastic. And in the

early '50s, when the space movies came out—*This Island Earth* [Joseph M. Newman, 1955] was a revelation—I was in heaven.

JL: The visual effects and those vivid Technicolor colors still hold up.

JD: Plus it was written on the level of a ten year-old. It's fabulous! I saw *Invaders From Mars* [William Cameron Menzies, 1953] and then *Forbidden Planet* [Fred M. Wilcox, 1956] when they came out. If you saved up enough Quaker Oats box–tops you could get into that for free...

JL: You're only five years older than I am and it makes such a difference to the films you actually saw in a movie theater.

JD: It makes a tremendous difference, because from '53 to '58 were a kind of golden years for science fiction movies.

JL: I saw *The 7th Voyage of Sinbad* [Nathan H. Juran] at the Crest Theater on Westwood Boulevard in 1958. But those other films I saw on television in black and white.

JD: Well, that was the beginning for you, but I had already been watching sci-fi and horror films for a long time at the movies. They were marketed to kids. You'd maybe have one friend, or two, who liked monster movies, but you really didn't know many people who liked them, so you felt a little isolated. But when you went to the supermarket and you saw *Famous Monsters of Filmland* magazine on the shelf next to *Lady's Home Journal*, you realized: "My God, there must be other people like me out there!" I spent years writing letters to *Famous Monsters*, trying to get my name in it. If you could get your name in it, you were immortal! I wrote letters about everything: all the movies I'd seen, who were my favorite monsters, whatever.
I finally got to the point where I wrote about the *worst* movies I'd ever seen. It was published in the magazine as an article titled "Dante's Inferno!" And when Forrest J Ackerman sent me the magazine, annotated with "Go, Joe! Go!" it was the greatest thing that had ever happened to me. I was 12 or 13. Then I read the article and, of course, he'd completely re-written it. He used words like "symbiotic"—things I didn't even understand. But nonetheless, I felt like, "Wow! I'm part of a community." There was this feeling of solidarity with other kids like me. Now there are online fan communities, but there wasn't anything like that then. If you wanted to find out about a movie, you had only the TV guide. If you went to the library, the movie books were very scholarly and serious and not interesting to kids. The great boon of *Famous Monsters* was that it got people interested in film history.

JL: Yeah, it had articles not just about actors, but on writers, directors, technicians... like Willis O'Brien, Ray Harryhausen, Jack Pierce, Fritz Lang, Tod Browning, Lon Chaney, Richard Matheson, James Whale, and on and on.

JD: *Famous Monsters of Filmland* put all those disparate strands together in a way comprehensible to kids.

JL: Most horror magazines and websites now are just about maiming and killing. People are really into gore!

"It's confronting death without having to really die."

JD: It's all spectacle. It's pure, transgressive spectacle. It involves the same kinds of emotions that the Romans experienced when the Christians were thrown to the lions. Except in movies, it's safe, we're not really killing anybody. Now extreme gore is an accepted part of the way films are made. If you have a gory death scene, you can build a whole film around it, like *The Final Destination* [David R. Ellis, 2009].
People are so jaded. They've seen every plot, they've seen every twist, they've seen every gore effect. They've seen it all! And there are many things competing for their attention now that didn't exist when we were growing up. Plus, they know nothing about film; they know nothing about film history. They don't know who Jimmy Stewart was! They don't know!

JL: It kind of freaks me out.

JD: And you say, "How ignorant of them," but the fact is, in order to know about something you have to see it! The Marx Brothers—who are they? Laurel and Hardy? Nobody programs them. People don't want to see them.

JL: My kids grew up with all the old movies, so I was so shocked when my daughter brought a bunch of girls home for a sleepover and she wanted to put *The Women* [George Cukor, 1939] on for them. The girls refused to watch it because it was in black and white! It was very upsetting to me.

JD: The Marx Brothers, Harold Lloyd, Buster Keaton, and all that kind of stuff is only going to be kept alive in universities. They are no longer part of popular culture. This stuff runs only on cable or satellite. It's considered niche programming.

JL: Why do you think that so many vampire, werewolf, and zombie movies are now being made?

JD: It's an astonishment to me—particularly because I was loyal to the genre when

people thought it was trash, and now it has become mainstream. The fact is that the motion picture industry has become a glorified B-movie factory. Nowadays, the studios mine all the old, low-budget serials and monster titles, give them massive budgets, and cast them with big stars.

JL: Well, that's directly because of Spielberg and Lucas!

JD: Exactly! But there was a moment during the *Jaws* and *Star Wars* period in the '70s, when it seemed like movies were going to grow up. Look at what the studios made in those decades. But now it's like the suits realized: "Wait a minute! We can just make fantasy films with no content and they will all show up all over the world! So now it's all elves and *Lord of the Rings*, special effects in *Transformers*... it's non-content film. Films that aren't *about* anything.

JL: *Gremlins* [Joe Dante, 1984] was a case where there was a new fantasy film with a political subtext. And the wonderful malevolence of the Gremlins was so subversive! And *Gremlins 2: The New Batch* [Joe Dante, 1990] had some brilliant stuff in it. I saw that movie a hundred times—because my son Max adored it. But there are extraordinary moments in that. Really funny, brilliant, and dark...
Okay, enough about you. Let's talk about some specific monsters: The Mummy.

JD: The bromide about the Mummy was that you just need to walk away, and if you walked fast, you could get away from him. But when I was a kid, even though he was slow, he always got his victims. So it seemed to me that he had this magical power.

JL: And vampires?

JD: They're back. And now they're sexy and young, and they're...

JL: Mormon!

JD: Absolutely, the whole appeal of the *Twilight* thing is that they can't have sex. It's the abstinence thing—that's why parents are saying: "You should see these *Twilight* movies; they're really good!"

JL: So summing up, do you have any thoughts about why it is we like monsters?

JD: They're sources of melodrama; they're dangerous; they make people run in fear; they decimate; they kill; they do all the things that a bomb does. Maybe it's an embracing of death that starts at an early age. But basically, monsters do bad things and usually cause lots of death and heartache. Monsters are metaphors. Godzilla is a perfect example. Here is atomic war come to life, to be visited upon the people of Japan. That would be a good game: Name the monster movie and then the metaphor!

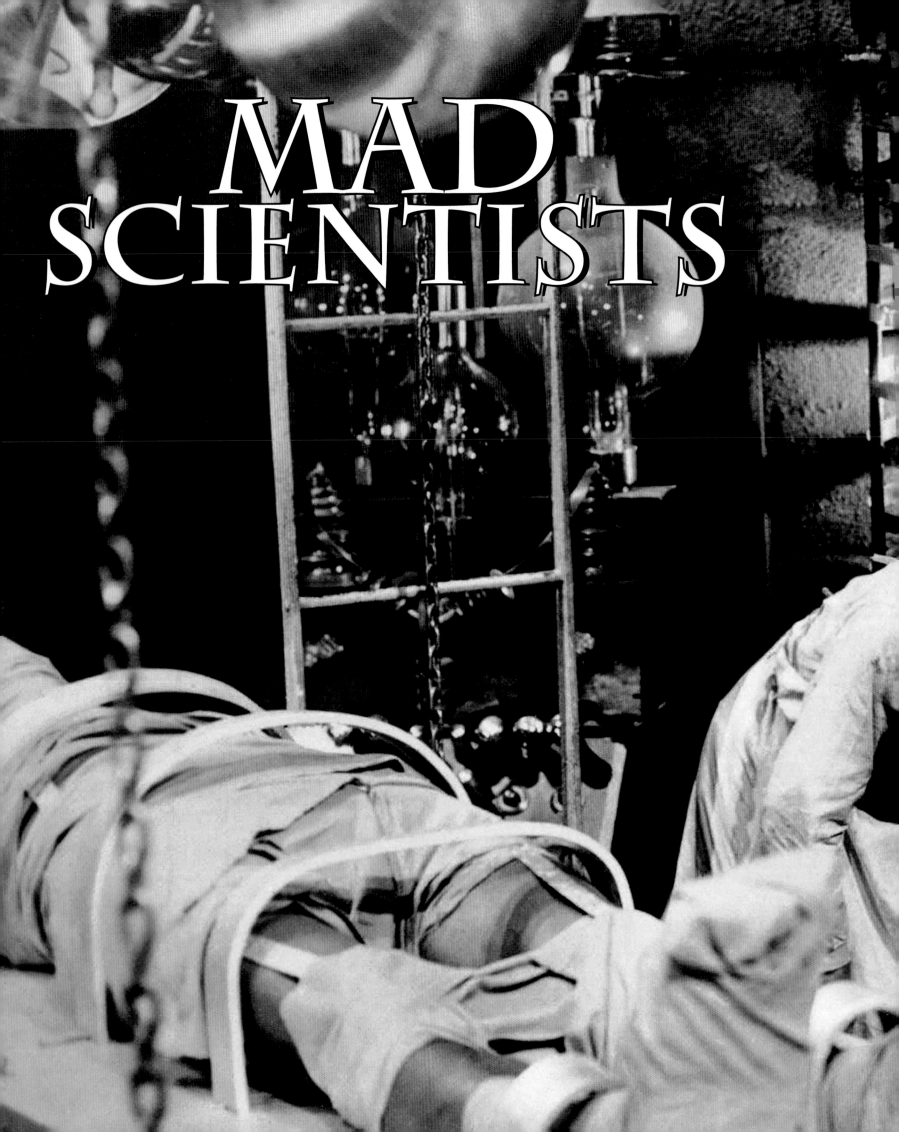

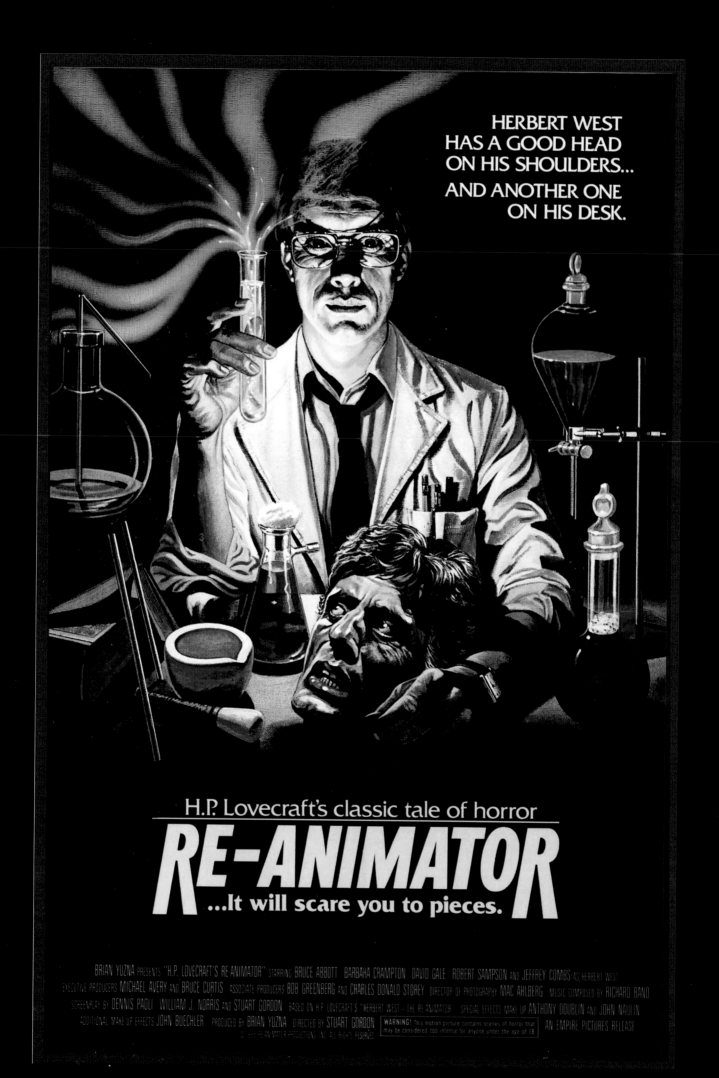

MAD SCIENTISTS

Scientific curiosity is the bedrock of progress. Sometimes, however, scientific research can be harmful to those conducting it; Madame Curie almost certainly died from the effects of the very radioactivity she discovered.

In *Die, Monster, Die!* [Daniel Haller, 1965], Boris Karloff's work with a radioactive meteor in the cellar of his house has catastrophic consequences for his entire family. In *The Invisible Man* [James Whale, 1933], Dr. Jack Griffin (Claude Rains) is driven mad by the injections of "Monocane," a drug he has discovered that makes him invisible. And woe to poor Dr. Jekyll, whose research into what we now call psychopharmacology releases his inner, murderous personality, his alter ego Mr. Hyde. Dr. Morbius (Walter Pidgeon) learns too late the power of the technology of the lost race of Krell in *Forbidden Planet* [Fred M. Wilcox, 1956] when it unleashes his subconscious thoughts as a living creature of pure energy. The terrifying Monster from the Id is only seen in outline when it is being blasted by lasers. This memorable and fearsome monster was animated by Joshua Meador, on loan to MGM from the Walt Disney Studios.

The insane Dr. Moreau from H. G. Wells' novel *The Island of Dr. Moreau* is a ruthless scientist performing radical surgeries on animals to create men. Wells' short novel was written in 1896 as an anti-vivisectionist tract and the three feature films based on the book have all emphasized the extreme sadism of Dr. Moreau. Dr. Moreau (Charles Laughton) in *Island of Lost Souls* [Erle C. Kenton, 1932], rules the "manimals" he's made by their fear of "The House of Pain"— the operating room where he struggles to cut out "the stubborn beast flesh." The Beast Man Sayer of the Law (Béla Lugosi) confronts the bullwhip-wielding Dr. Moreau with his plaintive, "We are not men. We are not beasts. We are things." The Beast Men finally revolt, turning Moreau's gleaming scalpels on their tormentor. Laughton's screams as he is dragged off to The House of Pain live long in the memory. This truly disturbing movie could be used as an "anti-genetic engineering" brochure in the present day!

▲ **Frankenstein's monster**—frontispiece illustration from the 1831 edition of *Frankenstein; or, The Modern Prometheus* by Mary Shelley.

The most famous mad scientist would have to be Henry Frankenstein (Colin Clive) in the classic 1931 Universal Picture, *Frankenstein* [James Whale]. His experiments to revive with electricity the creature he has pieced together from dead bodies created the definitive movie monster. As portrayed by Boris Karloff, in make-up by the great Jack Pierce, the Monster is both to be feared and pitied. Karloff's brilliant performance powerfully conveys the Monster's pain, innocence, and brutality.

The tremendous popular success of *Frankenstein* gave James Whale the freedom to create its extraordinary sequel, *The Bride of Frankenstein* [1935], which gave us not only Elsa Lanchester's unforgettable performance in the dual role of author Mary Shelley and the Bride of the Monster, but the maddest of all mad doctors, Doctor Septimus Pretorius (Ernest Thesiger).

Mad doctors tend to have bizarre obsessions; my personal favorite is the brain transplant. Dracula himself (Béla Lugosi) plans to put Lou Costello's brain into the skull of the Frankenstein Monster (Glenn Strange) in *Abbott and Costello Meet Frankenstein* [Charles Barton, 1948]. George

Zucco transplants the brain of a young man into a gorilla in *The Monster and the Girl* [Stuart Heisler, 1941] and Dr. Sigmund Walters (John Carradine) puts the brain and glands of a young woman into the skull of an ape, creating the attractive, yet mysterious Paula Dupree (Acquanetta) in *Captive Wild Woman* [Edward Dmytryk, 1943].

A "matter transportation device" has tragic results when a common fly is inadvertently dematerialized along with the scientist Andre Delambre (Al Hedison) conducting the experiment. When Andre rematerializes, he has a giant fly's head and one large claw in *The Fly* [Kurt Neumann, 1958]. Meanwhile, the little fly now has one tiny arm and a tiny human head! The scene of this little fly trapped in a spider web as a huge and hideous spider bears down on him (his tiny human face squeaking "Help me!") is one of the silliest, yet most upsetting, images in all of the horror films of the 1950s.

In David Cronenberg's excellent remake of *The Fly* [1986], scientist Seth Brundle (a wonderful performance from Jeff Goldblum) is doomed to repeat the experiment, with more profound but equally shocking and tragic results.

The experiments of Dr. James Xavier (Ray Milland) with X-ray vision also go badly awry. His vision grows more and more powerful until he goes mad and tears out his own eyes in *X* [aka *The Man with the X-Ray Eyes*, Roger Corman, 1963].

In *Altered States* [Ken Russell, 1980], Dr. Edward Jessup (William Hurt) and his colleagues experiment with sensory deprivation water tanks and drugs to achieve "biological devolution." Jessup emerges from his tank once as a

▲ *Dr. Jekyll and Mr. Hyde* [Rouben Mamoulian, 1931] Fredric March's Dr. Jekyll transforms into Mr. Hyde. March won a Best Actor Academy Award for this performance.

primitive man and once again as "conscious primordial matter."

In *Swamp Thing* [Wes Craven, 1982], Dr. Alec Holland works in the swamps with his sister doing bio-medical research. He is trying to create a plant/human hybrid that can live in extreme environments. It should come as no surprise that Dr. Holland ends up a hybrid plant person himsel

Dr. Stoner (Strother Martin) wants to turn his handsome assistant into a large snake in *SSSSSSS* [aka *SSSSnake*, Bernard L. Kowalski, 1973]. In both *The Incredible 2-Headed Transplant* [Anthony M. Lanza, 1971] and *The Thing with Two Heads* [Lee Frost, 1972], neither the recipien nor the donor of the extra head is very happy with th results! After his wife is decapitated in a car accident, Dr. Bill Cortner (Jason Evers) keeps her severed head alive in his basement lab in the country while he scouts stri joints for the right body to sew it onto! His wife (Virginia Leith), or rather he head, is now *The Brain Tha Wouldn't Die* [Joseph Green, 1962]. She develop telepathic communication with a hideous monster locked in the basement closet—the result of her husband's earlier failed experiments. Without givin too much away, just let me say that this film has one of the strangest endings in movie history.

The fundamentally conservative nature of the horror film tends to reinforce the reactionary idea that, "There are some things Man is not meant to know." Intellectual curiosity is punished and those who dare question conventional wisdom suffer the consequences. I think this would be a good place to point out that Galileo was right, and the Church wrong!

Opposite page: (1) *The Curse of Frankenstein* [Terence Fisher, 1957] Peter Cushing as the ruthless and cold Dr. Frankenstein with Christopher Lee as the victimized monster.

(2 and 3) *The Bride of Frankenstein* [James Whale, 1935] Elsa Lanchester as the mate Frankenstein has made for his monster; Ernest Thesiger, as Dr. Pretorius, displays his own creations—homunculi he keeps in jars!

(4) *Forbidden Planet* [Fred M. Wilcox, 1956] Walter Pidgeon as Dr. Edward Morbius, a scientist who has partially solved the remarkable secrets of the Krell, a vanished alien race.

◄ The Testament of Dr. Mabuse
[Fritz Lang, 1933]
The poster for Lang's film about the mad Dr. Mabuse, a criminal genius who seems to be controlling a crime wave from inside an insane asylum.

▶ Mad Love
[Karl Freund, 1935]
Peter Lorre as mad Dr. Gogol, a surgeon obsessively in love with Yvonne Orlac (Frances Drake). A wild story of crazed love and hand transplants, this is the first movie adaptation of Maurice Renard's story *The Hands of Orlac* [*Les Mains d'Orlac*, 1920].

▼ Metropolis
[Fritz Lang, 1927]
Rudolf Klein-Rogge as C. A. Rotwang, a mad scientist, showing off his new Machine-Man.

"Isn't it worth the loss of a hand to have created the man of the future, the Machine-Man?"

C. A. Rotwang, the inventor (Rudolf Klein-Rogge), *Metropolis*

Doctor Moreau

H. G. Wells's novel *The Island of Dr. Moreau* [1896] is a gruesome story of a mad doctor performing surgical experiments on animals, cutting out the "stubborn beast flesh" to make Beast Men. Wells loathed the first [1933] and best movie version, with its Hollywood addition of a female creature and hints of bestiality—an addition that carried over into later remakes.

▼ *Island of Lost Souls* [Erle C. Kenton, 1932] A rare photograph of a test make-up. A remarkable mixture of animal parts in a terrific design not seen in the finished film.

▲ *Island of Lost Souls* [Erle C. Kenton, 1932] Charles Laughton gives a fantastic performance as the sadistic Dr. Moreau. Here, he gives instructions to one of his Beast Men.

"We are not men!
We are not beasts!
We are things!"

The Sayer of the Law (Béla Lugosi), *Island of Lost Souls*

◄◄ *The Island of Dr. Moreau* [John Frankenheimer, 1996] A profoundly terrible movie with Marlon Brando at his most bizarre as Dr. Moreau. The other photo is of one of the Beast Men on the island in a nice make-up, wasted on this film!

▲ *The Island of Dr. Moreau* [Don Taylor, 1977] Burt Lancaster as Dr. Moreau in this lackluster remake.

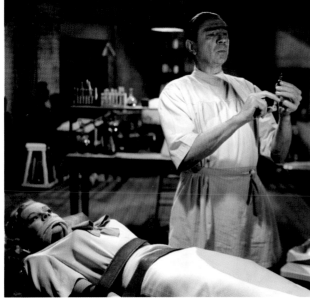

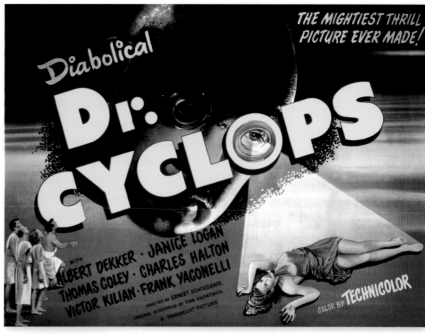

▲ Zombies on Broadway [Gordon Douglas, Gordon Dines, 1945]
Béla Lugosi as mad zombie expert Professor Renault, about to experiment on nightclub singer Anne Jeffreys. This comedy programmer must have one of the greatest titles in Hollywood history.

▲ Dr. Cyclops [Ernest B. Schoedsack, 1940]
Albert Dekker, as mad Dr. Alexander Thorkel, summons a group to his laboratory in the jungles of Peru, where he promptly shrinks them down to 12 inches high in his radiation chamber. His tiny prisoners manage to break one of the lenses in his eyeglasses, hence the title.

"Sometimes Professor Blake frightens me!

Student Sylvia Lockwood (Nancy Walters),
Monster on the Campus

▶ The Return of Dr. X
[Vincent Sherman, 1939]
Humphrey Bogart as Dr. Xavier, who needs a rare blood type to stay alive. Bogart's only horror film.

◀ Attack of the Puppet People [Bert I. Gordon, 1958]
John Hoyt is an insane doll maker who has invented a machine to shrink people to doll size for his amusement. A classic Gordon low-budget quickie, this one was rushed into production to capitalize on the success of 1957's *The Incredible Shrinking Man*.

▲ *Blood of the Vampire* [Henry Cass, 1958] Donald Wolfit as mad Doctor Callistratus, who does "blood deficiency" experiments on the inmates of a hospital for the criminally insane, in order to find a cure for his own anemic condition.

◄ *Monster on the Campus* [aka *Stranger on the Campus* and *Monster in the Night*, Jack Arnold, 1958] Arthur Franz, as Professor Donald Blake, becomes a Neanderthal monster stalking the campus after being exposed to the blood of a prehistoric fish called a coelacanth in his classroom.

▲ *The Tingler* [William Castle, 1959] Vincent Price, as pathologist Dr. Warren Chapin, discovers a parasite at the base of the spine, a "Tingler" that grows when its host experiences extreme fear. If the host does not scream, the Tingler's growth will kill them. Using this information, a friend of the doctor proceeds to frighten his mute wife to death. Vincent then removes the enlarged Tingler from the dead woman's body, but it escapes and makes its way into the very theater where we are watching the movie!!!

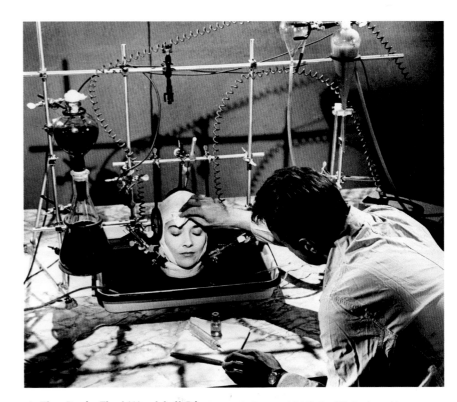

▲ *The Brain That Wouldn't Die* [Joseph Green, 1962] Dr. Bill Cortner (Jason Evers) attends to the head of his fiancée (Virginia Leith). He keeps her head alive in his basement while he searches for a voluptuous body to replace the one she lost in a car accident! An outrageous movie with a deeply twisted premise.

Dr. Fu Manchu

The creation of British author Sax Rohmer, evil genius Dr. Fu Manchu was a one-man "Yellow Peril," the embodiment of the West's fear and suspicion of the East.

▲ *The Mask of Fu Manchu* [Charles J. Brabin, 1932] Boris Karloff is magnificent as a lisping Fu Manchu in this lavish and delirious MGM production. Myrna Loy is a riot as Fah Lo See, Fu Manchu's nymphomaniac daughter.

▲ *Drums of Fu Manchu* [John English, William Witney, 1940] Henry Brandon as Fu Manchu in one of the greatest movie serials. Thrilling chases and narrow escapes abound as Sir Nayland Smith (William Royle) battles the wily oriental—once more played by a Caucasian in make-up.

◀ *The Face of Fu Manchu* [Don Sharp, 1965] Christopher Lee is a powerful Fu Manchu and Nigel Green an excellent Nayland Smith in this solid programmer. The first of five Fu Manchu pictures, of descending quality, starring Lee.

▶ *The Fiendish Plot of Dr. Fu Manchu* [Piers Haggard, 1980] Peter Sellers as Fu Manchu in this unfunny comedy. It is tragic that a film with a cast that includes Peter Sellers, Sid Caesar, Helen Mirren, David Tomlinson, and John Le Mesurier can be this bad.

A BEAUTIFUL WOMAN BY DAY—
A LUSTING QUEEN WASP BY NIGHT.

The WASP WOMAN

STARRING
SUSAN CABOT · FRED EISLEY · BARBOURA MORRIS
Produced and Directed by ROGER CORMAN · Written by LEO GORDON

▲ *Eyes Without a Face* [Georges Franju, 1960] Despite a sordid exploitation-movie plot (mad surgeon removes the faces from young girls to replace the face of his disfigured daughter), Franju crafted a film with moments of beauty within all the gruesome goings-on. Edith Scob as the doctor's daughter gives a haunting performance with her eyes—her face is mostly covered with a blank mask to hide her scarred features.

"Why are the mirrors in this strange house draped in black?"

Trailer for *Eyes Without a Face*

◀ *The Wasp Woman* [Roger Corman, 1959] Susan Cabot is the owner of a cosmetics company who injects herself with enzymes made from the "royal jelly" of a wasp queen as an anti-aging formula. Naturally, she becomes... The Wasp Woman! In the movie she has the head of a wasp, exactly the opposite of what is shown on the poster.

◄ *Atom Age Vampire*
[Anton Giulio Majano, 1963]
There is no vampire in *Atom Age Vampire*, just another mad doctor who must kill to stay alive.

► *Kiss Me Quick!*
[Peter Perry, Jr., 1964]
A "nudie-cutie" in which mad Dr. Breedlove's go-go girls dance for his alien visitor Sterilox from the "Buttless" galaxy. The Frankenstein monster and a rather raggedy Dracula also show up.

◄ *Voodoo Woman*
[Edward L. Cahn, 1957]
Mad scientist Tom Conway uses voodoo and modern science to create a creature in the African jungle. Another ridiculous monster suit from make-up man Paul Blaisdell.

► *X: The Man with the X-Ray Eyes* [Roger Corman, 1963] Ray Milland is Dr. James Xavier, whose experimental eyedrops allow him to see more than the human eye should. Once again, the moral is that we should not tamper with the natural order of things. Xavier ends up tearing out his own eyes! One of Corman's best films, with a terrific performance from Don Rickles as a carnival barker who sees a way to profit from Xavier's affliction.

INVISIBLE MEN

Classical myth is full of invisibility cloaks and mischief-making invisible gods. H. G. Wells' novel *The Invisible Man* [1897] was the first time a scientific approach to invisibility was proposed. Invisibility presented visually is the challenge of the movies below.

▲ ***The Invisible Man*** **[James Whale, 1933]** Claude Rains made his film debut in a role in which he was not seen but heard. Whale treated the story as a comedy, while Rains gave full throat to his character's growing megalomania. With groundbreaking special effects by John P. Fulton.

▲ ***Memoirs of an Invisible Man*** **[John Carpenter, 1992]** Chevy Chase never looked better as he regards himself in a mirror in a scene from Carpenter's very loose adaptation of the novel by H. F. Saint. A disappointing movie with good special effects.

▶ ***The Hollow Man*** **[Paul Verhoeven, 2000]** Kevin Bacon is the mad doctor who becomes invisible this time. At one point in Paul Verhoeven's over-excited movie there is even an invisible gorilla!

▲ ***The Nutty Professor*** **[Jerry Lewis, 1963]** Jerry Lewis is mild and shy Professor Julius Kelp, who transforms into nasty, smooth, lounge singer Buddy Love in Lewis' reinterpretation of Robert Louis Stevenson's *Dr. Jekyll and Mr. Hyde*. With stellar support from Stella Stevens and Kathleen Freeman, this is a funny and fascinating piece of self-analysis from the prolific actor/writer/director/producer.

◀ ***Die, Monster, Die!*** **[Daniel Haller, 1965]** A stunt man doubles for Boris Karloff as the unfortunate victim of radiation from a meteorite in this movie based on H. P. Lovecraft's story *The Color Out of Space* [1927].

▶ ***Carry On Screaming*** **[Gerald Thomas, 1966]** The *Carry On* gang in a plot similar to 1953's *House of Wax*. The usual *double entendres* and leering ensues. Fenella Fielding as Valeria Watt is a clear imitation of cartoonist Charles Addams' Morticia character, and the best thing in the movie.

SCIENCE RUNS AMOK to create a giant with two heads!

One brain wants to LOVE...
One brain wants to KILL!

...TWICE AS TERRIFYING AS ANY MONSTER OF FACT OR FICTION!

THE INCREDIBLE 2 HEADED TRANSPLANT

A John Lawrence Mutual General Production starring BRUCE DERN · PAT PRIEST · CASEY KASEM · ALBERT COLE
in THE INCREDIBLE TWO-HEADED TRANSPLANT also starring BERRY KROEGER Produced by JOHN LAWRENCE
Executive Producer NICHOLAS WOWCHUK · Associate Producer ARTHUR N. GILBERT · Directed by ANTHONY N. LANZA
and JOHN LAWRENCE · COLOR by DeLuxe · An AM...

◄ *The Incredible 2-Headed Transplant* [Anthony M. Lanza, 1971] A drive-in classic, in which mad doctor Bruce Dern transplants the head of a criminal onto the body of a big, mentally handicapped guy. Essentially remade as *The Thing With Two Heads* [Lee Frost, 1972], in which racist Ray Milland's head is attached to African American Roosevelt Grier's body, to Rosey's head's dismay. *The Thing With Two Heads* boasts an early cameo by Rick Baker in a two-headed gorilla suit.

"Frankenstein shocks the world as he mocks the devil!"

Trailer for *Frankenstein Created Woman*

▶ *Frankenstein Created Woman* [Terence Fisher, 1967] Peter Cushing as Dr. Frankenstein is still up to no good; this time the monster is played by Susan Denberg. Martin Scorsese likes this film because, "Here they actually isolate the soul... The implied metaphysics are close to something sublime." Marty was raised Roman Catholic, which is why I think he is so taken with this average Hammer film.

MAD DOCTOR PRICE

Along with Boris Karloff, Béla Lugosi, Peter Lorre, Peter Cushing, and Christopher Lee, Vincent Price became associated with horror and had a long career acting in genre films of every quality. Here are three of his maddest scientists.

◀ *Scream and Scream Again* [Gordon Hessler, 1970] Price plays a scientist trying to create a super race in this confusing movie. In a ghoulish running gag, every time a character wakes up in a hospital he is missing another part of his body.

▲ *The Abominable Dr. Phibes* [Robert Fuest,1971] Price has fun in this campy story of an organist avenging the death of his wife in an auto accident that also left him disfigured. Each murder of a doctor who failed to save her is inspired by one of the ten plagues of Egypt from the Old Testament.

▶ *Edward Scissorhands* [Tim Burton, 1990] Price as the kindly inventor who creates Edward Scissorhands (Johnny Depp) but dies before he can replace Edward's scissorhands with normal hands. Burton's most personal film, and Vincent Price's last movie.

◀▼ *Edward Scissorhands* [Tim Burton, 1990] Burton's original drawing of the character; Johnny Depp in costume and make-up as the character who represents Burton's feelings of isolation and alienation as a child in Santa Clarita, California. A visually inventive and witty film with a marvelous performance from the young Johnny Depp.

▲ *Abbott and Costello Meet Dr. Jekyll and Mr. Hyde* [Charles Lamont, 1953]
Dr. Jekyll's formula has found its way into the City of London's police force!

▲ *Horror Hospital* [Antony Balch, 1973]
Michael Gough as Dr. Christian Storm, who uses his health spa to perform lobotomy experiments on hippies, turning them into zombie slaves. Actually sounds better than it is.

"Do you think I made a mistake splitting his brain between the two of them?"

Dr. Frank-N-Furter (Tim Curry), *The Rocky Horror Picture Show*

▶ *The Rocky Horror Picture Show* [Jim Sharman, 1975]
Tim Curry in his star-making turn as Dr. Frank-N-Furter— "just a sweet transvestite from Transsexual Transylvania." The mad scientist has created boy toy, Rocky, in his quest for companionship. The movie version of Richard O'Brien's stage musical is still playing at midnight somewhere right now.

▲ *The Creeping Flesh* [Freddie Francis, 1973] Peter Cushing as Professor Emmanuel Hildern does not look too pleased with his visitor. Cushing is kept locked in his brother Christopher Lee's insane asylum doing experiments on the large humanoid skeleton he brought back from New Guinea. This movie is a piece of silliness in a handsome Victorian setting. My favorite plot device is that when the bones of the skeleton are put in water, they grow flesh and live once more!

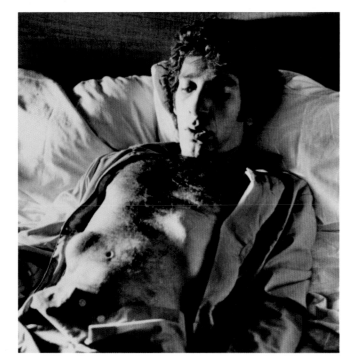

▲ **Shivers** [David Cronenberg, 1975] Cronenberg's first feature and already his "body-horror" aesthetic is evident. A doctor experiments with parasites for use in organ transplants and develops an organism that, once ingested, causes uncontrollable sexual desire. The organism spreads throughout a high-rise apartment complex, with violent results. David himself can be seen in the climax as one of the sexually berserk apartment dwellers.

▲ **Swamp Thing** [Wes Craven, 1982] Dick Durock as Swamp Thing in the first film based on the DC Comic book character. Durock wore this suit in a sequel and the subsequent television series. As H. L. Menken said, "No one ever went broke underestimating the American public."

▶ **Altered States** [Ken Russell, 1980] William Hurt emerges from a sensory-deprivation tank as "primordial matter" in Russell's wild movie, based on Paddy Chayefsky's only novel. Chayefsky also wrote the screenplay but had his name removed from the credits. I have to admit I like this movie, especially the sequence where Hurt, now regressed to an early, ape-like man, runs around the college campus and a zoo before reverting to his William Hurt self again. Miguel Godreau plays the "Primal Man" in make-up by Dick Smith.

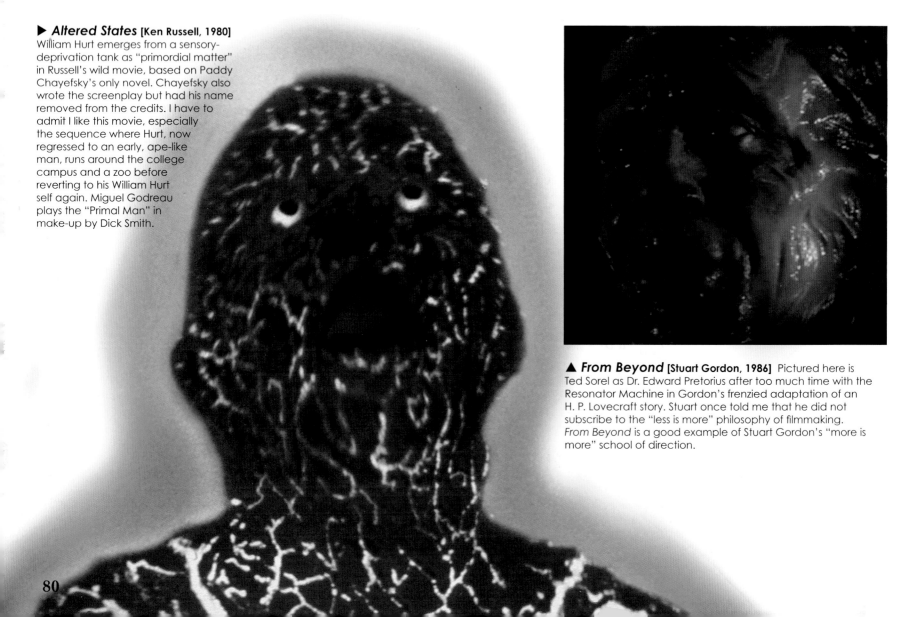

▲ **From Beyond** [Stuart Gordon, 1986] Pictured here is Ted Sorel as Dr. Edward Pretorius after too much time with the Resonator Machine in Gordon's frenzied adaptation of an H. P. Lovecraft story. Stuart once told me that he did not subscribe to the "less is more" philosophy of filmmaking. *From Beyond* is a good example of Stuart Gordon's "more is more" school of direction.

The Fly

The 1958 science fiction movie *The Fly* has an outrageous premise, but is played seriously by all involved. The idea of a wife putting her husband's head and arm into an industrial hydraulic press to deliberately crush him beyond recognition is such a dark concept to begin a film with, and the flashback to explain how we arrived at this point is so bizarre, one wonders how the hell 20th Century-Fox decided to make a movie based on the short story by George Langelaan in the first place! But aren't we glad they did?

"I'm an insect who dreamed he was a man and loved it. But now the dream is over... and the insect is awake."

Seth Brundle (Jeff Goldblum), *The Fly*

▲ *The Fly* [Kurt Neumann, 1958] Herbert Marshall, Vincent Price, and Charles Herbert discover the terrible truth in the horrifying climax of *The Fly*.

▲ *Return of the Fly* [Edward Bernds, 1959] The son of the mad scientist from the first film wants to vindicate his father's work. A bad idea.

▶ *The Fly* [David Cronenberg, 1986] Jeff Goldblum as mad scientist Seth Brundle [inset] in two stages of his metamorphosis into what he terms "Brundlefly." Cronenberg's movie is both gross and emotionally powerful.

81

"Mein Führer... I can walk!"

Dr. Strangelove (Peter Sellers),
Dr. Strangelove

▲ *Re-Animator* [Stuart Gordon, 1985] David Gale, as Dr. Carl Hill, holds his own severed head in his hands, about to perform a terrible pun on Barbara Crampton in the basement of Miskatonic University. Don't fret, she is rescued. Stuart Gordon's frenetic and terrific adaptation of the H. P. Lovecraft story *Herbert West—Reanimator* [1922].

▼ *Spider-Man 2* [Sam Raimi, 2004] After a lab explosion kills his wife, Dr. Otto Octavius (Alfred Molina) becomes arch-villain Doctor Octopus or "Doc Ock," using his mechanical tentacles to rob banks and cause trouble for Spider-Man in this even-bigger-budget sequel to Raimi's first *Spider-Man* [2002].

▲ *Dr. Strangelove* [Stanley Kubrick, 1964] Peter Sellers in the title role, an ex-Nazi scientist now working for the USA in this brilliant and blackest of black comedies. Sellers is dazzling as three different characters in the movie, the insane Dr. Strangelove, stiff-upper-lipped Group Captain Lionel Mandrake, and Merkin Muffley, the US President. As President Muffley says, "Gentlemen, you can't fight in here. This is the War Room!"

▲ *Gremlins 2: The New Batch* [Joe Dante, 1990] Christopher Lee as Dr. Catheter has something unpleasant on the end of his arm once the gremlins go out of control in Joe Dante's live-action cartoon sequel to his own *Gremlins* [1984].

▲ **Splice** [Vincenzo Natali, 2009] Delphine Chanéac, as Dren, confronts her "mother" Sarah Polley in this story of genetic engineering gone wrong. Another in a long line of "tampering with God's work" movies. The researchers are presented as pawns of an evil corporation. I doubt that the filmmakers are even aware of how reactionary their movie is.

◄▶ **Spider-Man** [Sam Raimi, 2002] Willem Dafoe, as Norman Osborn, tests a "strength enhancer" machine. It overloads and he becomes the Green Goblin, Spider-Man's arch enemy. Why the CEO of a major company couldn't get someone else to test the equipment I am still not sure.

DR. FRANKENSTEIN AND THE MONSTER

The collaboration of actor Boris Karloff, director James Whale, and make-up man Jack Pierce created one of the key icons of the 20th century. The image of Karloff's monster is deeply ingrained in the popular imagination, but Frankenstein and his monster have been portrayed in many different ways and by many different actors on stage, television, and in the movies.

▲ *Charles Ogle* [*Frankenstein*, **J. Searle Dawley, 1910**] The Thomas Edison Studios made the first film adaptation of Mary Shelley's novel *Frankenstein* with Charles Ogle looking suitably hideous in the title role.

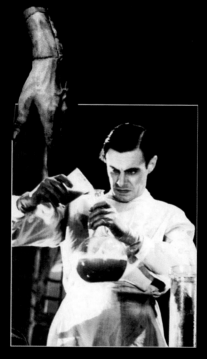

◀▲ *Boris Karloff, Colin Clive* [*Frankenstein*, **James Whale, 1931**] The monster and his maker in the first of the three films in which Karloff played the role.

▶ *Basil Rathbone* [*Son of Frankenstein*, **Rowland V. Lee, 1939**] Rathbone is Baron Wolf von Frankenstein, the son of Henry Frankenstein, in the second Universal film in which Karloff played the Monster. Reflected in Rathbone's mirror are Karloff as the monster and Béla Lugosi as Ygor.

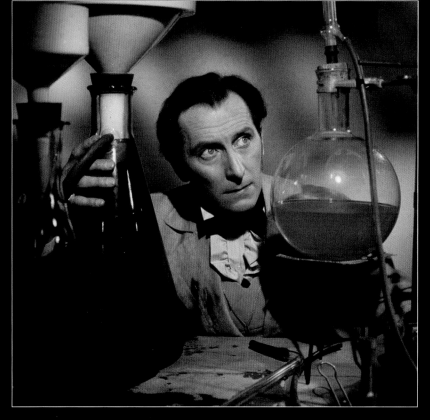

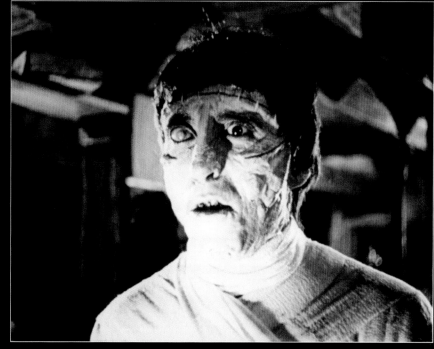

◄▲ **Peter Cushing, Christopher Lee** [*The Curse of Frankenstein*, **Terence Fisher, 1957**] This is Cushing's first appearance as Dr. Frankenstein, a character who became the focus of later Hammer Studios films. Christopher Lee's touching mime performance gave his monster great pathos.

"You're a good-looking fellow, do you know that? People laugh at you, people hate you, but why do they hate you? Because... they are jealous!"

Dr. Frankenstein (Gene Wilder), *Young Frankenstein*

▲ **David Prowse** [*Frankenstein and the Monster From Hell*, **Terence Fisher, 1974**] David Prowse is more famous as the man inside the Darth Vader costume who sounds just like James Earl Jones!

► **Gene Wilder, Peter Boyle**
[*Young Frankenstein*, **Mel Brooks, 1974**]
Wilder's neurotic Dr. Frederick Frankenstein and Peter Boyle's monster are at their most sublime singing "Puttin' On The Ritz" in Mel Brook's hilarious and affectionate homage to the Universal Picture's original *Frankenstein* trilogy.

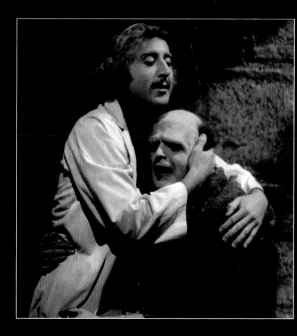

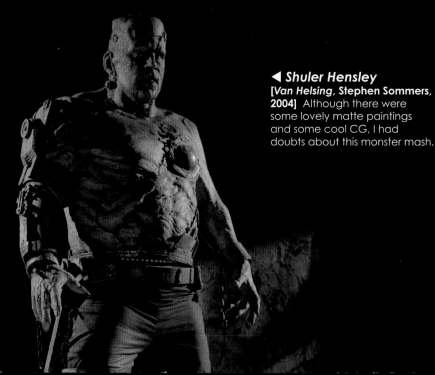

◄ **Shuler Hensley**
[*Van Helsing*, **Stephen Sommers, 2004**] Although there were some lovely matte paintings and some cool CG, I had doubts about this monster mash.

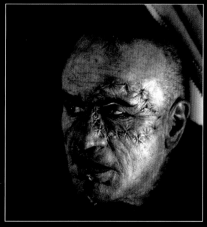

▲ **Kenneth Branagh, Robert De Niro** [*Mary Shelley's Frankenstein*, **Kenneth Branagh, 1994**] Branagh's Frankenstein is a little too frenetic for me, and De Niro's monster just looks uncomfortable. But Branagh is to be lauded for his attempt to be more faithful to the book.

DR. JEKYLL & MR. HYDE

Robert Louis Stevenson's novella *The Strange Case of Dr. Jekyll and Mr. Hyde* [1886] was adapted for the stage within a year of publication. The duality of man, that good and evil is in everyone, proved a fascinating subject and, as soon as the cinema was invented, there were Jekyll & Hyde movies. Personally, I am intrigued by the chemical aspects of the story; Stevenson was one of the first to discuss what is now called psychopharmacology.

▲ *John Barrymore* [*Dr. Jekyll and Mr. Hyde*, John S. Robertson, 1920] Barrymore had great success on stage with this role, shocking the audience with his rapid transformation in front of their eyes. The matinee idol known as "The Great Profile" created a Hyde that was terrifyingly hideous.

▲ *Fredric March* [*Dr. Jekyll and Mr. Hyde*, Rouben Mamoulian, 1931] Filmed before the Hays Code took effect in Hollywood, Mamoulian's film is explicit in its treatment of Miriam Hopkins' sexuality as Hyde's terrified mistress. March's Hyde became more ape-like with each transformation.

▲ *Spencer Tracy* [*Dr. Jekyll and Mr. Hyde*, Victor Fleming, 1941] A virtual remake by MGM of the earlier Paramount picture, with Ingrid Bergman in the Miriam Hopkins role. Although there is no romantic element in the novella, all of the dramatic adaptations add one.

▲ **Boris Karloff** [*Abbott and Costello Meet Dr. Jekyll and Mr. Hyde*, **Charles Lamont, 1953**] Boris Karloff somehow retains his dignity as Dr. Jekyll, despite the slapstick shenanigans of Bud and Lou.

▲ **Paul Massie** [*The Two Faces of Dr. Jekyll*, aka *Jekyll's Inferno*, **Terence Fisher, 1960**] Hammer Films' version of the Stevenson story is unusual in that it depicts Dr. Jekyll as dull and unattractive and Mr. Hyde as dashing and handsome.

▲ **Ralph Bates, Martine Beswick** [*Dr. Jekyll and Sister Hyde*, **Roy Ward Baker, 1971**] Another Hammer version, this time with Dr. Jekyll turning into a sexy and evil woman. Grave robbers Burke and Hare show up in this one to supply female bodies for Jekyll's experiments.

▲ **Tim Daly, Sean Young** [*Dr. Jekyll and Ms. Hyde*, **David Price, 1995**] Not a remake of the Hammer film, but a sex farce. Worth missing.

▲ **John Malkovich** [*Mary Reilly*, **Stephen Frears, 1996**] The interesting idea of telling the story from the point of view of a maid in Dr. Jekyll's household is squandered in this disappointing movie. Julia Roberts in the title role as the maid.

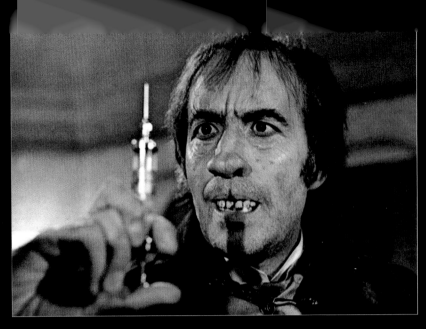

▲ **Christopher Lee** [*I, Monster*, **Stephen Weeks, 1971**] For some mysterious reason, Dr. Jekyll is renamed Dr. Marlowe and Mr. Hyde is Mr. Blake. Lee is excellent as both. Peter Cushing plays Frederick Utterson, Marlowe's lawyer. Make-up by Harry Frampton.

◄ **Oliver Reed** [*Dr. Heckyl and Mr. Hype*, **Charles B. Griffith, 1980**] Don't ask.

► **Jason Flemyng** [*The League of Extraordinary Gentlemen*, **Stephen Norrington, 2003**] Another terrible movie from a pretty good idea. Based on the graphic novel of the same name.

David Cronenberg

David Cronenberg on the set of *A History of Violence* [2005].

JL: David, how would you define a monster?

DC: A monster is a distortion of something that has a normal, non-threatening form. The monstrous form is threatening and disturbing because it is beyond the pale of what we consider normality. A monster is a deformation of what we consider normal and therefore safe.

JL: Do you remember your first encounter with a monster movie?

DC: *Bambi* [James Algar, Samuel Armstrong, 1942] was scary, and in *Bambi* it's the humans who are the monsters. As a kid I identified with Bambi. The hunters who would kill your mother are definitely monsters!

JL: What about the classic monsters like Frankenstein, Dracula, the Wolf Man?

DC: All those guys are deformations of normal humanity. Those are probably the scariest kind of monsters. But the shark in *Jaws* [Steven Spielberg, 1975] isn't a monster. It's an animal designed to kill you. It has no expression, its eyes are dead eyes. It is a killing machine. Does it qualify as a monster? Not really. Same with a T-Rex.

JL: What about Godzilla or a Cyclops or a dragon?

DC: Well, those are different because a Cyclops is a deformation of the human form. And there are some great monstrous creatures in, let's say, some of the *Harry Potter* films that are based on a *Tyrannosaurus rex*.

JL: But those dragons are magic!

DC: I think the further away from the human form a monster becomes, the more it becomes like a natural disaster. So, if you're eaten by a shark, it's almost like being hit by lightning. There's no ill will there. It's just a machine-like animal behaving normally. A natural occurrence.

JL: In *Jaws*, they did give the shark a personality. They made it malevolent.

DC: That's true… that was an attempt to mythologize the shark. To make the shark more than just a killing machine. And that's why *Jaws* was more successful than the movies about hundreds of piranhas who eat you up. The fact that there was one shark was the key. That's sort of a Moby Dick thing, to humanize and then mythologize an animal. When a monster is recognizably human, like a Cyclops, that's when the definition of monster and monstrous and monstrosity becomes very specific and very resonant.

JL: Okay. The Frankenstein Monster and the Wolf Man—I always find them sympathetic because they're victims.

DC: Yeah, there is a wonderful layering of those characters that makes them much more interesting. The same with vampires—there's just endless vampire films happening right now! But the more vampires are humanized, and even made beautiful, like in the *Twilight* movies, there comes a point where you treat them like… the disabled or something. They're humans but they have this disease problem. In other words, I guess you can go too far with the empathy. There has to be that sense of danger for a monster to really be a serious monster.

JL: What about the new craze for zombies? The flesh-eating, walking dead. What's that about?

DC: I think that's about video games, frankly. But once again they are deformations of normal humans and not only in the way they look, but also in their craving for human flesh.

JL: What do you mean by video games?

DC: In the early days of video games, the way that you could get around parental fear of having children enjoying killing people, was to have them not be people exactly. If they're anonymous creatures, it's okay to kill them. And really part of the fun of those movies and TV series is just the many different ways that you can kill a zombie. You don't have empathy with them, they're not sympathetic… everything shifts to sort of, like, "slaughter fun." It's actually quite different from the vampire thing.

JL: What are your thoughts on the Devil or demons or satanic possession?

DC: I have big problems with demons and the devil, since I don't believe in them. So, I've never dealt with anything like that in any of my films.

JL: A movie is supposed to create suspension of disbelief. I am an atheist; I am a Jew; I do not believe in Christ or the devil but, when I saw *The Exorcist* [William Friedkin, 1973] in the theater, it scared the shit out of me.

DC: *The Exorcist* was scary. It was very effective.

JL: Because it…

DC: Because it created a world that seemed real to you and they had a couple of priests in it who were characters you could identify with. The audience wants to be in the film, you know. If you haven't been able to make use of that desire as a filmmaker then you've failed. Because audiences come to the movies wanting that and if you shut them out of your movie, well, it's your fault. If you bring them into it, then, yes, you can absolutely create an ambience that is convincing. For the time of the movie the audience is living in that universe. And in that universe anything is possible. *The Exorcist* felt absolutely real and it drew you in slowly, slowly, before it started to hit you over the head. So, it was a very interesting example of suspension of disbelief.

JL: What drew you to *The Fly* [1986]? It's really about a mad scientist.

DC: I studied organic chemistry at the University of Toronto and I thought that I might be able to be like Isaac Asimov, a scientist and a writer. The fact that *The Fly* was based on some interesting and then-current hard science was what appealed to me. It wasn't magic. It wasn't supernatural. It was very physical. It was very body-oriented. And as an atheist, existentialist Jew myself, I really do think that the body is what we are, and that religion is a flight from that, fear of that…

JL: A lot of your movies deal with the human body…

DC: That's right.

JL: I thought that what happens to Jeff in *The Fly* was like a form of cancer. In fact, in a lot of your pictures, there are projections of cancer and aging…

DC: Yes, but isn't that intriguing? I mean, as you and I grow older, you can see what happens when someone, someone perhaps close to you, becomes monstrous. Monstrous in the sense that their body transforms as they age. And their mind, perhaps, starts to go in unpleasant ways. That's close-to-home monstrousness. The more fantastical a movie is, and I include demons and stuff, the further away it is from your body, from human reality.

JL: I saw *The Exorcist* with George Folsey, Jr. and Jim O'Rourke, who had been altar boys, both lapsed Catholics. It scared me, but when it was over I went home and went to sleep. Jim and George had nightmares for weeks!

DC: So, with *The Fly*, although you're not a scientist and you didn't go through the telepod, you are human and you have seen people become diseased or heard about people aging too rapidly or dying too soon. Any human in any culture can relate to what happens to the Jeff Goldblum character Seth Brundle in *The Fly*…

JL: So you don't consider him a mad scientist?

DC: No, not at all. Not at all mad. I have read fairly deeply into scientists and their life stories… They are a strange breed, but they're very human, and they're not mad at all. They're risk takers. I think most filmmakers can relate to scientists because we work with technology to create things that didn't exist before, to explore the world as we find it. Directing a movie is similar, in some ways, to a science experiment.

JL: It seems to me that all of the mad scientists and mad doctors in movies tend to illustrate the falsehood, "There are things Man is not meant to know." And you don't fuck with God's work. These films tend to be very conservative and reactionary and, although I hardly think of you as conservative or reactionary, all of the scientists in your films do end badly.

DC: Well, there's a reason for that. As George Bernard Shaw said: "Conflict is the essence of drama." It's dramatic compulsion that makes me do it. It wasn't God who made me do it!

JL: But the protagonists in your films do follow in the tradition of the scientist messing with "things he should not know."

DC: But you see it is the things that he *must* know. That's quite different…

JL: But in your films the "things he must know" end in violence and death.

DC: Yeah. Because it would not be very interesting if it didn't. That's what I mean by dramatic compulsion. It's to make it interesting and compelling for the audience.

JL: I don't think…

DC: Yes, there's a kind of an arrogance involved, but there's also a real desire to get to grips with the essence of human existence and the physical existence of Man and how that relates to the human spirit and to the human mind. My approach is more like

"Directing a movie is similar, in some ways, to a science experiment."

William Burroughs', that is to say, "Art is dangerous." Creation is a dangerous thing, but we must do it. We are compelled to do it. It is in the nature of Man to be creative. We transformed the planet as we evolved as human creatures. You don't stay out in the rain, you find shelter; you don't accept cold, you build a fire. Immediately you are not accepting the world as it is. To me that's just basic human activity. When you put this in a dramatic, scary but interesting context, you often end up with the scientist in a bad place because, in fact, a lot of scientists do end up in a bad place. Like the astronauts killed in the Space Shuttle explosion. Scientists are aware of the potential danger of exploring the things that they explore, but they feel an incredible compulsion to do so—a creative

David Cronenberg with the star of *The Fly* [1986].

compulsion and a desire for knowledge to understand the world. My movies often examine the price that is paid for that. But they're not really cautionary tales.

JL: Yes they are, David! Regardless of your intent, they are cautionary tales because they always end badly.

DC: Every medical discovery in the world has killed somebody, often a researcher or scientist…

JL: What's interesting about your version of *The Fly* is how attractive and funny and intelligent Goldblum's character is.

DC: There are many scientists who have suffered some disease by making themselves their own subject. And a way of distancing yourself from this terrible affliction that's hit you is to examine it like a scientist. To examine yourself as though you're your own patient or your own specimen.

JL: Why do we like horror films?

DC: I think it's a rehearsal for dealing with death…

JL: But that's what a rollercoaster is. A rollercoaster allows you to feel…

DC: No, no, I don't agree. You're talking to someone who has raced cars and motorcycles. Of course there's an element of "Oh my god I'm going to die,"—a good rollercoaster will give you that. And there's also the incredible sensation of speed and G forces and there's a kind of a liberating feeling in that. That's very exhilarating. It's not just a death-defying thing. As you know, if you go on a rollercoaster 20 times, you lose the fear.

JL: When you're racing a Formula One car David, there's real danger. I mean, you could flip over and die. You can really crash and burn. When you're on a rollercoaster you have all those sensations of speed and G force and falling, but you know you're safe. The theory is people go to horror films to experience that stuff, but be safe. But you don't think so?

DC: I don't think that seeing a horror film is the same as going on a rollercoaster ride. A rollercoaster ride is visceral and not meditative. A good horror film should have elements of both. A rollercoaster ride is devoid of philosophy, as far as I'm concerned.

JL: Okay, I give up. But why do people want to go see films that will terrify them?

DC: Well, they don't all. My family dentist once said to me, "Why should I go see your horror films? I have enough horror in my own life!"

Zombies

THEY WON'T STAY DEAD!

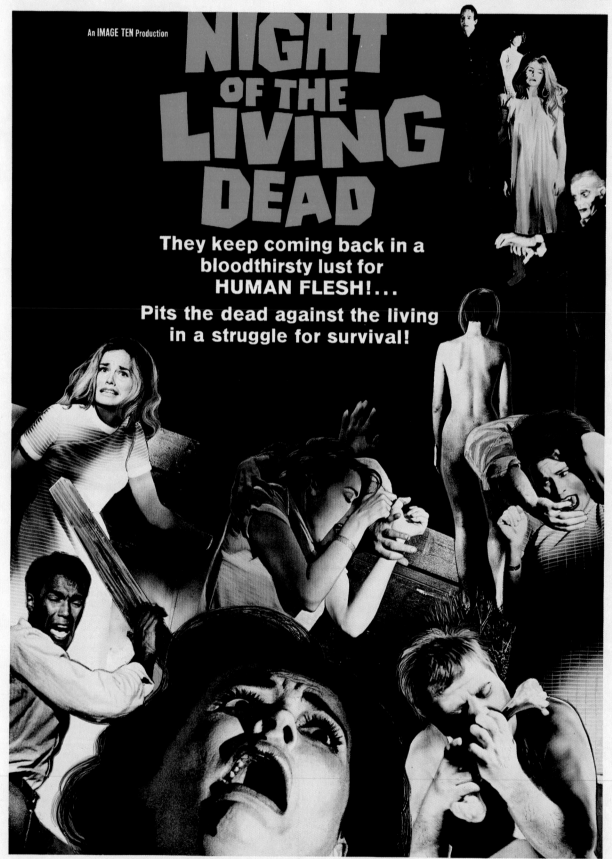

An IMAGE TEN Production

NIGHT OF THE LIVING DEAD

They keep coming back in a bloodthirsty lust for HUMAN FLESH!...

Pits the dead against the living in a struggle for survival!

Starring **JUDITH O'DEA · DUANE JONES · MARILYN EASTMAN · KARL HARDMAN · JUDITH RIDLEY · KEITH WAYNE**

Produced by Russel W. Streiner and Karl Hardman · Directed by George A. Romero · Screenplay by John A. Russo · A Walter Reade Organization Presentation — Released by Continental

68/321

Zombies

For decades, zombie movies drew on the traditional figures of Haitian Voodoo ritual. The clichéd image of a zombie was a tall, lean black man with glassy eyes. A prime example appears in *I Walked With A Zombie* [Jacques Tourneur, 1943], which is a much better movie than it sounds. Zombies were called the "Walking Dead" and they tended to shamble along. They may have been slow, but they just kept coming...

The mystical figure of Baron Samedi, Master of the Dead, a spirit (or Loa) that can be summoned by a Voodoo priest (or houngan), is always depicted wearing a top hat. Baron Samedi has been portrayed onscreen by Geoffrey Holder in the James Bond film *Live and Let Die* [Guy Hamilton, 1973] and by Don Pedro Colley in the blaxploitation/horror/gangster picture *Sugar Hill* [Paul Maslansky, 1974]. A Voodoo priestess is called a mambo (also the name of a popular Latin American dance).

In Haitian Voodoo, a houngan uses poisons and ritual burials to convince victims that they are dead. The houngan then uses their new zombies to pick sugar cane and for other menial tasks. Many claim that this practice continues today. In Voodoo and in the movies, zombies are symbols of exploitation and social decay.

Previous pages: Dawn of the Dead [aka *Zombi*, George A. Romero, **1978**] Romero's vision of the North American consumer; a fairly typical day at the mall.
Opposite page: Night of the Living Dead [George A. Romero, **1968**] Original poster for the little black and white movie from Pittsburgh, Pennsylvania that has had enormous impact on popular culture.

▲ ***Night of the Living Dead*** [George A. Romero, 1968]
On a scene still from his film, George gives me some good advice: "John—don't ever let the bastards in!"

Hammer Films' *The Plague of the Zombies* [John Gilling, 1966] places witchcraft (Voodoo)-created zombies at the center of a story of typically English class warfare, using the zombies as a menace and as slave labor.

Zombies are basically the Walking Dead. How the dead come to be walking varies. In Stuart Gordon's wild *Re-Animator* [1985], a concoction of glowing green liquid injected by syringe does the trick. In *An American Werewolf In London* [John Landis, 1981], the unfortunate lycanthrope David Kessler (David Naughton) is first visited by his increasingly decayed dead best friend Jack (Griffin Dunne), then surrounded by the gory victims of his "carnivorous lunar activities" who demand he kill himself. Apparently, when the "last remaining werewolf" is destroyed, his victims will cease being "undead." So are Jack and his companions zombies?

What about those poor unfortunates in all those movies who turn into flesh-eating crazies thanks to medical experimentation, atomic radiation, pollution, or some bizarre virus?

The term zombie has become a bit like pornography—even if we are unable to make a definitive description of exactly what a zombie is, we know a zombie when we see one!

The Spanish zombies in *Rec* [co-directed by Jaume Balagueró and Paco Plaza, 2007] or the British zombies in *Shaun of the Dead* [Edgar Wright, 2004], and *28 Days Later* [Danny Boyle, 2002] or the French zombies in *Paris by Night of the Living Dead* [Grégory Morin, 2009] and *La Horde* [Yannick Dahan, Benjamin Rocher, 2009], the New Zealand zombies in Peter Jackson's

Dead Alive [aka Braindead, 1992], and all those Italian zombies from Michele Soavi's Dellamorte Dellamore [aka Cemetery Man, 1994] to Lucio Fulci's Zombi 2 [1979] to the Japanese (I swear this is a real movie) Big Tits Zombie [Takao Nakano, 2010] to the all-American Zombie Strippers [Jay Lee, 2008], I think we can safely say that zombies are an international audience favorite.

My personal favorite zombie movie is King of the Zombies [Jean Yarbrough, 1941], a low-budget B movie from Monogram, in which the wonderful Mantan Moreland's supporting character, Jefferson "Jeff" Jackson, steals the picture as the only one who actually sees the zombies. He is then hypnotized by the villain to believe that he is a zombie, too. Once he thinks he is a zombie, his fear of the authentic zombies is replaced by feelings of camaraderie and good fellowship. Of course, when he discovers that he is not a zombie, he runs in terror from his former "brothers."

In the 1960s, movie zombies started to eat the flesh of the living, often feasting specifically on brains. In the very funny Return of the Living Dead [Dan O'Bannon, 1985] the zombies even speak! A police car is surrounded by hungry zombies who viciously attack the two cops inside and then gleefully eat their brains. The patrol car's radio crackles and a voice asks if they need assistance. One of the zombies clumsily takes the microphone and croaks, "Send more cops."

The Walking Dead is now no longer an all-encompassing term for zombies. In films like Return of the Living Dead and 28 Days Later [Danny Boyle, 2002], the zombies no longer shamble along, they can also run very fast. Assorted causes for their zombification have gone way beyond Voodoo to include atomic radiation, alien invasion, pollution, and weird Ebola-type viruses, sometimes natural, sometimes produced by the military. In Dead Alive, an outbreak of crazed, flesh-eating zombies in New Zealand is started by the bite of a "Sumatran Rat Monkey!"

In contemporary films, zombies are frequently agents of anarchy and represent the collapse of an orderly society. Films like 28 Days Later, Zombieland [Ruben Fleischer, 2009], and both versions of Dawn of the Dead [George A. Romero, 1978 and Zack Snyder, 2004], unleash berserk, flesh-eating zombies and suddenly, it's every man for himself as hordes of rotting corpses roam the streets and chaos reigns.

▲ **Live and Let Die** [Guy Hamilton, 1973]
Geoffrey Holder as Baron Samedi in this James Bond blaxploitation movie. The first time Roger Moore played Bond, James Bond.

Zombies have now evolved into modern agents of the Apocalypse. Based on a video game, the Resident Evil series of films stars Milla Jovovich as a former employee of an evil corporation who battles zombies through four movies and counting: Resident Evil [Paul W. S. Anderson, 2002], Resident Evil: Apocalypse [Alexander Witt, 2004], Resident Evil: Extinction [Russell Mulcahy, 2007], and Resident Evil: Afterlife 3D [Paul W. S. Anderson, 2010].

Maybe one of the reasons for the increasing popularity of the zombie movie is the aging population of the Western world. As the director David Cronenberg pointed out (see pages 88–9), "As we grow older, we transform into something monstrous. Our minds begin to fail us, as do our bodies themselves." Whether or not we like to admit it, we have all felt a horror of the aged and infirm. No one escapes the indignities and terrors of old age, physical decrepitude, and death. One day, the ravages of time will reduce all of us to shambling, drooling, "walking corpses" covered in lesions and clad in loose-fitting hospital robes. As Walt Kelly's brilliant comic-strip character Pogo discovered, "We have met the enemy, and he is us."

Opposite page: (1) **The Return of the Living Dead** [Dan O'Bannon, 1985] A very funny sequel to Romero's Night of the Living Dead [1968] that puts the blame for a zombie outbreak directly on the military. (2) **I Walked With a Zombie** [Jacques Tourneur, 1943]
Producer Val Lewton was given this title by RKO and told to make a movie out of it. What they got was a Voodoo version of Jane Eyre! (3) **The Omega Man** [Boris Sagal, 1971] The second film version of Richard Matheson's novel I Am Legend. Charlton Heston battles albino zombie vampires.
(4) **Shaun of the Dead** [Edgar Wright, 2004] Simon Pegg shines as he and a group of friends and loved ones deal with a zombie attack in contemporary London by seeking sanctuary at his favorite pub.

THEY'RE BACK FROM THE GRAVE AND READY TO PARTY!

THE RETURN OF THE LIVING DEAD

FEATURING MUSIC BY
T.S.O.L. • THE DAMNED • THE CRAMPS
THE JET BLACK BERRIES • 45 GRAVE
THE FLESH EATERS • SSQ • TALL BOYS

A Romantic Comedy.
With Zombies.

SHAUN OF THE DEAD

This September aim for the head.

The last man alive... is not alone!

CHARLTON HESTON THE ΩMEGA MAN

WALTER SELTZER PRODUCTION STARRING ANTHONY ZERBE • ROSALIND CASH
SCREENPLAY BY JOHN WILLIAM and JOYCE H. CORRINGTON
PRODUCED BY WALTER SELTZER DIRECTED BY BORIS SAGAL PANAVISION® TECHNICOLOR® FROM WARNER BROS. A KINNEY LEISURE SERVICE

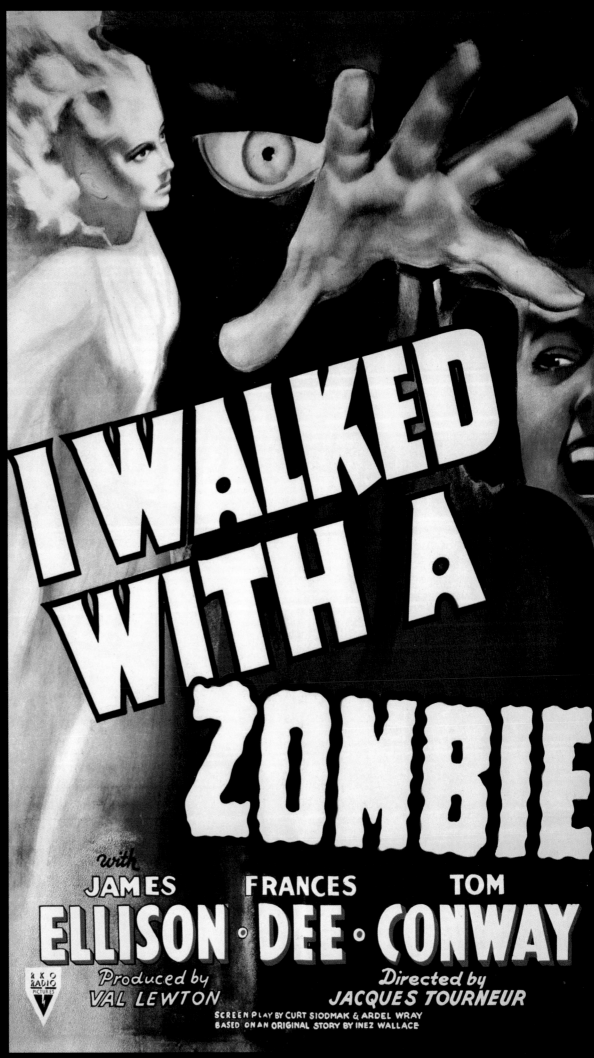

I WALKED WITH A ZOMBIE

with
JAMES ELLISON • FRANCES DEE • TOM CONWAY

RKO RADIO PICTURES

Produced by
VAL LEWTON

Directed by
JACQUES TOURNEUR

SCREEN PLAY BY CURT SIODMAK & ARDEL WRAY
BASED ON AN ORIGINAL STORY BY INEZ WALLACE

▲ *White Zombie* [Victor Halperin, 1932] Béla Lugosi as Murder Legendre, a white voodoo master on Haiti, who uses zombies as labor in his sugar cane mill. A rich plantation owner enlists Legendre's aid to help him with a sexual conquest. This is considered to be the first feature-length zombie movie.

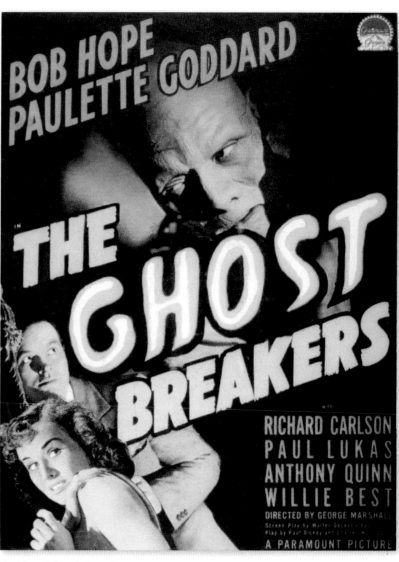

▲ *The Ghost Breakers* [George Marshall, 1940]
A Bob Hope comedy mystery with Willie Best and Bob taking turns being funny by being scared by Noble Johnson's genuinely creepy zombie. Remade by the same director as *Scared Stiff* in 1953 with Dean Martin and Jerry Lewis.

▲ *The Ghoul* [T. Hayes Hunter, 1933] Boris Karloff is the living dead in this, the first British horror film. Not really good, but an amazing cast: Karloff, Ralph Richardson, Ernest Thesiger, and Cedric Hardwicke.

▶ *I Walked With a Zombie* [Jacques Tourneur, 1943] Nurse Frances Dee with her patient and a zombie in the sugar cane field. I really don't want to tell you more, go see the movie!

▲ Revenge of the Zombies [Steve Sekely, 1943] A Monogram programmer; here we see John Carradine cower as the zombies (like the title says) get their revenge. An unusual group of racially integrated zombies for the time this movie was made.

▶ Zombies on Broadway [Gordon Dines, 1945] Béla Lugosi regards the same zombie that Frances Dee met in that sugar cane field on the Caribbean island of Saint Sebastian (see the photo below from *I Walked With a Zombie*)!

▶ Teenage Zombies [Jerry Warren, 1959] The poster's tagline—"A fiendish experiment performed with sadistic horror!"—could apply to any movie directed by Jerry Warren. Teenagers! Zombies! And a gorilla! What's not to like?

A FIENDISH EXPERIMENT PERFORMED WITH SADISTIC HORROR!

TEENAGE ZOMBIES

DON SULLIVAN KATHERINE VICTOR STEVE CONTE

PRODUCED & DIRECTED BY JERRY WARREN

◀ Zombies of Mora Tau [Edward L. Cahn, 1957] From the prolific Edward L. Cahn, a movie about a ship's crew of zombies who protect their sunken ship's treasure.

▶ The Dead One [aka *Blood of the Zombie*, Barry Mahon, 1961] Set in New Orleans. To inherit the family plantation, a woman uses Voodoo to make her brother a zombie and murder her rivals.

◀▼ The Incredibly Strange Creatures Who Stopped Living and Became Mixed-Up Zombies [Ray Dennis Steckler, 1964] Left: a photograph of one of the incredibly strange creatures who stopped living and became a mixed-up zombie. Below: the poster for this Fairway International SCHOCK Release.

▶ The Plague of the Zombies [John Gilling, 1966] Gilling's period Hammer film, with zombie slave labor being used by the upper class, is a zombie movie, of course, but like many British horror films, it is really about class.

▲ The Last Man on Earth [Ubaldo Ragona, Sidney Salkow, 1964] Shot in Rome pretending to be the USA. Vincent Price stars in the first (and most faithful) adaptation of Richard Matheson's *I Am Legend*. George A. Romero states that the zombies in this film inspired his "blue collar zombies." Released in 1964, the action takes place in the future—1968!

▲ *Sugar Hill* [Paul Maslansky, 1974] Those white gangsters should never have fooled around with a Voodoo priestess in the first place! Another AIP blaxploitation picture.

▲ *Rabid* [David Cronenberg, 1977] Zombies or vampires? Porn star Marilyn Chambers has a disturbing, penile parasite coming from her underarm. As I write this, David just finished making a movie about Freud and Jung, but you could make the argument that he's been making that movie for many years now!

▲ *Tales From the Crypt* [Freddie Francis, 1972] Peter Cushing as Arthur Grimsdyke (1907 – 1972) remembers an appointment he intends to keep. Cushing's bone structure made for an outstanding zombie (see page 307).

"If this picture doesn't make you scream and squirm, you'd better see a psychiatrist—quick!"

Trailer for *Shivers*

▲ *Shivers* [David Cronenberg, 1975] An entire apartment building's residents become sex-crazed zombies in Cronenberg's extreme situation comedy.

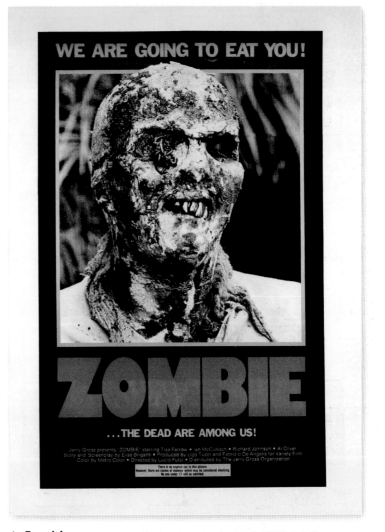

WE ARE GOING TO EAT YOU!

ZOMBIE

...THE DEAD ARE AMONG US!

Jerry Gross presents "ZOMBIE" starring Tisa Farrow • Ian McCulloch • Richard Johnson • Al Cliver
Story and Screenplay by Elisa Briganti • Produced by Ugo Tucci and Fabrizio De Angelis for Variety Film
Color by Metro Color • Directed by Lucio Fulci • Distributed by The Jerry Gross Organization

▲ *Zombie* [aka *Zombie Flesh Eaters*, Lucio Fulci, 1979] Fulci's gore fest had a terrific tagline: "We are going to eat you!" This film is infamous for the scene where a zombie pulls a woman by the hair, forcing a large wooden splinter into her eye.

▲ *Le Notti Del Terrore* [aka *Burial Ground*, **Andrea Bianchi, 1981**] Peter Bark, an adult dwarf with a bad wig, plays an adolescent boy who lusts after his mother in this grade Z Italian zombie picture. It's actually pretty funny if you're in a weird mood.

▲ *Day of the Dead* [**George A. Romero, 1985**] Sherman Howard as Bub, a zombie that seems to have some intellect and emotion. A bleak film, full of angry or psychotic characters and dead people who want to eat you.

▲ *An American Werewolf in London* [**John Landis, 1981**] Griffin Dunne as Jack Goodman does not look his best, and it will get worse. Jack is not happy being one of "the undead."

> # "Have you ever talked to a corpse? It's boring."
>
> Jack Goodman (Griffin Dunne),
> *An American Werewolf in London*

▼ *Evil Dead* [**Sam Raimi, 1981**] Raimi's very scary thrill ride. Five college students find a cabin in the woods and inside it a book called *Necronomicon Ex-Mortis*. With vines that rape and a whirling dervish, demonic POV, achieved through Sam's patented Shaky Cam. Crazy and frightening. And, oh yeah, there's this possessed girl in the cellar!

▲ *Evil Dead II* [**Sam Raimi, 1987**] Bruce Campbell suffering through whatever insane torments Sam Raimi could think of next in this reimagining of the first *Evil Dead*. This time Sam decided that instead of ripping the audience's heart out, he would tickle their funny bones. A brilliantly inventive movie—the Three Stooges do Grand Guignol!

▲ *Deadly Friend* [Wes Craven, 1986]
Kristy Swanson in the title role as a part-robot,
part-zombie avenger.

▶ *The Serpent and
the Rainbow*
[Wes Craven, 1988]
Wes went to Haiti to shoot
this adaptation of the
book by Wade Davis.
Here, Bill Pullman suffers
from chemically-induced
hallucinations. The movie
deals with Voodoo and
zombies at their source—
African and Christian
rituals mixed with drugs.

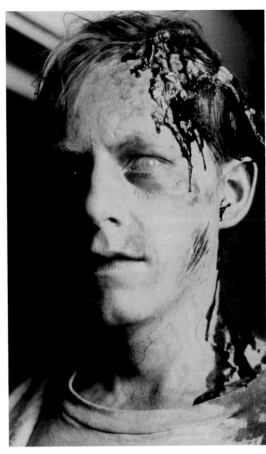

▲ *Pet Sematary* [Mary Lambert, 1989] Based
on the Stephen King novel, a variation of the
famous short story *The Monkey's Paw* by W. W.
Jacobs [1902]. Be careful what you wish for.

▶ *Michael
Jackson's Thriller*
[John Landis, 1983]
Michael surrounded
by zombies, before he
suddenly becomes
one himself! Then they
dance.

◄ Dead Alive [aka *Braindead*, Peter Jackson, 1992] Jackson's uproarious movie about zombies in Auckland is so gory it becomes Dada. With a cameo from Forrest J Ackerman.

▲ Death Becomes Her [Robert Zemeckis, 1992] A black comedy about cosmetic surgery, and our generation's fears of aging. Bruce Willis plays a doctor whose formula keeps both Meryl Streep and Goldie Hawn ambulatory long after their shelf life has expired.

"They're not dead exactly, they're just ... sort of rotting!"

Lionel Cosgrove (Timothy Balme), *Dead Alive*

▼ Army of Darkness [Sam Raimi, 1992] A demented mash-up of Mark Twain's *A Connecticut Yankee in King Arthur's Court* with the *Necronomicon Ex-Mortis*, Ray Harryhausen, and the Three Stooges! Bruce Campbell again plays Ash and, in a singularly bananas sequence, battles hundreds of little versions of himself. A surreal, nightmarish, and funny scene. Here, in a slapstick homage to Harryhausen, two Deadites are busy digging up more soldiers for their Army of Darkness.

▲ Cemetery Man [aka *Dellamorte Dellamore*, Michele Soavi, 1994] Anna Falchi as Rupert Everett's great love, only now she's dead and returned from the grave. An interesting story about the caretaker of a small cemetery in a small Italian town and his mentally handicapped friend who try to deal with the dead who refuse to stay in the ground.

◀ *Susan's Plan* [aka *Dying to Get Rich*, **John Landis, 1998**] Lara Flynn Boyle has a nightmare while taking a bath.

▲ *House on Haunted Hill* [William Malone, 1999] Some former residents of the House on Haunted Hill in Malone's stylish remake.

▲ *Undead* [Michael & Peter Spierig, 2005] An Australian zombie comedy. This time the zombie plague is caused by aliens.

◀ *Mortuary* [Tobe Hooper, 2005] After their father dies, the Doyle family moves into a mortuary to begin a new business and a new life. This turns out to be an extremely bad idea. From the director of *The Texas Chainsaw Massacre* [1974].

▶ *Dawn of the Dead* [Zack Snyder, 2004] A remake of the Romero classic [1978]. The living dead overwhelms an escape vehicle.

▶ *Flight of the Living Dead: Outbreak on a Plane* [Scott Thomas, 2007] Okay, I have to admit I've never seen this movie, but the title is funny. Maybe the pitch was: "Like *Snakes on a Plane*, but with zombies!"

◀ *Fido* [Andrew Currie, 2006] Billy Connolly is a zombie who becomes more than just a house pet in this Canadian comedy, set in the 1950s.

▶ *Gay Zombie* [Michael Simon, 2007] Okay, I haven't seen this one, either. Maybe the pitch was: "Like *Harry Met Sally*, only they're gay men and one of them is a zombie!"

◀ *I Am Legend* [Francis Lawrence, 2007] The third movie made based on Richard Matheson's outstanding novel *I Am Legend*. There is some terrific stuff in this film and Will Smith gives a strong performance. The realization of a Manhattan empty of people is very well done. But it all goes wrong in the third act with too many computer-animated zombies.

▲ **28 Weeks Later** [Juan Carlos Fresnadillo, 2007]
Zombification by virus... Rose Byrne is hoping that the zombie guy doesn't notice her in this sequel to Danny Boyle's *28 Days Later* [2002], which had a great opening sequence with plague-carrying monkeys.

▲ **Resident Evil: Extinction** [Russell Mulcahy, 2007] An ugly lady zombie from the third movie in the *Resident Evil* franchise. Every *Resident Evil* movie is basically Milla Jovovich kicking zombie ass. You could take random scenes from each of these films and cut them together and I don't think anyone would notice.

"Have you come in contact with... the infected?"

Scarlet (Rose Byrne), *28 Weeks Later*

▶ **Grindhouse**
[Robert Rodriguez, Quentin Tarantino, 2007] I think this is Quentin Tarantino as Lewis but I'm not sure. It definitely is someone infected with whatever it is that makes you melt! Rodriguez's wacky movie reminded me of watching those triple features on Hollywood Boulevard in the 1970s and, I believe, that was exactly his intention.

▶ **The Walking Dead**
[Frank Darabont, 2011]
One of special-effects company KNB's zombies from this popular and surprisingly graphic television series.

THE MONSTER CARRY

See page 320 for key

Sam Raimi

Sam Raimi on the set of *Drag Me to Hell* [2009].

JL: Sam, how would you define a monster?

SR: Something that represents our deepest, darkest fears in a physical form—for the movies.

JL: Do you believe in ghosts or anything supernatural?

SR: No, but I believe there are many things that are even more fantastic, as proven by science, out in the cosmos with the Hubble telescope: How gravity and time works backwards and the sub-atomic worlds. There are so many fantastic things.

JL: But that's a sense of wonder, not fear. Those aren't physical things that can hit you on the head.

SR: No, I wish there were some good old-fashioned monsters walking around.

JL: What about human monsters, like in *Psycho* [Alfred Hitchcock, 1960] or *The Silence of the Lambs* [Jonathan Demme, 1991]?

SR: I definitely believe that they're out there. And they make the subjects of terrifying movies. It's too real for me to be involved in as a filmmaker. I get too freaked out. I think all horror moviemakers are cowards at heart, but that area really terrifies me and I don't find it entertaining to work in, even though I do love *Pyscho*.

JL: What about *The Texas Chainsaw Massacre* [Tobe Hooper, 1974]?

SR: That's so brilliant.

JL: That's about crazy people.

SR: I found it very upsetting. As a filmmaker, I couldn't get involved in a project like that—but it was masterfully directed. In many ways it was like *Psycho* because it dealt with the most disturbing and monstrous aspects of human behavior, yet it was handled by a superb storyteller. That's a very unsettling combination.

JL: Deborah [my wife, Deborah Landis] can watch and enjoy your *Evil Dead* movies [*Evil Dead*, 1981, *Evil Dead II*, 1987, and *Army of Darkness*, 1992, all directed by Sam], she can see any movie with monsters. But she refuses to watch a movie like *The Boston Strangler* [Richard Fleischer, 1968], *The Silence of the Lambs*, or *Psycho* because those people exist.

SR: I get very disturbed watching those films. They have a very deep effect on me.

JL: What about Mike Myers in *Halloween* [John Carpenter, 1978], or Freddie Krueger [in *A Nightmare on Elm Street*, Wes Craven, 1984], these unstoppable killing machines who are clearly not human?

SR: Mike Myers was sort of a combination of the two. He was a great movie monster—with the artificiality of that blank Captain Kirk mask that he had—but there was also something very real about him. He could be any one of us tipped over the edge, putting on a mask, and doing terrible things. Mike Myers was both a movie monster and real person for me.

JL: I see Mike Myers as a supernatural figure, because he's unkillable. Even when he's shot point-blank, he gets up and walks away.

SR: You're right. That is how Carpenter presents him: as a ghost. In the beginning of the movie he's just this unbalanced guy...

JL: He's escaped from a lunatic asylum.

SR: And by the end he has supernatural powers. He's everywhere.

JL: What are some of your favorite monster movies?

SR: I really like *King Kong* [Merian C. Cooper, Ernest B. Schoedsack, 1933]; I think that's a great monster movie. I love the fact that the monster has a soul, because it really makes it rich and emotional—very deep. I'm a big fan of your movie, *An American Werewolf in London* [1981]. It's funny, it's scary, and it has a great love story. I like it when movies have a few different elements and they all work. It's hard to orchestrate that, but I like it when movies are rich and they have a lot of dimensions to them.

JL: In *King Kong* and *American Werewolf* both the leads are victims. They're sympathetic, even though they're the monsters.

SR: They are, and both films have tragic endings. The monster had a soul and it dies. It scared you, but you felt for him.

JL: What about Frankenstein's Monster?

SR: It's the same exact thing. I love Karloff's Frankenstein—James Whale's *Frankenstein* [1931]— and I loved *The Bride of Frankenstein* [James Whale, 1935] even more.

JL: Yeah, Doctor Pretorius is my favorite mad scientist of all mad scientists. What about *The Wolf Man* [George Waggner, 1941]?

SR: I liked *The Wolf Man* very much, and Lon Chaney, Jr. gave a great performance.

JL: Larry Talbot was another victim. What about Ray Harryhausen's creatures?

SR: Those are some of my favorite monsters of all time! I was very influenced by *Jason and the Argonauts* [Don Chaffey, 1963]. Every Harryhausen set piece in that film was absolutely brilliant. I love the skeletons that attack Jason. To this day, my mind boggles that Harryhausen could control and plot the movements of seven skeletons.

JL: And without video playback.

SR: Yes! How did he keep track, three seconds into a shot, on frame number 85, where skeleton number six was swinging his blade, and how fast he should be moving?

JL: It took him months to animate those three minutes. And you paid homage to that sequence in *Army of Darkness*. What's your favorite Harryhausen monster?

SR: Wow. I think Talos, (the bronze giant in *Jason and the Argonauts*). He might be the most frightening thing I've ever seen in the movies. I love (composer) Bernard Herrmann's music and those horrible groans of metal when the monster turns his head.

JL: The sound effects are incredible.

SR: And the way that Harryhausen limited Talos' ability to move. When he comes to life so slowly, it's awful!

JL: It's interesting that Talos has no expression. He's a bronze statue. He never changes, but the emotion conveyed when Jason and his men pull that hatch out of his heel and his lifeblood pours out…

SR: Yeah, you feel almost sorry for the guy. Almost. One of my favorite monsters, in the vein of Talos, is Gort [the robot in *The Day the Earth Stood Still*, Robert Wise, 1951]. Another faceless creature.

JL: Did you see that movie on television, or in the theater?

SR: I saw it at Camp Tamakwa, in Algonquin Park, Canada. They would show old 16mm prints, and they got that for a Saturday night.

JL: How old were you?

SR: I was probably 15 years old. It was great because you'd see the reel changes. The projector would run out and you'd have to wait for the second reel to be put up. It really gave you an appreciation of this being a film. I don't mind reel breaks because they give you time to think about what you just saw. It's like: "Oh, that was just an illusion but it was so powerful! I wonder what they're going to do next?"

JL: In your picture *Evil Dead*, isn't there a witch, possessed by demons?

SR: That's right. Evil spirits get inside the kids and possess them.

JL: Do you believe in God or the Devil?

SR: I don't believe in the Devil, but I do believe in a form of God.

JL: Some kind of higher intelligence?

SR: Some cosmic intelligence, yeah.

JL: You do this great thing in *Evil Dead II*— which is one of my favorite movies—where you make the action completely insane, just ridiculous, and it totally works! Like that sequence with Ash and his hand; it's a cartoon! It's totally insane, but it also makes you believe that Bruce's hand (Bruce Campbell, who plays Ash) has a complete will of its own.

SR: Thanks!

JL: You also did something in *Drag Me to Hell* [2009] that made me laugh so hard because it was so damn silly and out of left field.

SR: What?

JL: The anvil gag in the garage.

SR: Oh, that Roadrunner bit, yeah.

JL: It was like, "Who keeps an anvil suspended on ropes in their garage?" I thought, "Sam knows that's nuts. He did it deliberately."

SR: I did it for you!

JL: That was so funny. It really made me laugh.

SR: Thanks, man. That's very kind of you. Making you laugh is a big, big deal to me. (Laughs.)

JL: There was also one jump scare really got me in that film.

SR: When the witch (played by Lorna Raver) is in the back seat of the car?

JL: No, when the scary old lady appeared on Alison Lohman's cell phone. That really worked! I'm a good audience because I'm a sucker, but also, that gag was so very unexpected but completely plausible.

"I made *Evil Dead* just to break into the business…"

SR: I think one of the best scares I've ever seen was in *American Werewolf*. It was the dream within a dream; it was so powerful. I just shrieked and jumped out of my seat!

JL: I was inspired by Luis Buñuel's *The Discreet Charm of the Bourgeoisie* [1972]. That movie goes along for quite some time with this one character, and then he wakes up! So everything we just watched was a dream, but then someone else wakes up! And so on. Buñuel keeps surprising and confusing you. You think: "Wait a minute! His dream was in her dream. But who's dream are we in now? And is this reality or still a dream?" The dream within a dream within a dream is such a great concept. I just borrowed that and created a jump scare out of it.

SR: I remember the collective shriek in the theater when I saw *American Werewolf*, and I remember great roars of laughter, back and forth, back and forth.

JL: Well you do exactly that, Sam. You've had great success with that, too! Okay, now I have another question: Why are zombies so popular right now?

SR: I love George A. Romero! *Night of the Living Dead* [1968] was a big influence on me. At the time, that was the scariest movie that I had ever seen and it freaked me out. Romero shows us how to take the walking dead and one little house, and make a whole movie for no money. He's the one that gave me the formula for the *Evil Dead* movie.

JL: *Night of the Living Dead* had almost a documentary quality. Most fantasy films are set in a fantasy place. *The Wolf Man* was made in 1941, at the height of World War II. It takes place in England during the war and there are horses and carriages and no mention of the Nazis or German bombings! It was filmed on the back lot of Universal—it's like, where the fuck is this place?

SR: *Night of the Living Dead* had a docu-horror feel. It took place in our real world.

JL: Exactly. George A. Romero's zombies weren't big black guys with staring white eyes. They were ordinary folks. George calls them "Blue Collar Zombies." He had real people eating human flesh!

SR: Oh that bit is awful—the cannibalism.

JL: Politically, the movie was so smart.

SR: And the protagonist was expendable. When that first zombie attacks the girl, it was like, "No, wait! I'm following that girl! Anything can happen here! What's with this filmmaker?" You're in unstable hands once that's happened.

JL: Hitchcock did exactly that in *Psycho*. The movie is about Marion Crane, who is played by a movie star, Janet Leigh. We're in her story for 30 minutes and then she's brutally murdered and suddenly it's about Norman Bates! At the time it was very shocking for the audience.

SR: Plus in *Night of the Living Dead*, I had never seen a movie with a black male lead alone in a cabin with a white woman before. That probably created a bit of extra tension in the audience, whether they knew it or not. Social tension.

JL: I think the gore had a bigger impact on the audience than the subtleties of the politics. Although the irony of the ending is hard to miss. Anyway, Sam, you're associated with monsters and fantasy, but I get the feeling you're not that big a fan of the genre!

SR: Well, I made *Evil Dead* just to break into the business, not because I was a horror movie fan. I had not liked horror movies up until that point because they scared me so badly! My friend Rob Tapert [producer of *Evil Dead*] told me: "We can probably only raise about $100,000, and the only kind of movies that are made for that little are these cheap Italian horror movies for the drive-in. Can you make a horror movie?'

JL: We all started in exploitation—me, you, Francis Ford Coppola, Joe Dante—there is a long list. You knew that it didn't matter how bad the movie was, if there's a monster in it you could get it distributed.

Ghosts

Ghosts

The easiest Halloween costume to make is that of a ghost—all you need is a white bed sheet over your head. I suppose this comes from the custom of wrapping a corpse in a winding sheet. Certainly, pulling a sheet over a patient's face is a clear signal that the doctors have given up!

People who have lost loved ones are easy prey for "mediums" that claim they can communicate with those who, as Hamlet said, "shuffle off this mortal coil." The great magician Harry Houdini, devastated by the death of his mother, attended enough séances to be appalled by the blatant tricks and scams mediums used to convince people of their special skills in contacting the "dear departed."

The outrageous medium, Madame Arcati (Margaret Rutherford) in David Lean's movie of Noel Coward's comedy *Blithe Spirit* [1945] is not so far away from the medium depicted in Sam Raimi's *Drag Me To Hell* [2009]. Both summon up the spirits of the deceased and both are unable to control the spirits they summon.

Ghosts are literally the spirits of the dead. They can manifest themselves in many ways. And every way you can imagine a ghost to manifest itself has been exploited in the movies. *The Uninvited* [Lewis Allen, 1944] begins with

▲ **The Ghost of Banquo** by **Théodore Chassériau [1819-1856]** depicts the scene in William Shakespeare's *Macbeth* at the banquet when only Macbeth can see the ghost of the murdered Banquo.

Ray Milland's narration, "They call them the haunted shores, these stretches of Devonshire and Cornwall and Ireland which rear up against the westward ocean. Mists gather here, and sea fog, and eerie stories. That's not because there are more ghosts here than in other places, mind you. It's just that people who live hereabouts are strangely aware of them." Disregarding his own voice-over, Ray and his sister, played by Ruth Hussey, buy an empty house on a cliff overlooking the sea. While they wander around looking into the rooms, their terrier Bobby refuses to go up the stairs to the second floor. One room smells "like mimosa" and Ruth casually puts down the bunch of flowers she has just picked. Ray and Ruth do not notice, but we are shown the flowers quickly wilt and die. Suffice to say, the house is haunted. *The Uninvited* is romantic and frightening. It's also one of the few pictures to clearly show the ghost that still manages to keep us in suspense. I recommend that you see it.

Poltergeists are spirits that cause a physical disturbance, either by making loud noises, tossing objects around, or actually attacking people. In *Poltergeist* [Tobe Hooper, 1982], the spirits of long-dead Native Americans, whose burial ground has been built over by a housing development, make it very clear that they are unhappy with the situation. In *The Entity* [Sidney J. Furie, 1982] Barbara Hershey is repeatedly raped by an unseen force.

In *The Shining* [Stanley Kubrick, 1980], an isolated hotel with a murderous past slowly drives its winter caretaker, a writer named Jack Torrance, mad. Jack Nicholson's intense performance as Torrance is scarier than the

Previous pages: The Devil's Backbone [Guillermo Del Toro, 2001] An orphanage during the time of the Spanish Civil War is haunted in Del Toro's wonderful ghost story.
Opposite page: Henry Robin and a Specter [1863] A man about to shoot himself is confronted by his own ghost in this photomontage by Thiébault.

ghosts Kubrick shows us. The most frightening moment in the film is when Jack's wife Wendy, played by Shelley Duvall, looks at the pages he has been working on in the typewriter. All she sees are the words "All work and no play makes Jack a dull boy," neatly typed, over and over and over again.

Many films center around a team of researchers investigating a supposed haunted house, with unpredictable, but always spooky, results. *The Haunting* [1963], Robert Wise's movie version of Shirley Jackson's classic ghost story "The Haunting of Hill House" creates unbelievable tension by showing us nothing. Jan de Bont's terrible remake [*The Haunting*, 1999] does not scare us because it shows us way too much. Another team of paranormal investigators attempt to unravel *The Legend of Hell House* [John Hough, 1973], which Richard Matheson adapted from his own novel. Matheson and Hough craft a rip-roaring shocker with an unexpected ending.

Perhaps the best known haunted house franchise in movie history began with *The Amityville Horror* [Stuart Rosenberg, 1979], a supposedly true story about a house on Long Island. The poster declared, "FOR GOD'S SAKE, GET OUT!" So far the movie has spawned eight sequels and a remake, so clearly no one has taken this warning seriously.

Movie ghosts aren't always out to terrify or destroy. Phantoms of a far gentler disposition feature in *Casper* [Brad Silberling, 1995], a live-action movie (albeit with computer-animated ghosts) based on the *Casper the Friendly Ghost* comic books and cartoons. In the comedy

▲ **The Shining** [Stanley Kubrick, 1980]
Jack Nicholson as Jack Torrance, driven insane by the ghosts of Overlook Hotel, breaks down the door in an attempt to kill his wife and child. Based on the novel by Stephen King.

Topper [Norman Z. McLeod, 1937] the ghosts are not only friendly but, as played by Constance Bennett and Cary Grant, handsome, glamorous, and fun.

The Innocents [1961], Jack Clayton's elegant adaptation of Henry James' novella *The Turn of the Screw*, features a very fine performance from Deborah Kerr as the governess who fears for her sanity, and superb use of deep focus in gleaming black and white CinemaScope by director of photography Freddie Francis. When Deborah Kerr is kissed on the lips by Miles (Martin Stephens), the little boy she is supposed to be looking after, I defy you not to get the creeps.

Set during the Spanish Civil War in the 1930s, *The Devil's Backbone* [Guillermo Del Toro, 2001] is the tale of a haunted orphanage. This is the first in Del Toro's trilogy of fantastic tales set during that period (the second is *Pan's Labyrinth*, 2006; the third is yet to come). *The Devil's Backbone* is a straightforward ghost story. The surprise discovery at the end of the film is who is telling the tale!

We have had sad ghosts, vengeful ghosts, mischievous ghosts, evil ghosts, and loving ghosts, but my favorite ghosts appear in the beautiful Japanese film *Kwaidan* [Masaki Kobayashi, 1964]. The title translates literally as "Ghost Story." Based on Japanese folk tales collected by Lafcadio Hearn, the film comprises four, unrelated stories. With magnificent production and costume design, the film is a visual delight with moments of real terror. My two favorite stories are "Hoichi, the Earless" and "In a Cup of Tea." A magnificent and (I've got to say it), *haunting* film.

Opposite Page: (1) *The Innocents* [Jack Clayton, 1961] Deborah Kerr as Miss Giddings, the governess. Beautifully photographed by Freddie Francis, this is one of the best ghost movies ever made.

(2) *The Orphanage* [Juan Antonio Bayona, 2007] Another disturbing ghost story, set in an orphanage in Spain. Produced by Guillermo Del Toro.

(3) *The Uninvited* [Lewis Allen, 1944] After watching this film, you will never smell mimosa again without looking anxiously over your shoulder.

◀ *Topper*
[Norman Z. McLeod, 1937] Cary Grant and Constance Bennett as the ghosts of George and Marion Kerby, killed in a car accident. This delightful comedy also stars Roland Young as Cosmo Topper, the only person who can see or hear them. Based on the novel by Thorne Smith.

▶ *Liliom*
[Fritz Lang, 1933] "God's Police" come to take Charles Boyer to heaven to face judgment in Lang's only French film. Based on the play by Ferenc Molnár.

GENE TIERNEY
REX HARRISON
GEORGE SANDERS
The Ghost and Mrs. Muir
EDNA BEST · VANESSA BROWN · ANNA LEE
ROBERT COOTE · NATALIE WOOD · ISABEL ELSOM · VICTORIA HORNE
20th CENTURY-FOX TRIUMPH!
JOSEPH L. MANKIEWICZ
FRED KOHLMAR

▶ *House on Haunted Hill*
[William Castle, 1959] Millionaire Vincent Price and his fourth wife invite five people to spend the night; those alive in the morning will receive $10,000 each. The entertaining 1999 remake, directed by William Malone is great fun and features a witty performance by Geoffrey Rush doing his best Vincent Price.

◀ *The Ghost and Mrs. Muir*
[Joseph L. Mankiewicz, 1947] This romantic comedy has a very strange happy ending. When Gene Tierney grows old and dies, she can finally be united with the ghost of Rex Harrison's dashing sea captain!

▲ The Canterville Ghost
[**Jules Dassin, 1944**] Based on a short story by Oscar Wilde. Charles Laughton hams it up in the title role.

A Christmas Carol by Charles Dickens was published on December 17th, 1843 and television has broadcast some version of his story about miser Ebenezer Scrooge and his visitations by the Ghosts of Christmas Past, Present, and Yet to Come every December since 1949. "And God bless Tiny Tim!"

▲ A Christmas Carol
[**Edwin L. Marin, 1938**]
Reginald Owen as Scrooge is confronted by the ghost of his former business partner Jacob Marley, played by Leo G. Carroll.

▲ A Christmas Carol [aka *Scrooge*, **Brian Desmond Hurst, 1951**] Alastair Sim as Scrooge is shown his own grave by the Ghost of Christmases Yet to Come.

▲ Scrooge [**Ronald Neame, 1970**] Albert Finney's Scrooge is confronted by Death in this musical version. A great cast cannot overcome the terrible songs (with the exception of "Thank You Very Much," sung by a fellow dancing on Scrooge's coffin).

▶ The Muppet Christmas Carol
[**Brian Henson, 1992**]
A surprisingly faithful adaptation with Michael Caine as a first-rate Scrooge.

▲ From Beyond the Grave [**Kevin Connor, 1973**]
An anthology horror film from Amicus and producer Milton Subotsky. Peter Cushing runs an antique shop called Temptations Ltd., and woe to those who enter. Here, Ian Bannen already regrets his purchase.

◀ Scrooged
[**Richard Donner, 1988**] A modern comedy take on Dickens' story. Pictured here are Bill Murray as selfish TV exec Frank Cross with David Johansen of the New York Dolls as a New York Cab Driver Ghost of Christmas Past.

◀ The Haunting
[Robert Wise, 1963]
Claire Bloom and Julie Harris react to the very loud sounds made by "something" in the hallway outside their bedroom door in this Robert Wise classic.

▶ Halloween
[John Carpenter, 1978]
Michael Myers disguised as a ghost in John Carpenter's influential slasher film. Carpenter also wrote Halloween's much-imitated score. Is Michael Myers, in fact, a ghost himself? (See pages 240–1.)

"It was an evil house from the beginning —a house that was born bad."

Dr. John Markway (Richard Johnson), The Haunting

▲ Kwaidan [Masaki Kobayashi, 1964] Kwaidan means "ghost story" in Japanese, and this beautiful anthology film is comprised of four Japanese folk tales compiled by Lafcadio Hearn. Pictured is "Hoichi the Earless," a blind musician who has an intense and agonizing encounter with the ghostly subjects of his songs.

▶ Ghostbusters II
[Ivan Reitman, 1989] The sequel to Reitman's blockbuster comedy Ghostbusters [1984]. Co-scripter Dan Aykroyd (with Harold Ramis) originally conceived the premise as a vehicle for himself and close friend John Belushi. Both movies have rousing scores by Elmer Bernstein [Ghostbusters] and Randy Edelman [Ghostbusters II].

◀ Beetlejuice [Tim Burton, 1988] Michael Keaton in the title role is hilarious in Tim Burton's imaginative supernatural comedy.

◄ The Fog
[John Carpenter, 1980]
In this good-old-fashioned spook story, the ghosts of a ship's crew, deliberately shipwrecked off the coast of a small town 100 years ago, return to exact their revenge. The phantoms emerge from a supernatural fogbank.

▼▶ The Shining
[Stanley Kubrick, 1980]
The creepy, twin little-girl ghosts and a vision of the grisly way they died. Stephen King was dissatisfied with Kubrick's film of his book and wrote the teleplay for the TV mini-series version, directed by Mick Garris in 1997.

▲ The Amityville Horror [Stuart Rosenberg, 1979]
Based on the best selling "true story" about a haunted house in Long Island, New York, *The Amityville Horror* was sold with the wonderful tagline, "FOR GOD'S SAKE, GET OUT!"

▲ Poltergeist [Tobe Hooper, 1982]
Steven Spielberg produced this all-American suburban ghost story. JoBeth Williams' initial delight at invisibly moving kitchen chairs turns to terror when her daughter stares into a television showing nothing but static and announces, "They're here."

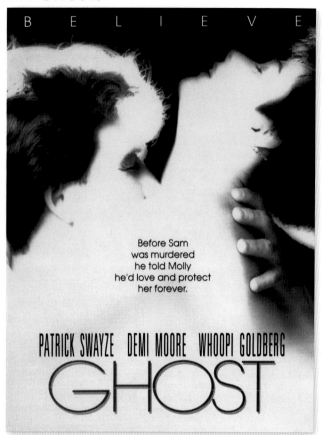

BELIEVE

Before Sam was murdered he told Molly he'd love and protect her forever.

PATRICK SWAYZE   DEMI MOORE   WHOOPI GOLDBERG

GHOST

▲ *Ghost* [Jerry Zucker, 1990] The ghost of Patrick Swayze uses fake medium Whoopi Goldberg to warn his widow Demi Moore of danger. This silly romantic movie was a tremendous box-office success.

"I see dead people."

Cole Sear (Haley Joel Osment), *The Sixth Sense*

▲ *The Sixth Sense* [M. Night Shyamalan, 1999] Moving performances from Haley Joel Osment, Bruce Willis, and Toni Collette help make this clever tale of a little boy who can communicate with the dead so powerful.

▶ *The Changeling* [Peter Medak, 1980] George C. Scott, Melvyn Douglas, and Trish Van Devere are terrific in Medak's shivery ghost story set in Seattle. Supposedly based on screenwriter Russell Hunter's true experiences living in an old mansion in Denver, Colorado.

"How did you die, Joseph? Did you die in this house? Why do you remain?"

THE CHANGELING

GEORGE C. SCOTT · TRISH VAN DEVERE
THE CHANGELING
MELVYN DOUGLAS · JOHN COLICOS · JEAN MARSH · RUSSELL HUNTER
WILLIAM GRAY & DIANA MADDOX
JOEL B. MICHAELS and GARTH H. DRABINSKY · PETER MEDAK

◀ *The Ring* [Gore Verbinski, 2002] The American remake of a 1998 Japanese movie based on Kôji Suzuki's novel *Ring*. Naomi Watts stars in the story of a cursed video tape that dooms all who watch it.

◀ *Sleepy Hollow* [Tim Burton, 1999] Johnny Depp stars in Burton's take on the famous short story "The Legend of Sleepy Hollow" by Washington Irving.

▲ *Paranormal Activity* [Oren Peli, 2007] Shot in seven days for very little money in his own home by writer/director Oren Peli; this film clearly demonstrates that sometimes less is more. An intensely scary experience, *Paranormal Activity* is a real crowd-pleaser.

▲ *Pirates of the Caribbean: The Curse of the Black Pearl*
[Gore Verbinski, 2003] The first of the hugely successful franchise based on the ride at Disneyland. Pictured is Geoffrey Rush as Hector Barbossa, the captain of a crew of ghostly pirates.

▲ *Ju-on* [aka *The Grudge*, Takashi Shimizu, 2003] Shimizu also directed the American remake of his own film which, for me, was not as scary or ethereal as his original. The *Ju-on* series began with two direct-to-video films that evolved into both Japanese and American theatrical movies.

▶ *The Grudge 2* [Takashi Shimizu, 2006] Shimizu's American remake of his own Japanese film stars Sarah Michelle Geller. She brings the curse from the first movie, created by a murdered housewife in Nerima, Japan, to Chicago, Illinois.

121

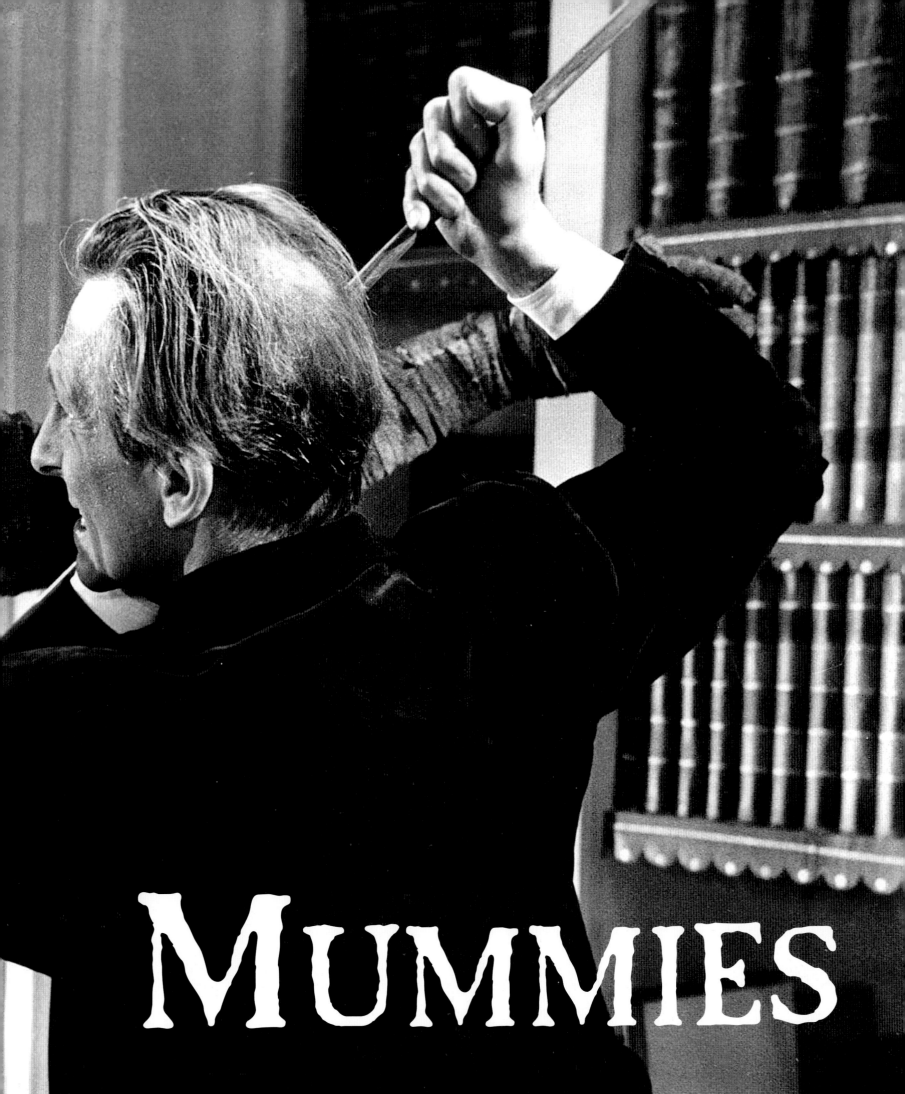

Mummies

MUMMIES

In 1922, archeologist Howard Carter's expedition discovered the tomb of Tutankhamun in Egypt. The fabulous treasures of "King Tut's Tomb" created a worldwide sensation and renewed the public's fascination with ancient Egypt.

Universal Studios's tremendous success with *Frankenstein* [1931] and *Dracula* [1931] had them looking for a third Universal Monster to exploit. They settled on *The Mummy* [Karl Freund, 1932], yet another story about a living corpse. Universal even used the same music for the opening credits of *The Mummy* as they did for *Dracula*, Tchaikovsky's *Swan Lake*!

Boris Karloff again sat patiently while make-up man Jack Pierce created yet another classic monster. Using cotton, collodion, clay, and spirit gum on Karloff's face and hands, Pierce then wrapped him in singed linen bandages and coated it all with dust. Karloff only had to go through this once (the Mummy only appears in one memorable scene in his burial dressing), but he referred to this make-up as the worst and "most trying day" he had ever endured on a movie. The film is a romance, with Karloff's priest Imhotep being mummified and buried alive for daring to fall in love with the Princess Ankh-es-en-amon. Centuries later, his sarcophagus is discovered and opened. When one of the archeologists reads aloud from the life-giving Scroll of Thoth, the Mummy Imhotep awakens, in one of the great moments in fantasy cinema. The terrified archeologist (Bramwell Fletcher) can only scream and say, "He went for a little walk."

▲ *Christopher Lee* as Kharis *The Mummy* [Terence Fisher, 1959], after he's been shot, but before he's impaled.

The Universal *Mummy* sequels became increasingly silly, as the Mummy (now called Kharis) became just a shuffling automaton. And now it could be anyone under those bandages—Lon Chaney, Jr., Tom Tyler, and stunt man Eddie Parker all took turns as Kharis.

In the late 1950s, the then-booming Mexican film industry started to produce its own Mummy movies—Aztec Mummy movies. Meanwhile, the UK's Hammer Films bought the rights to Universal's *Mummy* and made their own *The Mummy* [Terence Fisher, 1959] with Christopher Lee in the title role.

Stephen Sommers' big-budget remake of *The Mummy* [1999] was heavy on the CG and an international hit. It, too, spawned sequels, one of which, *Tomb of the Dragon Emperor* [Rob Cohen, 2008] was shot in China and brought us action hero Jet Li as the mummified first Emperor of China.

None of the many Mummy films produced since the Universal original have captured the sense of love and sorrow, dignity and decay of Karloff's performance.

My vote for the best, non-Karloff Mummy movie goes to Don Coscarelli's wonderfully insane *Bubba Ho-tep* [2002]. Based on the novella by Joe R. Lansdale, it tells the story of what really happened to Elvis Presley. It features an ancient Mummy that sucks the souls from his victims in a rude way, as well as fantastic performances from Bruce Campbell and Ossie Davis. The movie breathes fresh life into what had become a tired concept.

"My love has lasted longer than the temples of our gods. No man ever suffered as I did for you!"

Imhotep (Boris Karloff), *The Mummy*

▲ *The Mummy* [Karl Freund, 1932] Boris Karloff with Zita Johann in a trance as the reincarnation of his lost love, the ancient Princess Ankh-es-en-amon.

▼ *The Mummy's Ghost* [Reginald Le Borg, 1944] The second time Lon Chaney, Jr. played Kharis the Mummy.

◄ *The Mummy's Curse* [Leslie Goodwins, 1944] Lon Chaney, Jr. wears the wrappings and drags his foot as Kharis for the last time.

NEW THRILLS! NEW TERROR!

LON CHANEY

THE **MUMMY'S CURSE**

PETER COE   KAY HARDING
MARTIN KOSLECK   VIRGINIA CHRISTINE
KURT KATCH

◄ *Curse of the Faceless Man* [Edward L. Cahn, 1958] A petrified gladiator is found in the ruins of Pompeii and soon "something" starts killing people. Could this man of stone still be alive? What do you think?

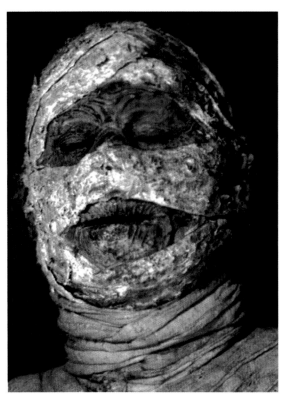

◀ *Abbott and Costello Meet the Mummy* [Charles Lamont, 1955] Veteran Hollywood stunt man Eddie Parker plays Klaris the Mummy in this, the 28th and last film Abbott and Costello made for Universal Pictures.

▶ *The Mummy* [Terence Fisher, 1959] The American poster for Hammer Films' "All New! In Technicolor" version of *The Mummy*.

NERVE-SHATTERING SHOCK!

THE MUMMY

ALL NEW! in TECHNICOLOR

PETER CUSHING · CHRISTOPHER LEE
YVONNE FURNEAUX   Directed by TERENCE FISHER

Screenplay by JIMMY SANGSTER · MICHAEL CARRERAS · ANTHONY NELSON KEYS
A HAMMER FILM PRODUCTION
A UNIVERSAL INTERNATIONAL RELEASE

▲ *The Curse of the Mummy's Tomb*
[Michael Carreras, 1964] Actor Fred Clark had great fun playing American showman Alexander King, who wants to exhibit the newly discovered Egyptian Mummy Ra-Antef (played by Dickie Owen).

▶ *The Mummy's Shroud* [John Gilling, 1967] Christopher Lee's regular stunt double Eddie Powell played the Mummy this time.

127

◀ *Blood From the Mummy's Tomb* [Seth Holt, 1971] Valerie Leon, in the dual role of Margaret Fuchs and the ancient Egyptian Queen Tera, poses with her sarcophagus in yet another Hammer Mummy movie featuring reincarnation.

▲ *The Monster Squad* [Fred Dekker, 1987] A fun and "family friendly" mash-up of all the classic Universal monsters; Dracula, the Wolf Man, the Frankenstein Monster, the Gill-man, and the Mummy were all redesigned so as not to infringe on the copyrighted make-up designs. The Mummy was played by an extremely thin Michael MacKay.

"Death is only

▲ *Bubba Ho-tep* [Don Coscarelli, 2002] The true story of what really happened to Elvis Presley. The Mummy was played by Bob Ivy. Bruce Campbell as Elvis and Ossie Davis as President John F. Kennedy are both outstanding.

▲ *The Mummy Returns* [**Stephen Sommers, 2001**] Rachel Weisz, as Evelyn O'Connell, screams at a mummy.

the beginning"

Imhotep (Arnold Vosloo), *The Mummy*

▶ *The Mummy* [**Stephen Sommers, 1999**] In this Universal Studios' remake "Ardeth Bay" (Oded Fehr) is a separate character from the Mummy. The Mummy, High Priest Imhotep, was played by Arnold Vosloo and a lot of very expensive CG done by the folks at George Lucas's Industrial Light & Magic.

▲ *The Mummy: Tomb of the Dragon Emperor* [**Rob Cohen, 2008**] Brendan Fraser's character Rick O'Connell's third Mummy adventure, this time in China. Jet Li's eyes are staring out of the Mummy face of Chinese Emperor Han.

Guillermo Del Toro

Guillermo Del Toro wearing the hand of Hellboy on the set of *Hellboy II: The Golden Army* [2008].

JL: Guillermo, how would you define a monster?

GDT: A freak of nature. Something that is unnatural. I think the difference between a monster and every other thing in horror is that the monster is a biological entity, it's alive.

JL: What about a ghost?

GDT: A ghost is not a monster.

JL: What about a monster's ghost? What about a ghost that kills people? You're saying monsters have to be physical beings?

GDT: Or beings that come out of nature. They can be related to physics, like the Monster from the Id [in *Forbidden Planet*, Fred M. Wilcox 1956]. The Id is a monster.

JL: What about Frankenstein's Monster?

GDT: Yes, Frankenstein created a monster.

JL: What about zombies?

GDT: Zombies would be monsters. Monsters have to be physical in some way.

JL: So, would Sissy Spacek in *Carrie* [Brian De Palma, 1976] be a monster?

GDT: I don't think *Carrie* is a monster movie; it's a horror movie.

JL: Aha! Are there any monsters in David Cronenberg's movies?

GDT: The only Cronenberg monster movies are *The Fly* [1986] and *The Brood* [1979], because all the little freaks are monsters. And, to some extent, *Rabid* [1977], because the Marilyn Chambers character becomes a vampire monster. A monster is anything that can be deformed, that can be altered, but has some root in nature. Godzilla is a monster, the Gill-Man [from *Creature From the Black Lagoon*, Jack Arnold, 1954] is a monster.

JL: What about monsters from space?

GDT: They can be monsters, as long as they are physical entities.

JL: Can a robot be a monster?

GDT: I think you can have a monster robot, or a robot monster.

JL: You're like me, Del Toro, you like monsters.

GDT: Yeah, I love them.

JL: You grew up in Guadalajara. What were your favorite monsters, as a child?

GDT: Frankenstein's creature—the Boris Karloff version [1931]—The Gill-Man, and the monster in *Alien* [Ridley Scott, 1979]. In fact, these are still my favorite monsters.

JL: Why do you love the Alien monster?

GDT: Because it broke every rule about how to shoot a man in a suit. The suit was designed to break the silhouette of the man inside, and Ridley Scott had him walking on all fours, or backwards.

JL: I love that monster, but I didn't like that metallic tongue with teeth thing that came out of its mouth. It just didn't feel organic to me.

GDT: I loved that! Anyway, those are my first three. Then would come the werewolf in *The Wolf Man* [George Waggner,1941]. I used to dress up as Lon Chaney, Jr.'s Wolf Man when I was a kid. I'd go to school dressed as a wolf man! I had the Wolf Man mask, but I didn't buy the Don Post werewolf hands. I bought the gorilla hands, because they were better-looking. So I went with the gorilla hands, gorilla feet, and the werewolf mask to my secondary school.

JL: What did your parents think of that?

GDT: They let me do it! And I bought the cheap artificial hair and would put it under my checkered shirt, and the other kids beat the crap out of me! (Laughs.)

JL: What is it that you find most intriguing about werewolves?

GDT: The blackout is the most interesting part.

JL: You mean that the werewolf has no memory of what happened the night before when he changes back to being human?

GDT: Yeah, like David waking up in the zoo pen in *An American Werewolf in London* [John Landis, 1981]. And how incredibly earnestly Lon Chaney, Jr. suffered in *The Wolf Man*.

JL: Curt Siodmak (screenwriter of *The Wolf Man*) was the first to push the idea of the werewolf as a victim.

GDT: And one of the great sufferers ever is Lon Chaney, Jr. You really wanted to tell him that everything was going to be all right. What attracts me most about the Wolf Man myth was the sympathetic nature of the character.

JL: When Dr. Jekyll drinks his formula, he becomes Mr. Hyde, who is a manifestation of Jekyll's lust and bad thoughts. Whereas the werewolf is Other, it's completely not you, it's like you become this separate beast.

GDT: The Wolf Man becomes a werewolf in spite of himself.

JL: The werewolves in *The Wolf Man* and *American Werewolf* are victims; Frankenstein's monster is a victim…

GDT: The Gill-Man in some ways.

JL: He's a total victim!

GDT: Yeah. He's like King Kong in many ways.

JL: Whereas the Alien is a predator.

GDT: Yeah, but what I love about the Alien is what I love about insects: Remote perfection.

JL: How do you feel about vampires?

GDT: My favorite vampire movie is *Nosferatu*.

JL: The Murnau, [1922], or the Herzog [1979]?

GDT: Both. And I also loved Willem Dafoe in *Shadow of the Vampire* [E. Elias Merhige, 2000] and Barlow (the vampire in Tobe Hooper's *Salem's Lot*, who was made up to resemble Nosferatu, 1979). That physicality is what I like the most.

JL: Vampires live forever, as Béla Lugosi [in *Dracula*, Tod Browning, 1931] says, "To die, to really die, that would be glorious." And then there's the sexual side of vampires; there's also this weird AIDS and blood transfusion thing. What did you think of Kathryn Bigelow's *Near Dark* [1987]?

GDT: I loved it. For me, the vampire myth in the Carpathian Mountains with the castle and the cape was always very remote. It's much more interesting set in an urban or suburban environment, like *Salem's Lot* or *I Am Legend* [Francis Lawrence, 2007].

JL: What about Christopher Lee's Dracula?

GDT: I love him! He is a righteous, arrogant figure; a guy that believes he deserves everything by lineage.

JL: Exactly. John Carpenter said that Dracula is all about the European aristocracy literally feeding off everybody.

GDT: Christopher Lee's Dracula exudes entitlement. Everybody talks about how sexual his Dracula was, but I think it was just very forthright. He went for it straight.

JL: One of the reasons people talk about it being sexual is that it's only relatively recently that vampires bite great chunks out of their victims. When Lugosi's and Lee's Dracula made those polite little punctures, their victims swooned. They became orgasmic!

GDT: Yeah. The whole sexual subtext of the vampire, I'm not denying. Also there was a lot less wardrobe for the ladies in the Hammer films; they were a lot more scantily clad!

JL: OK, so what about mad scientists, mad doctors, like Dr. Moreau? *Island of Lost Souls* [Erle C. Kenton, 1932]? Have you ever seen it?

GDT: I love it! I have a homage in *Blade II* [2002]: The "House of Pain!"

JL: *Island of Lost Souls* is one of my favorite horror movies. What do you think of witches and warlocks—movies like *The Devil Rides Out* [Terence Fisher, 1968]?

GDT: I don't think those are monster movies; those are supernatural movies.

JL: Do you think ghosts are scary?

GDT: Well, I have two simple rules that define horror for me: The things that create fear are either things that shouldn't be, but are, or things that should be, but are not. I'll give you an example (of the first rule): Your father died a week ago, you walk into your house and he's sitting at the dining table, completely still. That generates fear. An example of the second rule is: The scene in *Poltergeist* [Tobe Hooper, 1982], where the woman turns around, then turns back, and all the chairs are piled up in the kitchen: that shouldn't be, but is.

JL: But you don't consider anything supernatural to be monstrous?

GDT: Like I said, I'm willing to make an exception with vampires and werewolves because they have a physical manifestation. But in traditional tales of vampires—in many, many countries—the vampire is a spirit; it doesn't have a physical body. A monster has to have physicality.

JL: But what about a demon that grabs you and causes you bodily harm? I can picture a scene where people are in a room: there are terrible sounds, the walls are bending inwards, it's getting increasingly terrifying, and they're having this same argument! (Laughs.)

GDT: Yes! I think that there are many ways a ghost can physically manifest itself, but it doesn't have a body. We're going to go by my rules! I'll tell you: Most of the time a monster has a natural or physical body that has something to do with science, or biology, gone awry.

JL: What about the character of Regan in *The Exorcist* [William Friedkin, 1973], when she's possessed by Satan?

GDT: She's not a monster!

JL: Isn't Satan a monster?

GDT: No, he's a spirit! He's a spiritual entity.

JL: What about gnomes, or fairies, or elves, or leprechauns?

GDT: They're not monsters. Not for me.

JL: But they have physical bodies!

GDT: They are not monsters; they come from a completely different lore.

"Horror films are a rollercoaster of the soul."

JL: OK, well, now that you've destroyed half of my book, I'm going to go ahead and call them monsters anyway! Let's talk about *Psycho* [Alfred Hitchcock, 1960] and *The Texas Chainsaw Massacre* [Tobe Hooper, 1974], *Peeping Tom* [Michael Powell, 1960], movies like that.

GDT: Yeah, those are about psychopaths. Are they in your book?

JL: Psychopaths are *human* monsters! They're the only monsters that scare me. I'm not really scared by any monster in a movie, any monster as you define them, or any monster as I'm broadly defining them: Werewolves, vampires, they don't scare me; they do not exist. But people are crazy, they do terrible things, and they scare the shit out of me!

GDT: Has there ever been a monster movie that scared you?

JL: While actually watching the movie—absolutely! I'm a great audience, a real sucker for the sudden "BOO!" I've always maintained that *The Exorcist* is the greatest horror film because, although I don't believe in Jesus or Satan, during the course of the film I was scared.

GDT: *Alien* must have scared you.

JL: Actually, when I saw it the first time, I kept thinking: "This is a remake of *It! The Terror From Beyond Space* [Edward L. Cahn 1958]" and *Planet of the Vampires* [Mario Bava, 1965]! It was like a haunted house movie in space. But it's beautifully made. I love the scene with John Hurt… you know, the chest-burster?

GDT: Yeah.

JL: What made that scene work, isn't the chest-burster itself—that's kind of a dumb-looking puppet—but the moment when it actually bursts out of him—the horror on the actors' faces, their reactions, are so real. But I think *Aliens* [James Cameron, 1986] is a better movie than *Alien*. It was brilliant of James Cameron to make *Aliens* an action movie. Forgive me. I know that's sacrilegious.

GDT: No, no, it isn't! I'm just trying to define what a monster movie is. Hitchcock never did a horror film except for *The Birds* [1963]. That truly had a supernatural agent at work; it may not be ghosts, but it was supernatural. And to my mind, Spielberg did two great horror films: one was *Duel* [1971], because he elevated that truck to the state of a mechanical monster; and the other one was *Jaws* [1975], because he gave that shark intelligence and motivation… That is a monster movie that has haunted me for my entire life. I used to love the sea before I saw *Jaws*—I still love it, I still scuba dive, I snorkel, but I'm always nervous!

JL: Okay, the last question—and this is the one that everyone has given me radically different answers to. It's the one I expected the same answer to, but they've all been very different: Why do you think people like going to see scary movies?

GDT: I think it is part of our nature as myth-making mammals to tell stories of the dark and what lives in it. The earliest storytellers, seated around the campfire, were trying to make sense of the world. They needed to create angels and demons, and beauty and monsters. Fear can be a very powerful, spiritual experience, and we look for it. People say going to a horror movie is like a rollercoaster ride and I partially agree. But the rollercoaster analogy is limited. On a ride, you're only scared of being physically damaged. Horror films are a rollercoaster of the soul.

JL "Horror films are a rollercoaster of the soul." That's wonderful!

GDT They have a sort of purging effect. For a while, they allow you to believe in the supernatural in a stupidly rational world.

JL: Why do you think the audience for these films is mostly young people?

GDT: Because I think that horror movies destroy the illusion of order and sanity in the world. Order and sanity is a very adult concern. No one knows better the fragility and vulnerability of the real world than kids. At its worst, horror is a very repressive genre. But at its best, it's an incredibly anarchic and iconoclastic one. Kids identify with that.

JL: Muchas gracias, mi amigo!

GDT: You are more than welcome!

Myths, Legends, & Fairy Tales

Myths, Legends, & Fairy Tales

The world's myths, legends, and fairy tales have provided the movies with a plethora of monsters. Walt Disney introduced many of us to folk and fairy tales in his beautifully animated movies. In fact, the first ever feature-length, animated film is Disney's *Snow White and the Seven Dwarfs* [1937].

As captivating as Snow White is, it is the jealous and wicked Queen we all remember. The elegant and sensual Queen who turns herself into an Old Crone to give Snow White the poisoned apple was unforgettably voiced by an uncredited Lucille La Verne. Disney's films were often genuinely scary, as in *Sleeping Beauty* [1959], when actress Eleanor Audley gave voice to the evil fairy Maleficent's splendid line: "Now you must deal with me and all the powers of Hell!" as she magically transforms into a gigantic fire-breathing dragon to do battle with the dashing Prince.

The delightful Disney version of Carlo Collodi's classic book *The Adventures of Pinocchio* [1881], released as *Pinocchio* [1940], was also not without its dark side. The sequence when Pinocchio and his friend Lampwick's bad behavior causes them to "make asses of themselves" and they turn into donkeys, is as startling and sinister as any transformation scene in a werewolf movie.

The traditional French fairy tale "Beauty and

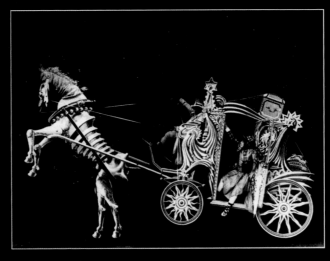

▲ *Cinderella* [Georges Méliès, 1899] An early Méliès "trick film."

the Beast" has been made into a number of movies. The best one is Jean Cocteau's magical *La Belle et la Bête* [1946]. The Beast, played by Jean Marais, is so glorious, that at the "happy ending," his metamorphosis into the handsome human prince is a bit of a let-down. The Disney *Beauty and the Beast* [1991] is a full-on operetta, with witty songs by Howard Ashman and Alan Menken and outstanding voice work by Paige O'Hara as Beauty and Robby Benson as the Beast.

The Irish fairies known as leprechauns have starring roles in movies in which they are good, like the charming *Darby O'Gill and the Little People* [Robert Stevenson, 1959] and movies where they are evil, like the series of films that started with *Leprechaun* [Mark Jones, 1993]. Warwick Davis has played the malicious little magical bastard in six Leprechaun films so far, with no end in sight! Davis has also written an entertaining autobiography called *Size Matters Not* [Arum Press, 2010], in which he talks about his little person roles in countless fantasy films, including *Willow*, *Star Wars*, *Harry Potter*, and more.

Elves and dwarfs feature in all of *The Lord of the Rings* trilogy of films [Peter Jackson, 2001, 2002, 2003]. Based on the books by J. R. R. Tolkien, the trilogy contains thousands of fantasy beings including giants, trolls, fairies, wizards, ambulatory

Previous pages: Belle (Josette Day) soothes the savage Beast (Jean Marais) in Jean Cocteau's classic fairy tale adaptation *La Belle et la Bête*.
Opposite page: (1) *Jason and the Argonauts* **[Don Chaffey, 1963]** Talos, the gigantic Man of Bronze that comes to life

when Hercules takes a javelin-sized pin from the treasure he guards. Ray Harryhausen's animation is extraordinary as Talos somehow moves as a Man of Bronze would move. Here, Talos, like the ancient Colossus of Rhodes, waits to grab Jason's ship, *Argo*.
(2) *Jason and the Argonauts* **[Don Chaffey,**

1963] Jason (Todd Armstrong) fighting the Hydra, the seven-headed dragon that guards the Golden Fleece. Another scene lit up by Harryhausen's breathtaking stop-motion animation. **(3)** *Legend* **[Ridley Scott, 1985]** Princess Lily (Mia Sara) reaches out to a unicorn in Scott's beautiful-looking fairy tale.

talking trees, demons, goblins, and an army of Orcs. Through a powerful motion-capture performance by Andy Serkis, the emotionally tortured creature Gollum stands out from the rest of the extraordinary array of mythical characters on display.

The one-eyed giants called Cyclops show up occasionally in films based on both Greco-Roman and Arabian Nights mythology. My favorites are the incredible Cyclops that live on the Island of Colossa in Ray Harryhausen's first feature film shot in color, *The 7th Voyage of Sinbad* [Nathan H. Juran, 1958]. I saw this movie at the age of eight and it changed my life in the same way that the original *King Kong* [Merian C. Cooper, Ernest B. Schoedsack, 1933] changed Harryhausen's (see my conversation with Ray on pages 148-9). I was enchanted, not only by the impressive Cyclops, but also by the fabulous dragon, and especially the skeleton brought to life by the wicked magician Sokurah (played in a wonderfully hammy turn by Torin Thatcher). Towards the beginning of the film, Sokurah turns the Princess' handmaiden into a dancing Snake Woman, Ray's favorite monster from this particular voyage of Sinbad's.

Harryhausen took Sinbad on two more voyages, *The Golden Voyage of Sinbad* [Gordon Hessler, 1973] and *Sinbad and the Eye of the Tiger* [Sam Wanamaker, 1977], both movies adding even more mythological monsters to the Harryhausen menagerie, including ghouls, a one-eyed centaur, a griffin, and a multi-armed statue of Kali that comes to life to sword-fight Sinbad and his crew.

The poet Homer gave us the Cyclops in the

▲ *A Midsummer Night's Dream* [Max Reinhardt, William Dieterle, 1935] Anita Louise as Titania, Queen of the Fairies and James Cagney as Bottom the Weaver, who has been given the head of a jackass by Puck (Mickey Rooney), in this lavish, Warner Brothers production of the play by William Shakespeare.

Odyssey, and *Ulysses* [Mario Camerini, 1955] starring Kirk Douglas in the title role, is a good retelling of the hero's epic voyage to his homeland of Ithaca following the fall of Troy. An Italian wrestler named Oscar Andriani plays the Cyclops, who is tricked by wily Ulysses into getting drunk so that once more we can watch a poor Cyclops have something sharp jammed into his only eye. Also based on Greek mythology is *Jason and the Argonauts* [Don Chaffey, 1963], which allowed Harryhausen to create more of his remarkable creatures to illustrate the story of Jason and his quest for the Golden Fleece. On Jason's adventure, we meet the colossal bronze statue Talos, brought to life by the hubris of Hercules, the flying Harpies sent to torment the blind Phineas for misusing his gift of prophecy, the many-headed Hydra who guards the Golden Fleece, and the "Children of the Hydra's teeth"— screaming skeleton warriors. The Gods themselves watch Jason's adventures from Mount Olympus and occasionally intercede on his behalf (as Hera does by sending the sea god Triton to hold back the Clashing Rocks, enabling Jason's ship *Argo* to pass through unharmed).

Harryhausen's final foray into Greek myth was the story of Perseus, told in *Clash of the Titans* [Desmond Davis, 1981]. Here, Pegasus the flying horse, giant scorpions, the snake-haired Medusa, and the Kraken compete for our attention. The movie was remade in 2010 [Louis Leterrier] with CG effects and mediocre 3D. But at least we got to hear once more those delicious words: "Release the Kraken!"

◀ *The Thief of Bagdad* [Ludwig Berger, Michael Powell, Tim Whelan, 1940]
Mary Morris as the Silver Maid, an exotic—and deadly—mechanical toy made by the evil Jaffar to assassinate the Sultan of Basra. This lavish fantasy began shooting in London but moved to Hollywood to finish when the war broke out.

▼ *The Golden Voyage of Sinbad* [Gordon Hessler, 1973] The second in Harryhausen's Sinbad trilogy. Here, a living stone statue of Kali, the Hindu Goddess of death, sword fights Sinbad (John Phillip Law, in the white turban) and his crew.

▲ *Alice in Wonderland* [Norman Z. McLeod, 1933]
There have been at least 22 feature films based on Lewis Carroll's classic children's story. This Paramount Pictures version is suitably bizarre. Here is Charlotte Henry as Alice, with Polly Moran as the Dodo Bird. W. C. Fields played Humpty Dumpty, Gary Cooper the White Knight, and Cary Grant was the Mock Turtle!

"Where is Belle? Where is Belle?"

The Beast (Jean Marais), searching for Belle in his magic mirror, *La Belle et la Bête*

▼ *Beauty and the Beast* [Gary Trousdale, 1991]
Disney's delightful musical, with witty songs by Howard Ashman and Alan Menken. Robby Benson and Paige O'Hara gave the Beast and Beauty their voices. Based on Jeanne-Marie Leprince de Beaumont's story, first published in 1757.

▲ *La Belle et la Bête* [Jean Cocteau, 1946]
Cocteau's magical film combines Jeanne-Marie Leprince de Beaumont's story with *La Chatte Blanche* by Catherine d'Aulnoy, published in 1697! Surreal and gorgeous, Cocteau's movie is truly romantic in the best sense of the word. Josette Day is Belle and Jean Marais is the fabulous Beast.

GORGONS

◀ The Gorgon
[Terence Fisher, 1964]
Hammer Films ignores Greek mythology and sets this in a rural German village in 1910. Prudence Hyman is Megaera the Gorgon who, at the time of the full moon, turns victims to stone with a single glance. With Peter Cushing as Dr. Namaroff and Christopher Lee as Prof. Karl Meister.

▶ 7 Faces of Dr. Lao
[George Pal, 1964]
Tony Randall as Medusa (one of seven parts Randall plays in the film), a deadly exhibit in the Circus of Dr. Lao.

◀ Clash of the Titans
[Desmond Davis, 1981]
Ray Harryhausen's Medusa, Ray Bradbury's favorite Harryhausen creature. In a tense, torch-lit sequence, Perseus (Harry Hamlin) stalks Medusa, hoping to use her severed head to turn the Kraken to stone.

◀ Perseus and the Gorgon
[Jim Henson, 1998]
A good retelling of the Greek myth on *Jim Henson's The Storyteller*, an excellent, but short-lived, television series.

▶ Percy Jackson & The Lightning Thief [aka *Percy Jackson & the Olympians: The Lightning Thief*, Chris Columbus, 2010]
Uma Thurman as Medusa in Chris Columbus's attempt to create another franchise like he did with the *Harry Potter* books by J. K. Rowling. This one is based on *The Lightning Thief*, the first novel in the *Percy Jackson & The Olympians* series by Rick Riordan.

▲ Clash of the Titans [Louis Leterrier, 2010] The remake, based on Harryhausen's design for his Medusa. This film suffered from being made 3D in an imperfect post-production process.

CYCLOPS

▲ **The Three Stooges Meet Hercules** [Edward Bernds, 1962] The Three Stooges encountered this unusual, giant, two-headed Cyclops in this slapstick adventure.

▲ **Ulysses** [Mario Camerini, 1955] Kirk Douglas stars as Ulysses in this Italian movie that is fairly faithful to Homer's *Odyssey*. Italian wrestler Oscar Andriani made an impressive Cyclops.

▲ **Krull** [Peter Yates, 1983] Bernard Bresslaw as Rell the Cyclops in this odd fantasy film. Bresslaw is unrecognizable in his make-up; otherwise you would remember him as a regular in the *Carry On* movies! Peter Yates was a wonderful director, but this is not one of his best.

▶ **The 7th Voyage of Sinbad** [Nathan H. Juran, 1958] One of the awe-inspiring Cyclops that live on the Island of Colossa in the first of Harryhausen's *Sinbad* trilogy. When roasting one of Sinbad's crew on a spit, he licks his lips in anticipation of his meal! One of the screen's greatest fantasy creations.

▲ **The Chronicles of Narnia: The Lion, the Witch and the Wardrobe** [Andrew Adamson, 2005] Howard Berger, Gregory Nicotero, and Nikki Gooley won an Academy Award for Best Make-up for their work on this film.

▲ *The Wonderful World of the Brothers Grimm* [Henry Levin, George Pal, 1962] Laurence Harvey and Karlheinz Böhm as Wilhelm and Jacob, the Brothers Grimm in this Cinerama spectacular. Henry Levin directed the framing story of them writing their famous tales, and George Pal directed the fairy tales. With delightful stop-motion animation by Wah Chang and Gene Warren in the George Pal tradition. Years later, I was shocked to discover that the deranged killer in *Peeping Tom* [Michael Powell, 1960] was one of the Brothers Grimm!

▲ *The Brothers Grimm* [Terry Gilliam, 2005] Mackenzie Crook not looking well in Terry Gilliam's very different vision from George Pal's. Matt Damon and Heath Ledger played the Brothers Grimm.

"The gods of Greece are cruel! In time all men will learn to live without them!"

Jason (Todd Armstrong), *Jason and the Argonauts*

▲◀◀ *Jason and the Argonauts* [Don Chaffey, 1963] Here are just three of Jason's encounters with the marvels of Greek myth in Harryhausen's wondrous movie. Above: The Argonauts fight the winged Harpies sent by Zeus to punish blind Phineas for misusing his gift of prophecy. Left: The grateful Phineas gives Jason an amulet, which summons the god Triton, shown here holding back the Clashing Rocks so that the *Argo* may pass unharmed. Above left: The teeth from the slain Hydra (see page 134) are sown by wicked King Aeetes and, up from the ground, sprout skeleton warriors that attack Jason and his men. This four-minute sequence took Ray more than four months to animate!

Trolls

▲ **Time Bandits** [Terry Gilliam, 1981]
Peter Vaughan as Winston the Ogre in Gilliam's wonderful and very witty fantasy. This one is a must see.

▲ **Bridge to Terabithia** [Gábor Csupó, 2007] Based on Katherine Paterson's novel about kids who invent their own fantasy world called Terabithia.

▶ **Troll** [John Carl Buechler, 1986]
A wicked troll king shows up in San Francisco. An interesting piece of trivia about this film, is that Michael Moriarty plays a character named Harry Potter!

◀ **Labyrinth**
[Jim Henson, 1986]
Rob Mills (Ron Mueck, voice) as Ludo, one of the many terrific fantasy creatures that populate Jim Henson's fairy tale. David Bowie played Jareth, the Goblin King.

▲ **The Troll Hunter** [aka *Trolljegeren*, André Øvredal, 2010] Told through the first-person camera of a "documentary" crew, this is an exciting and funny story about the existence of monstrous Trolls in Norway and the secret government agency keeping them under control.

Gremlins [Joe Dante, 1984] Dante's wonderful, dark, fairy tale comedy. When cute little Mogwai Gizmo (above) gets wet, eggs sprout from his back and produce many more Mogwai. However, these Mogwai, like Stripe (right), are downright dangerous. The enormous success of *Gremlins* allowed Dante to make the even more adventurous *Gremlins 2: The New Batch* in 1990. *Gremlins* is a marvelous mix of the sweet and the sinister.

"How come a cute little guy like this can turn into a thousand ugly monsters?"

Sheriff Frank (Scott Brady), *Gremlins*

▲ **The NeverEnding Story II: The Next Chapter** [George T. Miller, 1990] The second of three films based on Michael Ende's book. Above is a living mountain and below Jonathan Brandis encounters a griffin. All three films are chock-a-block with monsters suitable for children.

▲ **The Golden Voyage of Sinbad** [Gordon Hessler, 1973] A one-eyed centaur fights a griffin near the Fountain of Destiny on the lost continent of Lemuria, in the second of Ray Harryhausen's *Sinbad* trilogy.

▲ **Harry Potter and the Prisoner of Azkaban** [Alfonso Cuaron, 2004] Harry Potter encounters a griffin, one of the many fantastic creatures that populate the Harry Potter movies.

"Release the Kraken!"

Calibos (Neil McCarthy), *Clash of the Titans* [1981]

▲ *Clash of the Titans* [Desmond Davis, 1981] The Kraken comes for Princess Andromeda in a staging reminiscent of many classic paintings of the Greek myth. Will Perseus and Pegasus get there in time to save her?

▲ *Clash of the Titans* [Louis Leterrier, 2010]
The oddly designed Kraken in the remake. Notice how tiny Pegasus appears next to the gigantic monster.

▲ *Pirates of the Caribbean: Dead Man's Chest* [Gore Verbinski, 2006]
Disney's Kraken destroys a merchant ship in the second of the *Pirates of the Caribbean* franchise.

▲ *Leprechaun in the Hood* [Rob Spera, 2000] Warwick Davis stars as the evil little bastard in this, the fifth in the six Leprechaun movies in the franchise so far. This one is the blaxploitation edition.

▶ *Darby O'Gill and the Little People* [Robert Stevenson, 1959] Jimmy O'Dea as King Brian of the Leprechauns stands on a sleeping Sean Connery as Michael McBride in this delightful Disney movie based on the *Darby O'Gill* books by Herminie Templeton Kavanagh. The great Albert Sharpe played Darby O'Gill. Using the Schufftan Process (forced perspective creating the illusion of size differential) the movie has amazing scenes of Darby among the "little people."

▲ *Erik the Viking* [Terry Jones, 1989] The size of this sea monster can be seen by comparison with Erik's ship in front of it. Loosely based on Jones' own book, *The Saga of Erik the Viking*.

afternoons of a faun

▶ *7 Faces of Dr. Lao* [George Pal, 1964] Tony Randall as Pan himself, here on display in Dr. Lao's circus tent. Pan plays his pipes and arouses the dormant sexuality of a young widow (Barbara Eden) in an unusually erotic scene for a "family" movie.

◀ *The Chronicles of Narnia: The Lion, the Witch and the Wardrobe* [Andrew Adamson, 2005] James McAvoy as Mr. Tumnus, a faun who switches sides and becomes an ally to the Pevensie children. Based on the book by C. S. Lewis.

▶ *Exquisite Sinner* [Josef von Sternberg, Phil Rosen, 1926] An intriguing shot of Conrad Nagel as a faun playing his pipes, which was probably in a dream sequence in this lost silent film. The cast list has the equally intriguing credit, "Myrna Loy..... Living Statue."

▲ Time Bandits [Terry Gilliam, 1981] Sean Connery as King Agamemnon fighting the Minotaur in Gilliam's wonderful fantasy adventure.

▲ The Chronicles of Narnia: The Lion, the Witch and the Wardrobe [Andrew Adamson, 2005] A Minotaur, one of the many mythical creatures created by Howard Berger for this epic fantasy film (see page 307).

◀ Minotaur, the Wild Beast of Crete [Silvio Amadio, 1960] Rosanna Schiaffino in the Minotaur's clutches in this Italian sword and sandal movie.

◀▼ The Lord of the Rings [Peter Jackson, 2001-2003] Peter Jackson's Tolkien trilogy is jam-packed with fantastic beasts of all sizes and shapes. From left to right: Gollum, a brilliant motion-capture performance from Andy Serkis as the pathetic creature consumed with desire for the Ring; the fearsome Cave Troll in the Mines of Moria; one of the Orcs, the evil soldiers of Lord Sauron (Christopher Lee).

"We wants it! We needs it! Must have the precious!"

Gollum (Andy Serkis), *The Lord of the Rings: The Return of the King*

▼▲ Beowulf [Robert Zemeckis, 2007] Crispin Glover in a motion-capture performance as Grendel (above) and Angelina Jolie as Grendel's mother (below) in this CG version of the tale. There is a lengthy battle between Beowulf (Ray Winstone) and Grendel in which Beowulf is naked. The lengths to which the director has to go to make sure his genitals are not seen are truly hilarious.

▲ Pirates of the Caribbean: At World's End [Gore Verbinski, 2007] Bill Nighy as Davy Jones. His amazing tentacled face is a completely computer-generated animation. A fabulous-looking character.

"Do you fear death?"
"You have no idea."

Davy Jones (Bill Nighy) to Jack Sparrow (Johnny Depp),
Pirates of the Caribbean: At World's End

▼ Pan's Labyrinth [aka *El Laberinto del Fauno*, Guillermo Del Toro, 2006] Doug Jones as the Faun in del Toro's remarkable movie. Ten-year-old Ivana Baquero gives a sensitive, very real performance as Ofelia, the young girl who is the star of the film.

▲ How the Grinch Stole Christmas [Ron Howard, 2000] Jim Carrey gives a terrific performance in Rick Baker's Academy Award-winning make-up for the Grinch. From the classic children's book by Dr. Seuss. I personally prefer Chuck Jones' 1966 animated television version, which was marvelously narrated by Boris Karloff.

147

Ray Harryhausen

Ray Harryhausen, the author, and the skeleton from *The 7th Voyage of Sinbad* [1958], used again in *Jason and the Argonauts* [1963]; London, 2010.

Photo by Mark Mawston

JL: Ray, I know you don't like the term "monster."

RH: I don't like the term "monster," because that's not what we do. All our creatures are misunderstood creatures, because they usually come from another world.

JL: So what does the word "monster" mean to you?

RH: I associate the word "monster" with some sort of insane creature that growls and is physically distorted. I don't like to use the word. It has to do with things like Frankenstein and Dracula and horrible people who do horrible things.

JL: Well, some of your creatures do horrible things.

RH: They don't do horrible things. They're just out of their element!

JL: Hmm.

RH: (Laughs.)

JL: Doesn't Medusa do horrible things?

RH: Well, that's her nature! She's a snake woman! (Laughs.)

JL: All right, let me think about it…

RH: She was cursed by Hera (queen of the Greek gods).

JL: What about the Cyclops?

RH: I don't know about the Cyclops…

JL: The Cyclops in *The 7th Voyage of Sinbad* [Nathan H. Juran, 1958]. The Cyclops tries to eat people!

RH: (Laughs) But that's his nature! He's not a monster!

JL: Are there creatures in other people's movies that you are particularly fond of?

RH: Not that I'm *fond* of…

JL: I know what you're fond of: King Kong!

RH: Oh yes, but he was neither man, nor beast, as they said in the script. He was a throwback of some sort. Most gorillas have straight eyebrows, so I slanted Mighty Joe Young's eyebrows so that he would look a little different than a normal gorilla.

JL: I had a problem with Peter Jackson's *King Kong* [2005]. Peter just made him a big gorilla, not at all a mythical beast, just a very big gorilla. Do you like fantasy films in general?

RH: Oh, I love them. They stretch the imagination.

JL: What are some of your favorites… that you didn't make?

RH: (Laughs) Well I thought *Jurassic Park* [Steven Spielberg, 1993] was fascinating.

JL: And you wouldn't call them monsters, just dinosaurs.

RH: Dinosaurs are not monsters; they're just a product of their time!

JL: It's just that when they're out of their time, they are forced to behave badly.

RH: They behave badly because they don't know what they're doing. They don't normally live in this world.

JL: That's a good answer. What about something like in *One Million Years B.C.* [Don Chaffey, 1966], where you have dinosaurs living with humans?

RH: Well, we don't make these pictures for paleontologists. If you just have a bunch of dinosaurs running around barking at each other, there's no drama. You have to include humans!

JL: What about the movie *Creation*? The Willis

O'Brien project that was never realized. Wasn't that just dinosaurs?

RH: Well, I think they had more than dinosaurs. They had people in it, too.

JL: What was the Irwin Allen movie you worked on?

RH: That was *The Animal World* [1956].

JL: That had drama in it, and no people.

RH: Well, it was a brief sequence. (The BBC-TV series) *Walking With Dinosaurs* doesn't have any people in it. It's more realistic, but they tried to make dinosaurs that would be acceptable for paleontologists, and we're making movies just to entertain! You can't entertain with a dinosaur just chewing on another dinosaur!

JL: Do you think you're more interested in fantastic beings, or in beings that have a basis in reality?

RH: I think the whole point of any fantasy film is to stretch the imagination, because when one lives in a dream world like me, it's always "what if this could happen?"

JL: Do you think that creatures can be manifestations of people's fantasies or fears?

RH: Sometimes, but *Dr. Jekyll and Mr. Hyde* was more about the dual personalities that we all have.

JL: What about Dr. Moreau, with his genetic experiments? Would you call him a monster?

RH: Dr. Moreau was an early one in genetic experiments and now they are coming to pass. Lord knows what they will create—I don't know!

JL: I know *King Kong* [Merian C. Cooper, Ernest B. Schoedsack, 1933] is the movie that inspired you.

RH: Oh it did. It was an inspiration because it was so different than any other movie.

JL: Do you remember when you saw it?

RH: I was 13. A few marbles have lost their way… maybe they rolled under the davenport…

JL: No, seriously, I know you know. Tell me when you saw it.

RH: I saw it back in 1933, when it first came out. At Grauman's Chinese Theater on Hollywood Boulevard. In Los Angeles, where I grew up.

JL: Was there a live show before the movie?

RH: There was a stage show. Sid Grauman was a great showman at that time. Sid had this great prolog with live actors, and then Kong came on.

JL: Kong himself came on?!

RH: No John. The movie! Although they did have a big bust in the lobby. The prolog got you in the mood to accept the fantasy, which was, at the time, very extreme.

JL: Really? There had been *The Lost World* [Harry O. Hoyt, 1925], the silent picture, and that had been a tremendous hit.

RH: There was, but most people didn't remember it. And Max Steiner's great music made *King Kong* much more impressive than *The Lost World*, which probably had only a piano accompaniment.

JL: How important is music to movies?

RH: I think music is very important to fantasy films, particularly movies that don't rely on very profound dialog. Our fantasies are mostly action pictures, and music enhances them. It makes everything bigger than life, which is the function of good film music.

JL: When you were planning scenes, did you think of the music? When you worked with Bernard Herrmann, did you talk about the score beforehand?

RH: No, no, no, no. You have to leave it to somebody like Bernard Herrmann. Different people write different kinds of music. Herrmann specialized in rousing action music while a composer like Miklos Rozsa wrote romantic music.

JL: You've done movies based on books by Jules Verne and H. G. Wells. Who is your favorite fantasy author?

RH: I couldn't choose a favorite. I like Wells; he was very profound. I liked his book, *The Island of Dr. Moreau*. Did you ever see the picture that Charles Laughton starred in?

JL: Yes, *Island of Lost Souls* [Erle C. Kenton, 1932] is great. That movie had wonderful make-up.

RH: Oh, very good make-up. I don't know who did the score, but it wasn't a complete score.

JL: I don't remember the music. I just remember the monsters! Béla Lugosi was one of them, "The Sayer of the Law!" Do you have a particular favorite of your creatures?

RH: I can't have, because the others get jealous (laughs). I like the complicated ones. They're much more interesting to animate. Like the Hydra in *Jason and the Argonauts* [Don Chaffey, 1963], and Medusa in *Clash of the Titans* [Desmond Davis, 1981]. The sword fight with the Seven Skeletons in *Jason and the Argonauts* as well.

JL: How long did the Seven Skeletons sword fight take you to animate?

RH: It took about four and a half months to put it together. I was the only animator on it. I had to time all the swords, so that when an actor brought his sword down and stopped, a skeleton's blade would be there to meet it.

JL: What are some of the fantasy films, other than *King Kong* and *Island of Lost Souls*, that had a big impact on you?

RH: *Jurassic Park* [Steven Spielberg, 1993] was very impressive. Phil Tippett and Dennis Muren did wonderful work on that. And I liked *Close Encounters of the Third Kind*, too [Steven Spielberg, 1977]. There's a space monster I particularly love in *Forbidden Planet* [Fred M. Wilcox, 1956]. A great movie!

> ## "The whole point of any fantasy film is to stretch the imagination."

JL: I love the creature in that: "The Monster from the Id."

RH: Yeah. It was a fascinating concept and very well done.

JL: You've already said it, but I would like you to tell me again. You never call your creatures monsters because…?

RH: Well monsters, I think, in most people's minds, are these bad men who go around scaring everybody.

JL: Doing bad things.

RH: Doing insane things! (Laughs.)

JL: Whereas, a creature…

RH: A creature, like the one in *20 Million Miles to Earth* [Nathan H. Juran, 1957] comes from a different planet, and he is not aggressive until somebody is aggressive to him—the farmer jabs him with a pitchfork! That, of course, upsets his ego. (Laughs.)

JL: What do you think of actors who are famous for their fantasy roles, like Boris Karloff, or Christopher Lee?

RH: Well, Boris Karloff was perfect for *Frankenstein*. And he's still the most profound Frankenstein's Monster, I think. He wasn't just frightening.

JL: But in your films, there are moments where you want people to be frightened.

RH: Well, yes. But that's the way you stage a film. As a director, you have to think about how you're going to stage it so you get the most effective appearance, visually.

JL: You know, I was thinking about it, and in your films, even more than a sense of fear, you often impart with a sense of wonder.

RH: Well, we try to do that. I hope that the strangeness of the subject matter also helps create a feeling of wonder.

Ray animating the dragon from *The 7th Voyage of Sinbad* [1958] on a miniature set.

Dragons & Dinosaurs

Dragons & Dinosaurs

What's the difference between a dragon and a dinosaur? "Dragons" are legendary creatures with reptilian traits. The term "Dinosaurs" refers to a diverse group of animals that were on Earth from the beginning of the Triassic period to the end of the Cretaceous. That was a long time ago. So for the purposes of this book, which is about monsters in the movies, I think I can safely lump them together in one chapter. Especially since humans and dinosaurs did not coexist and most movies featuring dinosaurs have people running for their lives away from them.

Winsor McCay, the brilliant newspaper cartoonist (creator of the amazing comic strip *Little Nemo in Slumberland*), wanted an animated film to use in his vaudeville act. With thousands of drawings, McCay created *Gertie the Dinosaur* [1914], in which the dinosaur Gertie would respond onscreen to McCay's live commands from the stage. Gertie is probably cinema's first dinosaur.

The first major movie to feature dinosaurs was an adaptation of Sir Arthur Conan Doyle's novel *The Lost World* [Harry O. Hoyt, 1925]. This starred Wallace Beery as Professor Challenger and showcased the groundbreaking stop-motion animation of Willis O'Brien. *The Lost World*'s climactic scenes, in which a brontosaurus brought back by Challenger escapes and wreaks havoc on the streets of London, would inspire literally hundreds of movies in the future.

The rampaging dinosaur in *The Lost World*

▲ **Evil defeated:** St. George and the Dragon, a tinsel picture from the 19th century.

ends up swimming in London's River Thames; 36 years later, *Gorgo* [Eugène Lourié, 1961] and son wade down the Thames, making their way back home to the sea. *Gorgo* is one of those movie dinosaurs that relies more on the imagination of the filmmakers than on any science or research into the fossil record.

In 1924, Fritz Lang directed *Die Nibelungen: Siegfried* and *Die Nibelungen: Kriemhild's Revenge* [also 1924]. Based on the same 12th-century epic poem, *The Song of the Nibelungs*, that Richard Wagner based his Ring Cycle operas on, the first film has a marvelous dragon for Siegfried to slay. As I am sure you all remember, Siegfried bathes himself in the dragon's blood, and if you're curious about the proper way to bathe in dragon's blood, Lang shows us how.

The Russian film *Ilya Muromets* [aka *The Sword and the Dragon*, Aleksandr Ptushko, 1956] features a ferocious dragon created, like the one in *Siegfried*, as a full-size mechanical puppet for the lead actor to fight.

Since both dinosaurs and dragons are hard to come by for motion-picture work, filmmakers have used a number of methods to bring them to the screen, including full-size puppets, like those in *Siegfried* and *Ilya Muromets* and, later, sophisticated animatronics in *Jurassic Park* [Steven Spielberg, 1993] and its sequels. Traditional, hand-painted cell animation was used in the *Rite of Spring* sequence in Walt Disney's *Fantasia* [Bill Roberts, Paul Satterfield, 1940], while CG animation featured in *How to Train Your Dragon* [Chris Sanders, Dean DeBlois, 2010]. *Jurassic Park* and its sequels also makes extensive use of CG.

To save money, live lizards, iguanas, and alligators with fins attached to them were shot in slow motion in an attempt to convey great size

---

Previous pages: ***One Million Years B.C.*** **[Don Chaffey, 1966]** Raquel Welch as Loana in the claws of a pterodactyl! A Hammer color remake of the black and white Hal Roach original [1940], with special effects by Ray Harryhausen.

Opposite page: ***The Beast From 20,000 Fathoms*** **[Eugène Lourié, 1953]** Harryhausen's influential dinosaur-on-the-loose movie. Tagline: "They couldn't escape the terror! And neither will you!"

and weight in movies like *One Million B.C.* [Hal Roach, Hal Roach Jr., 1940], the remake of *The Lost World* [Irwin Allen, 1960], and *Journey to the Center of the Earth* [Henry Levin, 1959].

My preference in dinosaurs and dragons is for ones made with stop-motion animation, as in the silent *Lost World*, *King Kong* [Merian C. Cooper, Ernest B. Schoedsack, 1933], *The Beast of Hollow Mountain* [Edward Nassour, Ismael Rodríguez, 1956], *The Wonderful World of the Brothers Grimm* [Henry Lavin, George Pal, 1962], *Dinosaurus!* [Irvin Yeaworth, 1960], *Jack The Giant Killer* [Nathan H. Juran, 1962], and the wonderful Loch Ness Monster in *7 Faces of Dr. Lao* [George Pal, 1964]. Another, simpler technique to bring these enormous creatures to life is just to use men in dinosaur costumes stomping around miniature sets. This was done in *Gorgo* [1961], and Japanese movies like the original *Godzilla* [Ishirô Honda, 1954] and all of its sequels and imitations.

Stop-motion animator Ray Harryhausen has created some of my favorite dragons and dinosaurs. There is the majestic dragon of *The 7th Voyage of Sinbad* [Nathan H. Juran, 1958] and the unforgettable Hydra that guards the Golden Fleece in *Jason and the Argonauts.* [Don Chaffey, 1963].

Ray's *The Beast From 20,000 Fathoms* [Eugène Lourié, 1953] was the first of the many monsters unleashed by the atomic bomb. Based on a Ray Bradbury short story, "The Fog Horn," in which a lonely, prehistoric beast rises from the sea mistaking a lighthouse foghorn for a mating call, the enormous success of *The Beast From 20,000 Fathoms* provided the incentive for Toho Studios in Tokyo to produce their own gigantic-beast-rising-from-the-sea movie, *Godzilla*, in

1954. *Godzilla*'s sequel, *Godzilla Raids Again* was retitled *Gigantis, the Fire Monster* for its US release in 1955.

Harryhausen made more realistic dinosaurs in Hammer's remake of *One Million Years B.C.* [Don Chaffey, 1966]. Ray also gave us the indelible image of Raquel Welch in a fur bikini carried off by a mama pterodactyl to feed to her hungry chicks. In Harryhausen's *The Valley of Gwangi* [Jim O'Connolly, 1969], cowboys discover dinosaurs in a hidden valley and capture an allosaurus, which they put on display in a bullring. It breaks free, and dies trapped in a burning cathedral.

Ishirô Honda's Japanese dragon (or is he a dinosaur?) *Godzilla* [1954] was an international sensation and has been followed by countless sequels and one ill-conceived, big-budget Hollywood remake [Roland Emmerich, 1998]. Godzilla himself has had a fascinating relationship with Japan. Originally a symbol of the destruction caused by the two atomic bombs dropped on Japan during World War II, Godzilla has gone from being Japan's ultimate villain, to the country's friend and protector. Godzilla has been joined by *Rodan! The Flying Monster!* [Ishirô Honda, 1956], a sort of jumbo

▲ **The Lost World** [Harry O. Hoyt, 1925] The first film version of Sir Arthur Conan Doyle's classic book. Wallace Beery played Professor Challenger in this silent movie, with stop-motion animation by the great Willis O'Brien.

pterodactyl, and a golden, three-headed flying dragon from outer space named *Ghidorah, the Three-Headed Monster* [Ishirô Honda, 1964] among others. The great Eiji Tsuburaya supervised almost all of Toho Studios' giant monster films, his special effects distinguished by his trademark miniatures: entire cities built to scale to be knocked down, stomped on, and blown up.

Paleontologists keep discovering new dinosaurs and I am sure that moviemakers will, too. And I for one, look forward to meeting them.

Opposite page: **(1)** *Gertie* [aka *Gertie the Dinosaur*, **Winsor McCay, 1914**] Pioneering cartoonist Winsor McCay toured in vaudeville with his hand-drawn animation, giving the onscreen dinosaur verbal commands from the stage.

(2) *The Ghost of Slumber Mountain* [**Willis O'Brien, 1918**] The poster for the 19-minute-long, stop-motion animation that got O'Brien the job of animating the dinosaurs for *The Lost World* [Harry O. Hoyt, 1925], which led to his masterpiece, *King Kong* [1933].

(3) *Goliath and the Dragon* [aka *La Vendetta di Ercole*, **Vittorio Cottafavi, 1960**] This Italian sword and sandal epic not only features a good dragon, it also has an unexpected Broderick Crawford as King Eurystheus!

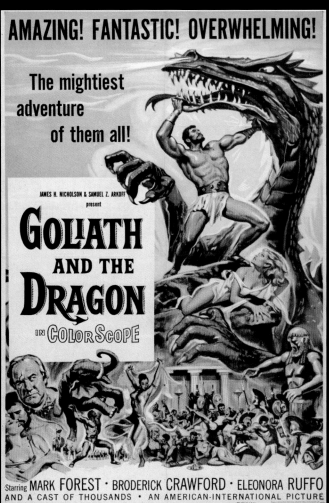

◀ *Die Nibelungen: Siegfried* [Fritz Lang, 1924] Paul Richter as Siegfried bathes in the blood of the dragon he has just slain to make himself invincible. However, a falling leaf lands on his shoulder, leaving one vulnerable spot. The first of the two films Lang made based on the medieval epic poem *The Song of the Nibelungs*.

▼ *Fantasia* [Bill Roberts, Paul Satterfield; *Rite of Spring Sequence* directors, 1940] Walt Disney and conductor Leopold Stokowski's ambitious attempt to bring classical music to the masses, and the first motion picture to ever be released in Stereophonic Sound. To illustrate Igor Stravinsky's *Rite of Spring*, they created a beautifully animated history of the evolution of life on Earth, from amoebas to the extinction of the dinosaurs. A daring and still fascinating work.

◀ *King Kong* [Merian C. Cooper, Ernest B. Schoedsack, 1933] Ann Darrow (Fay Wray), high up in the tree where Kong has put her for safety, looks on as he battles a *T. Rex*. Brilliantly staged, with innovative use of sound effects (by Murray Spivack). A classic sequence from Willis O'Brien's stop-motion tour de force.

▲ Unknown Island [Jack Bernhard, 1948]
Photographed in Cinecolor, this movie used men in ridiculous dinosaur suits. Pictured is a prehistoric giant ape (probably Ray "Crash" Corrigan) who seems to be tickling a *Tyrannosaurus Rex*.

▲ The Land That Time Forgot [Kevin Connor, 1975] A workmanlike adaptation of Edgar Rice Burroughs' book about a World War I German U-Boat and its captives discovering an island where dinosaurs still roam. This Amicus production used big, clumsy dinosaur suits and full-size props, like this one attacking Doug McClure, for the primeval beasts.

▲ Ilya Muromets [aka *The Sword and the Dragon* and *The Epic Hero and the Beast*, Aleksandr Ptushko ,1956] Boris Andreyev as Ilya Muromets about to slay a dragon. Roger Corman recut and dubbed this Russian film and I saw it on television many times as a kid, not knowing exactly what to make of the words not matching the actors' mouth movements. The first Soviet movie shot in CinemaScope.

▶ The Beast of Hollow Mountain [Edward Nassour, Ismael Rodríguez, 1956] From a story by Willis O'Brien, who used the name "El Toro Estrella" for his writing credit! This particular shot is too close and clearly shows the cowboy is a puppet. O'Brien did not do the stop-motion animation for this film, which is very similar to his original screenplay *The Valley of the Mist*, later made by O'Brien's protégé Ray Harryhausen as *The Valley of Gwangi* [Jim O'Connolly, 1969].

◀ Dinosaurus! [Irvin Yeaworth, 1960] The puppet double for the little boy Julio rides the puppet *apatosaurus* in this dumb movie. Surprisingly, *Dinosaurus!* was photographed by the great Stanley Cortez. Scenes from the film show up in *Schlock* [me, 1973].

▶ Rodan! The Flying Monster! [Ishirô Honda, 1956] Ishirô Honda is at it again! Tagline: "The Super-Sonic Hell-Creature No Weapon Could Destroy!" Rodan looks much less like a European dragon than the poster portrays him.

"It's disgraceful to think of putting this fabulous creature on display in a cheap circus."

Professor Bromley (Laurence Naismith) in *The Valley of Gwangi* [1969]

▲ Jack the Giant Killer [Nathan H. Juran, 1962] The Kerwin Mathews puppet astride the flying dragon animated by Jim Danforth in this *The 7th Voyage of Sinbad* imitation.

◀ The Wonderful World of the Brothers Grimm [Henry Levin, George Pal, 1962] The lovely dragon that terrorizes Buddy Hackett and Terry-Thomas in the "Singing Bone" sequence of this Cinerama movie.

▲ The Valley of Gwangi [Jim O'Connolly, 1969] Based on an original, unproduced script by Willis O'Brien, Harryhausen finally realized his mentor's vision and put cowboys and dinosaurs together in the Old West. Here, the captive Gwangi is being transported to be put on public display.

▲ *The Magic Sword* [Bert I. Gordon, 1962] Gordon's best film. But any movie with Basil Rathbone as an evil wizard and Estelle Winwood as a sorceress can't help but be watchable. Gary Lockwood (murdered by HAL in *2001: A Space Odyssey*) as Sir George faces the fire-breathing, two-headed dragon to save Princess Helene (Anne Helm).

▲ *Sleeping Beauty* [Les Clark, Eric Larson, Wolfgang Reitherman, 1959] Prince Phillip faces the fire-breathing dragon that the wicked fairy Maleficent has become. If you visit Disneyland Paris, below the Castle there is a full-size audioanimatronic dragon lurking. Both the Castle and the Dragon are based on the ones in this movie.

▲▶ *Gorgo* [Eugène Lourié, 1961] Lourié seemed to specialize in giant dinosaur pictures, this time it's British. Gorgo's mom is pictured here, trashing London's Tower Bridge.

▲ *Atragon* [aka *Undersea Warship*, Ishirô Honda, 1963] The lost continent of Mu threatens the world, but a Japanese World War II captain has secretly built Atragon, the greatest submarine ever (to rebuild the Japanese Empire) and uses it to fight back against the Empress of Mu. Oh yeah, the submarine is also attacked by a sea serpent. An entertaining and jingoistic Japanese fantasy film with an amazing militaristic score by Akira Ifukube.

◀ *Gamera vs. Barugon* [aka *War of the Monsters*, Shigeo Tanaka, 1966] Gamera is one of the wackier giant Japanese monsters, a gigantic flying turtle! Gamera fights Barugon, a giant lizard who can shoot a "freeze ray" out of his mouth. I love this wild publicity photo.

▲ *The 7th Voyage of Sinbad* [Nathan H. Juran, 1958] The superlative dragon the evil Sokurah (Torin Thatcher) keeps chained to protect his cave. Sinbad (Kerwin Mathews) releases the dragon to fight the Cyclops, but then orders his crew to fire a giant crossbow they've constructed and this beautiful dragon dies on the beach.

159

INVINCIBLE...INDESTRUCTIBLE!

What was this awesome BEAST born fifty million years out of time?

SEE: A MIGHTY CITY TRAMPLED TO DESTRUCTION!
SEE: MISSILES AND ATOM BOMBS POWERLESS!
SEE: CIVILIZATION RIOTING WITH FEAR!

American International Pictures presents

in COLOR

REPTILICUS

CARL OTTOSEN · ANN SMYRNER Original Story by · SID PINK · IB MELCHIOR & SID PINK · Produced and Directed by · SIDNEY PINK
A CINEMAGIC, INC. PRODUCTION · AN AMERICAN INTERNATIONAL PICTURE

▲ *Reptilicus* [Poul Bang, Sidney W. Pink, 1961] Made in Denmark. How they thought the audience would accept the incompetent marionette flailing around an awful miniature Copenhagen I do not know.

> "You swore to all of us that we were not going to harm the dinosaur!"
>
> Wade (Steven Keats), *The Last Dinosaur*

▶ *The Land That Time Forgot* [Kevin Connor, 1975] Not even Doug McClure can save Bobby Parr from being carried off by a rather stiff, full-size, prop pterodactyl in the "lost world" of Caprona.

◀ *One Million Years B.C.* [Don Chaffey, 1966] A Mama pterodactyl is about to feed Raquel Welch to her hungry chicks. Ray Harryhausen did the effects in an unusual "work for hire" at this stage of his career.

◀ *The Last Dinosaur* [Alexander Grasshoff, Tsugunobu Kotani, 1977] A Japanese/US coproduction with appalling men-in-dinosaur-suits special effects. Richard Boone plays a big game hunter who... Oh, never mind.

▶ *Amazon Women on the Moon* [Joe Dante, 1987] Jack the Ripper was really the Loch Ness Monster! A "re-enactment" from the *Bullshit or Not?* segment, starring Henry Silva.

▲ *The Private Life of Sherlock Holmes* [Billy Wilder, 1970] Wilder's bittersweet love letter to Sherlock Holmes. Here, Holmes (Robert Stephens) and Gabrielle Valadon (Geneviève Page) encounter the Loch Ness Monster—actually a disguise for a secret British submersible being tested in the loch. Holmes' brother Mycroft (Christopher Lee) informs Sherlock that the beautiful Gabrielle is notorious German spy Ilse von Hoffmanstal!

▶ *The Water Horse: Legend of the Deep* [Jay Russell, 2007] Based on Dick King-Smith's novel *The Water Horse*. A family film about a boy and his Loch Ness Monster.

▶ *Dragonslayer* [Matthew Robbins, 1981]
Phil Tippett at ILM invented a stop-motion animation technique called "go motion" for the dragon in this fantasy film. With the wonderful Ralph Richardson as Ulrich of Craggenmoor. Ken Ralston designed the flying sequences for the Vermithrax Pejorative, still the most awesome dragon in the movies.

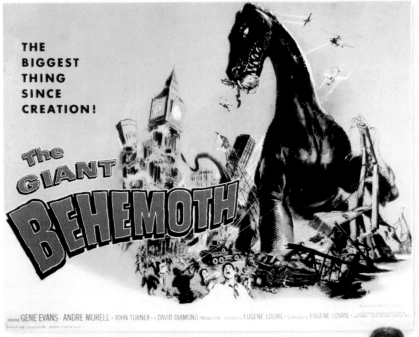

THE BIGGEST THING SINCE CREATION!

GENE EVANS · ANDRE MORELL · JOHN TURNER · A DAVID DIAMOND PRODUCTION · Directed by EUGENE LOURIE · Screenplay by EUGENE LOURIE

▶ *Q, the Winged Serpent*
[Larry Cohen, 1982]
The Aztec god Quetzalcoatl is living at the top of Manhattan's Chrysler Building and grabbing people off of rooftops to eat! Michael Moriarty (an extraordinary performance), plays a petty crook who discovers the monster's lair and wants the city to pay him for the information. Stop-motion animation by David W. Allen and Randy Cook. Another bizzarro movie from Larry that really works.

▲ *The Giant Behemoth* [Douglas Hickox, Eugène Lourié, 1959] Willis O'Brien and Pete Peterson did the stop-motion monster in LA, while the production itself was filmed in London. A prehistoric monster swims up the Thames and… Hey, wait a minute… hasn't this been done before?

▶ *The NeverEnding Story*
[Wolfgang Petersen, 1984]
Noah Hathaway as Atreyu with Falkor, his flying "luckdragon" (voiced by Alan Oppenheimer). An epic fantasy from the director of *Das Boot* [1981].

"All major theme parks have had delays. When they opened Disneyland in 1956, nothing worked!"
"But, John. If the Pirates of the Caribbean breaks down, the pirates don't eat the tourists!"

John Hammond (Richard Attenborough) to
Dr. Ian Malcom (Jeff Goldblum), *Jurassic Park*

◀ **Jurassic Park**
[Steven Spielberg, 1993] One of Stan Winston's dinosaurs up to no good.

◀ **Evolution** [Ivan Reitman, 2001] David Duchovny eyes a dinosaur in the mall in this sci-fi comedy from Ivan Reitman.

▶ **Eragon**
[Stefen Fangmeier, 2006] Another talking dragon movie. This one is based on the novel by Christopher Paolini. Rachel Weisz is the voice of Saphiria the dragon.

▲ **The Lost World: Jurassic Park** [Steven Spielberg, 1997]
The incredible, life-size audioanimatronic *Tyrannosaurus Rex* in the second of the three *Jurassic Park* movies.

▶ **Dragonheart** [Rob Cohen, 1996] Fairy tale foolishness; although Sean Connery's voice is ideal for the voice of Draco, the dragon pictured here, in conversation with knight Dennis Quaid.

162

▲ **Godzilla** [Roland Emmerich, 1998] Godzilla sniffs Matthew Broderick in this misguided remake.

▲ **Dragon Wars** [aka *D-War*, Shim Hyung-rae, 2007]
Korean fantasy, in which a dragon attacks Los Angeles.
You could be fooled by the poster into thinking this
could be fun. I was.

▶ **Avatar** [James
Cameron, 2009]
Jake Sully (Sam
Worthington) in his
Na'vi avatar body
riding a Toruk, one of the
many fantastic examples
of the flora and fauna
of Pandora.

▶ **Land of the Lost**
[Brad Silberling, 2009]
A Will Ferrell comedy
vehicle based on the Sid
and Marty Krofft children's
television series. This action
shot makes it look more
exciting than it is.

▶ **Alice in Wonderland**
[Tim Burton, 2010]
The Jabberwocky!
"The jaws that bite, the
claws that catch!"

▲ **The Mummy: The Tomb of the Dragon Emperor** [Rob
Cohen, 2008] One of the sequels to *The Mummy* [1999]. This is the one
with the cool-looking, three-headed dragon.

MONSTROUS APES

MONSTROUS APES

In *King Kong* [Merian C. Cooper, Ernest B. Schoedsack, 1933], theatrical showman Carl Denham (Robert Armstrong) has captured the giant ape, brought him to Manhattan, and billed him as "The Eighth Wonder of the World." The opening-night audience thrills with anticipation waiting for the curtain to rise on what promises to be the Broadway sensation of the decade. Two women wonder what Mr. Denham has in store for them this time. One remarks that she heard it was "some kind of gorilla." As two men climb over them on their way to their seats, the other woman replies, "Ain't we got enough of them in New York already?"

King Kong is the greatest fantasy film of all time. When Ray Harryhausen saw *King Kong* at Grauman's Chinese Theater on Hollywood Boulevard, he was stunned by Willis O'Brien's stop-motion animation of Kong and the prehistoric denizens of Skull Island. O'Brien became Harryhausen's mentor and hired him to assist on the later stop-motion gorilla picture, the romantic *Mighty Joe Young* [Ernest B. Schoedsack, 1949].

What is it about apes and particularly gorillas that makes them the go-to monster for the movies? Even haunted-house comedies always had a guy in a gorilla suit running around.

Monkeys have obvious similarities to human beings, something that has fascinated people for centuries. But gorillas themselves are relatively new to us. When the first gorilla cadaver was stuffed and brought to Europe from Africa in the late 1840s, the ape's massive size and obvious power shocked many people.

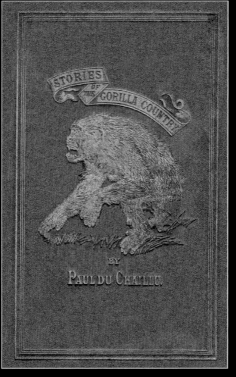

▲ Stories of the Gorilla Country [1867]
Cover of the first edition of Paul du Chaillu's book about his adventures with the gorillas of Africa. (From the Author's collection.)

Popular books, like Paul du Chaillu's *Stories of the Gorilla Country* [1867] helped to create the myth of gorillas as ferocious raiders, carrying off women from native villages. This theme of the gorilla as rapist became a popular motif in western art: the French sculptor Emmanuel Frémiet's bronze *Gorilla Carrying off a Woman* won the Medal of Honor at the Paris Salon in 1887. Popular culture, including the movies, has continued to perpetuate the image of the rampaging giant ape, even though gorillas in the wild are the gentlest of herbivores.

Chimpanzees are known for their intelligence and "human-like" behavior. However, as adorable as baby chimps are, they grow up to be very big and very aggressive animals. Nevertheless, what audiences demanded were *gorillas*.

Filmmakers soon realized that putting a man in a gorilla suit was far more practical than working with a real gorilla. And soon a special breed of performer (often supplying their own ape suits) began playing gorillas in thrillers, horror films, and comedies.

Names like Emil Van Horn, Charles Gemora, George Burrows, Ray "Crash" Corrigan, and Bob Burns may not be familiar names nowadays, but their gorilla suits are, for each actor had his own, instantly recognizable one.

Gorilla suits were often more valued than the performers who owned them. The B-movie producer Herman Cohen was too cheap to fly ape-performer George Burrows to London to wear his gorilla suit for *Konga* [John Lemont, 1961], so Burrows reluctantly agreed to rent it to the production. The suit was worn by an unknown British stunt man.

Konga is a particularly wacky movie. Botanist Michael Webber (an over-the-top Michael Gough) injects a chimpanzee (portrayed by a real chimpanzee) with a serum that somehow changes the chimp into a highly aggressive gorilla. Webber's jealous girlfriend/assistant injects more serum into the chimp/now gorilla which causes it to grow big enough to rampage around London, destroying Tower Bridge and Big Ben in the process. George Burrows was furious when producer Cohen returned his gorilla suit heavily damaged by the miniatures and pyrotechnics used by the British crew. But perhaps Burrows' gorilla suit's lowest moment was when he wore it as the space monster Ro-Man in *Robot Monster* [Phil Tucker, 1953]. The ape body was used, but the head replaced by an extremely silly helmet, which can only be described as a goldfish bowl with an old TV antenna on top.

Crash Corrigan (and his costume) played the gorilla in *The Bride and the Beast* [Adrian Weiss, 1958]. The typically weird Ed Wood screenplay concerns a woman who must chose between her husband and a gorilla! The title character in *The White Gorilla* [Harry L. Fraser, 1945] is Crash Corrigan again, but this time his suit was dyed snow white. With his gorilla suit already dyed, Corrigan quickly appeared in the title role of *White Pongo* [Sam Newfield, 1945] as an albino gorilla who might just be the Missing Link. Corrigan's gorilla also turns up in *Captive Wild Woman* (see page 171), *The Bowery Boys Meet the Monsters* [Edward Bernds, 1954], and one of the few films directed by screenwriter Curt Siodmak, *Bride of the Gorilla* [1951].

Charles Gemora worked as a special-effects man at Paramount Studios for many years, with a sideline performing in the gorilla suits he used to design and manufacture. Gemora took care to make his suits as realistic as possible. He gives one of the great gorilla performances in *The Monster and the Girl* [Stuart Heisler, 1941], a peculiar mixture of mad-scientist, brain-transplant, gangster, and boy-and-his-dog movie that is one of my favorites. Gemora also played the murderous gorilla in *Murders in the Rue Morgue* [Robert Florey, 1932] and fooled around with the Marx Brothers in *At the Circus* [Edward Buzzell, 1939]. One of the craziest

moments in the films of Laurel and Hardy is in *Swiss Miss* [John G. Blystone, 1938] when Stan and Ollie are trying to carry an upright piano across a narrow wooden suspension bridge high over a canyon in the Swiss Alps, and Gemora's gorilla tries to cross in the opposite direction! After a struggle, the gorilla falls off the bridge, only to turn up at the very end of the movie on crutches, with his head bandaged and his leg in a plaster cast, and chase our heroes off into the sunset. Most wonderful of all is when Gemora's gorilla lumbers onto the stage in the glamorous nightclub in *Blonde Venus* [Josef von Sternberg, 1932] and removes his gorilla hands and then head to reveal Marlene Dietrich in a blonde Afro wig!

▲ *Gorille enlevant une Femme* [*Gorilla Carrying Off a Woman*] A bronze sculpture by Emmanuel Frémiet [1887]. (From the Author's collection.)

Emil Van Horn was another renowned gorilla impersonator. He had a less realistic costume than Gemora, but he performs energetically in *The Ape Man* [William Beaudine, 1943], co-starring with Béla Lugosi. He also makes a memorable appearance in W. C. Fields' surreal *Never Give a Sucker an Even Break* [Edward F. Cline, 1941].

Various studio make-up and costume departments manufactured ape suits over the years. But with "special effects make-up man" Rick Baker, the gorilla suit reached new levels of sophistication. His suit for the Bigfoot named Harry in *Harry and the Hendersons* [William Dear, 1987] was worn by Kevin Peter Hall, the very tall actor who later portrayed the Predator in *Predator* [John McTiernan, 1987]. Baker used remote radio controls to work the facial features on Harry which, combined with the terrific mime of Kevin Peter Hall, created a remarkably realistic character.

Baker himself wore the ape suit in John Guillermin's 1976 remake of *King Kong* and as the gorilla named Dino in *The Kentucky Fried Movie* [John Landis, 1977]. His apes for *Greystoke: The Legend of Tarzan, Lord of the Apes* [Hugh Hudson, 1984] and *Gorillas in the Mist* [Michael Apted, 1988] remain unsurpassed.

Why do apes continue to intrigue, amuse, frighten, and fascinate us? Look in the mirror.

Opposite page: (1) *The Monster and the Girl* **[Stuart Heisler, 1941]** Charles Gemora is the gorilla holding Ellen Drew in this lobby card for one of my favorite ape movies. George Zucco's scientist transplants the brain of an avenging farm boy into the skull of a gorilla.

(2) *Blonde Venus* **[Josef von Sternberg, 1932]** During the "Hot Voodoo" dance number, as the drums pound and the trumpet wails, a gorilla menacingly comes onstage. The gorilla removes its head to reveal the beautiful face of Marlene Dietrich (inset)!

(3) *Greystoke: The Legend of Tarzan, Lord of the Apes* **[Hugh Hudson, 1984]** The infant Tarzan, safe in the arms of apes that adopt and raise him in the jungle. The first part of the film, dealing with Tarzan in Africa, is great. Rick Baker made the magnificent apes.

▲ *Tarzan of the Apes* [Scott Sidney, 1918] Elmo Lincoln and friend in the first Tarzan movie. The names of the maker of that ape suit and the player inside it are unknown (at least to me). Based on the books by Edgar Rice Burroughs.

▲ *Murders in the Rue Morgue* [Robert Florey, 1932] Charles Gemora as Erik, the orangutan about to kidnap another woman for his master Dr. Mirakle (Béla Lugosi). Based on Edgar Allan Poe's *The Murders in the Rue Morgue* [1841], which many believe to be the first true detective story.

> # "Out of the underworld comes the Gorilla—strangler of men—kidnapper of women!"

Publicity tagline for *The Gorilla*

▲ *The Gorilla* [Alfred Santell, 1927] Based on the play by Ralph Spence, a spoof of popular stage thrillers like *The Cat and the Canary* [written by John Willard, 1922], this was a Broadway hit turned into a broad comedy film. Here, the title character holds Alice Day in a rather lascivious manner. An odd gorilla suit with a small head and very big hands.

▲ *The Monster and the Girl* [Stuart Heisler, 1941] His brain now inside this massive gorilla's head, Scott Webster regards his sleeping sister, Susan (Ellen Drew). Charlie Gemora's best gorilla-suit performance.

◄ *The Unholy Three* [Jack Conway, 1930] Charles Gemora as Hercules the gorilla and Lon Chaney as ventriloquist Professor Echo. A sound remake of the 1925 silent of the same title, this was Chaney's last film and only talkie. Lon spends most of the film in drag, disguised as Mrs. O'Grady!

▲ *Tarzan the Ape Man* [W. S. Van Dyke, 1932] C. Aubrey Smith and Maureen O'Sullivan in the clutches of a giant gorilla (Ray Corrigan). The first Johnny Weissmuller and Maureen O'Sullivan *Tarzan* movie, this film is where Cheetah and Tarzan's famous yodeling call originated. Produced before the Hays Code, so Weissmuller and O'Sullivan wear extremely scanty loincloths.

▲ *The Ape Man* [William Beaudine, 1943] Experiments by mad doctor James Brewster (Béla Lugosi) turn him into an ape man! He and his gorilla must obtain human spinal fluid to reverse this situation before it's too late. A Monogram Picture, so you know it's cheap.

◄ *Captive Wild Woman* [Edward Dmytryk, 1943] A publicity shot of Cheela the gorilla (Ray "Crash" Corrigan) holding Paula Dupree (Acquanetta). In the film, sexy Acquanetta becomes a gorilla (also Corrigan) and then sultry but deadly Paula Dupree. It is all very impractical.

▲ *Jungle Captive* [Harold Young, 1945] The sequel to *Jungle Woman* [Reginald Le Borg, 1944]. An unsettling, well executed make-up by uncredited maestro Jack Pierce.

◄ *Killer Ape* [Spencer Gordon Bennet, 1953] After years playing Tarzan, former Olympic Gold Medal-winning swimmer Johnny Weissmuller segued into playing Jungle Jim in low-budget pictures and a television series. I've not seen this Jungle Jim adventure, but the credits list Max Palmer as "Man Ape." I bet that's Max tussling with Weissmuller in this photograph.

"Am I dreamin' or did I just see a gorilla? And a beautiful dame!?"

Max O'Hara (Robert Armstrong), *Mighty Joe Young*

▼ *Mighty Joe Young* [Ernest B. Schoedsack, 1949] One of the Joe Young puppets animated by Willis O'Brien and Ray Harryhausen. A wonderful movie!

▲ *The Bowery Boys Meet the Monsters* [Edward Bernds, 1954] The monsters the Bowery Boys meet are a vampire, a robot, and a gorilla.

◄ *Alraune* [Arthur Maria Rabenalt, 1952] Scientist Erich von Stroheim builds a perfect woman except for her complete lack of morality. Here she is, the title character, as played by Hildegard Knef, posing in front of von Stroheim's caged ape.

MISSING LINKS

▲ **2001: A Space Odyssey** [Stanley Kubrick,1968] Daniel Richter as the ape (referred to as Moon Watcher in Arthur C. Clarke's novel) about to toss that bone into one of the most celebrated edits in motion picture history. The ape suits were designed and built by Stuart Freeborn (see page 307).

▲ **Half Human** [Ishirô Honda,1957] The prolific Ishirô Honda's next project after *Godzilla* [1954]; a Yeti-type creature is discovered in the Japanese Alps. A US version added scenes shot in LA with John Carradine and Morris Ankrum.

◀ **Trog** [Freddie Francis, 1970] One of those movies where you wonder if anyone ever went to the rushes. Joan Crawford's last film. Great fun if you are in a cruel mood, otherwise it's depressing.

◀ **Missing Link** [Carol & David Hughes, 1988] Peter Elliot as the last *Australopithecus robustus* (man-ape); his tribe has been slaughtered by the aggressive *Homo erectus* (humans) in this unusual docudrama narrated by Michael Gambon.

▲ **Skullduggery** [Gordon Douglas, 1970] A tribe of ape-like creatures, the Tropis, are used as slave labor in Papua New Guinea. When one of the Tropis is murdered, the trial focuses on whether or not the Tropis are animal or human. An interesting film, starring Burt Reynolds, with the excellent Tropis make-ups credited to Bud Westmore and Marvin G. Westmore.

▲ **Quest for Fire** [Jean-Jacques Annaud, 1981] An ambitious and unintentionally funny story of early man, especially the scene where Rae Dawn Chong teaches her mate the missionary position. Based on the novel by J.-H. Rosny [1911].

▶ Keep 'Em Flying [Arthur Lubin, 1941] Bud Abbott and Lou Costello join the Army Air Corps after being fired from the carnival and air show where they've been working. Lou meets this gorilla.

COMEDY GORILLAS

▲ The Chimp [James Parrott, 1932] A sublime Laurel and Hardy short. Stan and Ollie work for a circus that closes and are paid off with a flea circus and a gorilla wearing a tutu named Ethel (Charlie Gemora). Most of the action concerns them trying to sneak Ethel up to their room under the nose of their suspicious landlord (Billy Gilbert). The landlord is a very jealous man, especially so when he hears a commotion from upstairs and Ollie pleading: "Ethel! Will you take off that tutu and come to bed?" Did I mention that the landlord's wife is named Ethel?

▶ Never Give a Sucker an Even Break [Edward F. Cline, 1941] W. C. Fields, writing under the pseudonym Otis Criblecoblis, created this surrealistic and very funny film, about Fields pitching a film to producer Franklin Pangborn. Fields is pictured with a gorilla, played by Emil Van Horn.

▲ Dizzy Detectives [Jules White, 1943] The 68th short that the Three Stooges—Larry, Moe, and Curly—made for Columbia (they made 190 shorts altogether). The boys are drafted by the police to help solve the mysterious "ape-man" crimes that are terrorizing the city.

▼ At the Circus [Edward Buzzell, 1939] Harpo, Groucho, and Chico crooning with Charlie Gemora in this publicity photo.

▲ Road to Bali [Hal Walker, 1952] Bob Hope, Bing Crosby, and Dorothy Lamour star in this, the sixth of the seven *Road* movies, and the only one in color. Bob is being held by an amorous gorilla.

▲ **Robot Monster** [Phil Tucker, 1953] I'm not entirely sure what George Nader is trying to do to Ro-Man in this publicity shot for one of the all-time, strangely fascinating, terrible movies. I admire the sheer balls of putting a space helmet on a gorilla suit and thinking that would be okay as an alien monster. With music by a young, "gray-listed" Elmer Bernstein!

▲ **Bride of the Gorilla** [Curt Siodmak, 1951] A steamy melodrama, in which South American plantation manager Raymond Burr murders his boss to get to his wife, Barbara Payton, and is cursed by a witch doctor to turn into a murderous gorilla at night. Directed by the screenwriter of *The Wolf Man* [1941]. This time, Lon Chaney, Jr. is the cop on the case.

◀ **The White Gorilla** [Harry L. Fraser, 1945] Ray "Crash" Corrigan in his now white gorilla suit. Corrigan also plays Steve Collins and the Narrator. A triple threat.

▲ **Gorilla at Large** [Harmon Jones, 1954] In Technicolor and 3D! That's beautiful Anne Bancroft in the arms of George Barrows as Goliath the Gorilla. With a cast that includes Lee J. Cobb, Raymond Burr, and Lee Marvin, this one's a keeper!

◀ **Unknown Island** [Jack Bernhard, 1948] A great, hand-tinted publicity shot of the prehistoric, giant gorilla who has the best dialog in the picture.

pLANET OF THE APES

Based on the book by Pierre Boulle, *Planet of the Apes* [Franklin J. Schaffner, 1968] featured innovative, Academy Award-winning make-ups by John Chambers and a forceful performance by Charlton Heston as the stranded astronaut Taylor. The film spawned four sequels, two television series, and a remake in 2001. The screenplay by Michael Wilson and Rod Serling, and the ambitious art direction by William J. Creber and Jack Martin Smith, combined with Leon Shamroy's old-school camera work, make the first *Planet of the Apes* a milestone in movie science fiction.

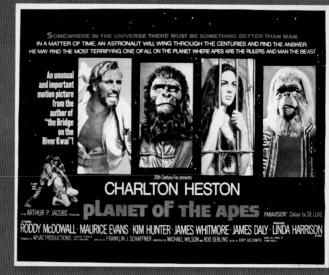

▲ **Planet of the Apes** [1968] The original ad art for Schaffner's science-fiction classic.

◀ **Planet of the Apes** [1968] Kim Hunter and Roddy McDowall as Zira and Cornelius, the chimpanzee scientists, whose curiosity leads to the disclosure of a terrible secret.

"Take your stinking paws off me, you damned dirty ape!"

George Taylor (Charlton Heston), *Planet of the Apes*

▲ **Planet of the Apes** [1968] Maurice Evans as Dr. Zaius, protector of the faith.

▲ **Planet of the Apes** [1968] Charlton Heston as the astronaut Taylor, being restrained by two gorillas.

▲ **Planet of the Apes** [1968] Gorillas pose for a picture with their hunting trophies.

The bizarre world you met in "Planet Of The Apes" was only the beginning... WHAT LIES BENEATH MAY BE THE END!

BENEATH THE PLANET OF THE APES

Starring JAMES FRANCISCUS · KIM HUNTER · MAURICE EVANS · LINDA HARRISON
Co-Starring PAUL RICHARDS · VICTOR BUONO · JAMES GREGORY · JEFF COREY · NATALIE TRUNDY · THOMAS GOMEZ
and CHARLTON HESTON as Taylor

G ALL AGES ADMITTED General Audiences

◀ **Beneath the Planet of the Apes** [Ted Post 1970] Ad art for the first Apes sequel, which ends with the total destruction of the planet Earth!

▶ **Battle for the Planet of the Apes** [J. Lee Thompson 1973] Probably the lowest budget of the original *Apes* series of films. John Huston plays the Lawgiver!

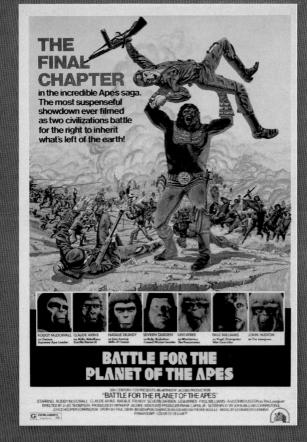

THE FINAL CHAPTER in the incredible Apes saga. The most suspenseful showdown ever filmed as two civilizations battle for the right to inherit what's left of the earth!

BATTLE FOR THE PLANET OF THE APES

▶ **Battle for the Planet of the Apes** [J. Lee Thompson, 1973] The Author as "Jake's Friend" in his role (mercifully cut out of the picture) as Babysitter to Caesar's son. Seen here giving said son a piggy-back ride.

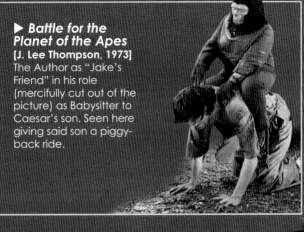

"Get your stinking hands off me, you damn dirty human!"

Attar (Michael Clarke Duncan), *Planet of the Apes* [2001]

◀ **Planet of the Apes** [Tim Burton, 2001] Tim Roth as General Thade throttles Mark Wahlberg as astronaut Capt. Leo Davidson.

▲ **Planet of the Apes** [Tim Burton, 2001] Michael Clarke Duncan as Col. Attar. Richard Zanuck, who was President of Production at 20th Century-Fox and the man who gave the green light to the original, produced this disappointing remake. With great ape make-ups by Rick Baker.

177

◀ *Konga*
[John Lemont, 1961]
Mad scientist
Michael Gough is
helpless in Konga's
giant grasp in this
publicity paste-up
photo.

▶ *Queen Kong*
[Frank Agrama,
1976] Obviously
Queen Kong was
a fan of *Konga*
and wanted a
photo of herself
by Big Ben, just
like Konga's.
And here it is.

"Due to the horrifying nature of this film, no one will be admitted to the theater!"

Publicity tagline, *Schlock*

◀ *Schlock* [John Landis, 1973] Shot in 1971
but not released until 1973, this was the first
collaboration between Rick Baker and me.
I would like a title card at the head of this film
that reads: "Made in 12 days for $60,000 by a
21 year old, so give me a break." Not good,
but it does have its moments.

▲ *Murders in the Rue Morgue* [Gordon
Hessler,1971] Jason Robards about to get his
throat cut in this loose adaptation of the Edgar
Allan Poe story. In this movie, the disfigured
murderer disguises himself as an ape that looks
suspiciously like the Stuart Freeborn apes from
2001: A Space Odyssey [1968].

▶ *The Abominable
Snowman*
[Val Guest, 1957]
Based on a BBC
teleplay called
The Creature by
Nigel Kneale, this
Hammer film about
an expedition to find
the Yeti starred
Peter Cushing and
Forrest Tucker.

▲ **The Man With Two Brains** [Carl Reiner,1983] A gorilla for use in a brain-transplant operation in mad scientist Dr. Alfred Necessiter's (David Warner) lab in his castle-condo, in this very funny Steve Martin movie. Steve plays Dr. Michael Hfuhruhurr.

▲ **Mighty Joe Young** [Ron Underwood, 1998] Charlize Theron and Bill Paxton with the amazing, full-size Joe Young built by Rick Baker for this remake.

▲ **Harry and the Hendersons** [William Dear, 1987] Kevin Peter Hall as Harry in another Academy-Award-winning make-up by Rick Baker.

▶ **The Mummy: Tomb of the Dragon Emperor** [Rob Cohen, 2008] I would not want to be in this guy's place, in the clutches of a very big CG Yeti.

King Kong

◀◀▲ *King Kong* [Merian C. Cooper, Ernest B. Schoedsack, 1933]
The original and still the greatest giant ape movie ever made. Here is ad art from the first of its many theatrical releases and an excellent shot of Kong carrying Fay Wray up to his mountain lair. Above is a close-up of Kong (see page 303).

▶ *Son of Kong*
[Ernest B. Schoedsack, 1933]
Carl Denham (the great Robert Armstrong) returns to Skull Island and finds a slightly-smaller-than-Kong, white gorilla. Made quickly to cash in on *King Kong*'s fantastic success. The ending really traumatized me, as a kid.

◀ *King Kong Escapes*
[aka *King Kong's Counterattack*, Ishirô Honda, 1967] Dr. Who invents a giant robot King Kong called Mechani-Kong and... oh, never mind.

▲ *King Kong* [John Guillermin, 1976] A close-up of Rick Baker as King Kong in the Dino De Laurentiis remake.

▲▶ *King Kong* [Peter Jackson, 2005] A close-up of Andy Serkis as King Kong in a motion-capture performance; (right) Naomi Watts and Kong share a rare quiet moment together.

"Oh no, it wasn't the airplanes. It was Beauty killed the Beast!"

Carl Denham (Jack Armstrong), *King Kong* [1933]

▲ *King Kong Lives* [John Guillermin, 1986] Peter Elliot as King Kong in the worst *King Kong* movie ever.

Rick Baker

Rick Baker at home (photo by the Author).

JL: Rick, what's your definition of a monster?

RB: I think I have a different concept of a monster than most people. I've always been fascinated by them, but I don't see them as bad. The kinds of monsters that I like are Frankenstein's Monster, Quasimodo, and guys like that. The ones I like are sympathetic.

JL: OK, but what *are* monsters?

RB: Monsters are creatures that don't exist in the real universe.

JL: Mythological monsters, like dragons and Cyclops…

RB: I like all those. I've always been attracted to things that aren't in the real world. Fantastic things, grotesque things. I don't like gory stuff…

JL: But you do a lot of gore effects! Didn't you tell me that when you were a teenager, you used to do make-up wounds on yourself, just to freak people out?

RB: Yeah I did, but that was just to get a reaction, an easy reaction. That's why I don't have that much respect for those kinds of make-ups because I know how easy it is to fool somebody with just the sight of blood. It's not as hard as doing a character, or to turn a young person, through make-up, into an old person.

JL: Your own interest in monsters seems to be aesthetic.

RB: It's a visual thing. I've always been fascinated by the way they look and how people designed and changed a human into something else.

JL: If I said to you, "I want to be made-up to look like me, but I want it to be scary," are there things, shortcuts, you can do…?

RB: There is kind of a formula to that.

JL: Like what?

RB: Angularity. Look at the werewolf in *An American Werewolf in London* [John Landis, 1981], your four-legged hound from hell. It had big scary teeth that are going to tear you up, but it's also sculpted in a very angular way. The brows are very angular and there are 45° angles all through it. There is something scary about 45° angles.

JL: Well, Dracula has got that going on.

RB: Yeah, with the widow's peak and the eyebrows shaved—I use 45° angles all the time.

JL: They always show the devil that way, and Mephistopheles has brows like that.

RB: Yeah, the devil's horns go up at 45°, as well as the ears. I don't know why 45° angles

are scary, but they are! I think some of the scariest make-ups, and the guy who was the best at making scary faces, was Lon Chaney, Sr. So many designs that I've done, and I know other make-up artists would say the same, were influenced by Chaney in *The Phantom of the Opera* [Rupert Julian, 1925]. Some of the faces he makes in that are great.

JL: And Chaney was using old stage make-up, with big limitations in what he could do because of the primitive materials he had to work with.

RB: A lot of the old make-up guys didn't have a lot of the tools that we have now, and that's part of the reason their efforts worked so well. They worked within specific limitations. They couldn't make 10,000 werewolves crawl on the ceiling, you know? There was a certain reality to their work. It was closer to what you could really believe.

JL: Do you have a favorite movie monster?

RB: Frankenstein is my favorite and the Boris Karloff version is by far the best. It was one of those movies where the mix of people involved—James Whale, Jack Pierce, and Boris Karloff—created magic.

JL: Karloff had an amazing face.

RB: He's got a great face, and the make-up Pierce designed for his face never looked as good on anyone else. And I don't think that anyone else was as good as Karloff either.

JL: OK, so you've done a lot of aliens.

RB: Aliens and werewolves. I did your movie [*An American Werewolf in London*], and I did *The Wolfman* [Joe Johnston, 2010], and I did *Wolf* [Mike Nichols, 1994]…

JL: Of course! What is it about werewolves that people are so interested in.

RB: Well, I think everybody seems to feel like there's a beast inside them somewhere.

JL: Like Jekyll and Hyde?

RB: It's that whole evil side coming out. But what I like about werewolf movies is the change in the appearance of the person. I'm interested in the transformation, more than the story itself. That animal and man combination has always fascinated me, going back to [French artist Charles] Le Brun. I always thought the combination of humans and animals was such a fun thing. That's why I liked *Island of Lost Souls* [Erle C. Kenton, 1932].

JL: The first film version of (H. G. Wells' novel) *The Island of Dr. Moreau*? I love that movie! The make-ups in that picture are great.

RB: Better than in any of the remakes.

JL: Why is that?

RB: Because my favorite make-ups are the

Baker making-up Griffin Dunne as "Dead Jack" for *An American Werewolf in London* [1981].

ones where the guys didn't have the tools that we have today! For *Island of Lost Souls*, they didn't have foam rubber or silicone so they couldn't make really crazy things, and I think they benefited from that. The Beast Men are these hairy, man-like creatures, but there's a reality to it.

JL: You flew to London to join me for Ray Harryhausen's 90th birthday event at the National Film Theater. [Steven] Spielberg, [James] Cameron, [George] Lucas, Tim Burton, Guillermo [Del Toro] all talked about how he inspired them. What is so special about Ray's work?

RB: He really does give those metal and foam rubber puppets life! He makes them characters… but also, I think a lot of this is that we're the generation which grew up with his films and saw them fresh and new. I would watch a Harryhausen movie and suffer through 20 minutes of bad acting just to see his effects. Since then, I've seen so many huge effects movies, with thousands of things doing all sorts of crazy action, to the point where it just has no impact and I don't care. But I can watch one of Ray's puppet animations with complete pleasure.

JL: Do you remember the big battle in the second *Lord of the Rings* movie [*The Two Towers*, Peter Jackson, 2002]? That was the first time I saw a CG movie with so much CG that wasn't in outer space. I thought: "This is great!" It was a way of realizing these enormous monsters on a vast scale. But now I've become so bored with CG effects. Things have gotten so elaborate, I just don't care.

RB: I know, just because you can have a thousand werewolves climbing upside-down on the ceiling, it doesn't mean that you should!

JL: You know what you showed me once that totally freaked me out? You were very gleeful. You had gotten a medical encyclopedia full of horrible photographs of medical anomalies, and one of them was of teeth growing out of a guy's leg. Do you remember that? It really freaked me out.

RB: When I first went to junior college, I found books on plastic surgery. Just talking about those kinds of things scares me. Seeing what can happen to you and that you can still be alive… There was one guy in particular that was in an airplane crash, who basically had no face, and no skin on the top of his head. They had drilled holes in his skull to let the pressure out, but the guy was alert and alive. I find that horrifying. What scares me is that it could actually happen to me. How would I deal with that when I looked in the mirror and that's what looked back at me?
   I think that's something that always fascinated me about make-up: that I could look through my eyes, and see a completely different person looking back at me in the mirror. I was painfully shy as a kid, but in make-up you can do things you can't do as yourself.

JL: I think that's true of Eddie Murphy.

RB: I think it's true of any actor. Everybody hates the process of being made-up—hours in the morning—but you're sitting there looking at yourself, and you can see that other face, the character's face, looking back.

JL: What clearly demonstrates that is costume. I've seen it millions of times. Once the actors get into their clothes, they know who the character is.

RB: Actors need that. When you walk onto a cool set and you're in this environment, and you're in make-up and costume, it's got to help! With all this movement to motion-capture and blue screen, I really think it affects the performance and reality of the moment.

"There is something scary about 45° angles."

JL: I am always impressed by the fact that actors, especially in fantasy films, so often have to react and respond to something that is not there. Some gigantic creature or cataclysmic event that will be put in later in post production.

RB: So many people say "If we don't do it today, it's not going to work." Then I'll say, "Did you see *Star Wars*? You know the band that's in the cantina was shot six months later in a whole different country, by a whole different group of people, and you would swear that they're there in that cantina."

JL: But that used to be standard! That's filmmaking!

RB: Yeah, that's what's missing now though, isn't it? (Laughs.)

Baker working wolf head in Piccadilly Circus for *An American Werewolf in London* [1981]. (See page 48.)

NATURE'S REVENGE

Whether it is rats, spiders, snakes, bees, sharks, or just big old mean dogs, we are all afraid of some animal out there. Movie makers, constantly searching for something to scare us with, have shamelessly taken advantage of our reasonable fears of bee stings, spider bites, and being devoured by sharks, by featuring these and other beasties in horror films.

Producers and directors can take a real creature and make it gigantic, like the crab in *Mysterious Island* [Cy Endfield, 1961] or the spider—"Crawling Terror, 100 Feet High"—in *Tarantula!* [Jack Arnold, 1955], or they can just unleash vast numbers of the critters we dread: bees in *The Swarm* [Irwin Allen, 1978]; or snakes in *Snakes on a Plane* [David R. Ellis, 2006]. If a vast, unstoppable army of ants in *The Naked Jungle* [Byron Haskin, 1954] isn't enough to scare you, then how about the REALLY HUGE ants of *Them!* [Gordon Douglas, 1954] or *Empire of the Ants* [Bert I. Gordon, 1977]? If the rats made you uneasy in *Willard* [Daniel Mann, 1971], schlock producer's logic says that the giant rats in *The Food of the Gods* [Bert I. Gordon, 1976] should *really* make you jump out of your seat.

I can imagine the writer's pitch now: "The great white shark that terrorized the beaches in

▲ *It Came From Beneath the Sea*
[Robert Gordon, 1955] To save time animating his stop-motion puppet, Ray Harryhausen gave it only six tentacles—so it was really a giant *hextapus* that pulled down the Golden Gate Bridge.

Jaws [Steven Spielberg, 1975] was puny! He just wasn't really that big! How about a Mega Shark?" "Yes! Yes!" shouts the producer. "And he could battle a Giant Octopus!" And that is how *Mega Shark vs. Giant Octopus* [Jack Perez as Ace Hannah, 2009] was born. In that film, the absurdly big Mega Shark destroys San Francisco's famed Golden Gate Bridge, which had obviously been repaired since 1955 when it was heavily damaged by the giant octopus in Ray Harryhausen's *It Came From Beneath the Sea* [Robert Gordon, 1955].

If worms give you the creeps, then the millions of flesh-eating bloodworms in *Squirm* [Jeff Lieberman, 1976] will make you do just what the title says. In *The African Queen* [John Huston, 1951] the audience shared Humphrey Bogart's character's revulsion when he came out of the water covered in leeches. If a few normal-size leeches generated such disgust, then an *Attack of the Giant Leeches* [Bernard L. Kowalski, 1959] is the only way to go.

It isn't always necessary to make something we naturally avoid, like a scorpion, into a colossal version of itself to frighten us. (*The Black Scorpion* [Edward Ludwig, 1957] did that with stop-motion animation by the great Willis O'Brien.) Sometimes a rabid dog [*Cujo*, Lewis Teague, 1983] or just an angry grizzly bear [*Grizzly*, William Girdler, 1976] is enough to terrify us without the use of special effects.

Usually, the giant animal monster is explained by some pseudo-scientific theory: it's a prehistoric beast frozen in ice, or a mutant, created by atomic radiation. The monster is sometimes

Previous pages: The Fabulous World of Jules Verne [aka A Deadly Invention, Karel Zeman, 1958] Czech filmmaker Karel Zeman's unique blend of live action, stop motion, and drawn animation reproduces the look of 19th-century etchings, which works wonderfully well in this fusion of two Jules Verne novels.
Opposite page: Creature From the Black Lagoon [Jack Arnold, 1954] Julie Adams and the Gill-Man (Ben Chapman) in an unusual color publicity still (the film is black and white).

created by toxic waste or by some covert corporate or government experiment gone terribly wrong. The man-eating piranha in Joe Dante's *Piranha* [1978] are the results of a misguided military experiment, while in the 2010 remake, *Piranha 3D* [Alexandre Aja], the vicious piranha are prehistoric fish freed from an underwater cavern by an earthquake. The change reflects the politics of the era in which each film was made.

Sometimes the reason for nature turning on us is unexplained. When Alfred Hitchcock's *The Birds* [1963] attack and kill, no reason is given for their behavior. The characters speculate on what could be making the birds turn suddenly homicidal, but the movie deliberately offers no solution to the mystery and ends on an uneasy, unresolved note.

Creature From the Black Lagoon [Jack Arnold, 1954] is a classic story of an ancient species destroyed by contact with modern civilization, essentially the plot of the first half of *King Kong* [1933]. The Gill-Man was designed by Millicent Patrick and is considered to be one of the greatest monsters in film history. The celebrated sequence where Julie Adams is swimming on the surface of the lagoon, unaware of the Creature as it swims beneath her, remains one of the most poetic in the genre. A B movie made almost entirely on the back lot of Universal Studios (except for the underwater sequences, shot in the crystal-clear waters of Wakulla Springs, Florida) *Creature From the Black Lagoon* was a great success and is still one of the best 3D movies ever made. Two sequels followed, in which the Gill-Man continued to be abused by the human leads.

▲ **Moby Dick** [John Huston, 1956] Captain Ahab (Gregory Peck) with harpoon in the jaws of the Great White Whale.

Other humanoid, water-based creatures include *The Monster of Piedras Blancas* [Irvin Berwick, 1959], the very silly fish-men of *Horror of Party Beach* [Del Tenney, 1964], and the infamous *Humanoids From the Deep* [Barbara Peeters, 1980]. Infamous because the producer, Roger Corman, had additional scenes shot in which the monsters were shown actually raping the nubile young girls hired to be topless and scream as the slimy fish-men, created by make-up maestro Rob Bottin, had their way with them. And to increase the sleaze factor, the movie ends with one of the rape victims giving birth to a baby fish monster by having it burst through her stomach in a geyser of blood, in blatant imitation of the "chest burster" scene in Ridley Scott's *Alien* [1979].

Underwater is not the only place we will find humanoid monsters—they also come from underground. The scary, carnivorous cave dwellers a group of women encounter in Neil Marshall's *The Descent* [2005] are very nasty indeed. Be warned, this is definitely not a movie for the claustrophobic. Deep in the bowels of the Earth can also be found *The Mole People* [Virgil W. Vogel, 1956], who are used as slave labor by a race of "Sumerian Albinos!"

Another movie that features an insatiable underground threat is Ron Underwood's *Tremors* [1990]. Kevin Bacon and Fred Ward play two contemporary cowboys trying to deal with the huge subterranean monsters they discover in a small town in the Nevada desert. *Tremors* is a textbook example of a well made and entertaining monster movie.

Opposite page: (1) *Mega Shark vs. Giant Octopus* [Ace Hannah, 2009] Mega Shark attacks the Golden Gate Bridge. Followed by *Mega Shark vs. Crocosaurus* [2010] and *Sharktopus* [2010]. What can I say?

(2) *Night of the Lepus* [William F. Claxton, 1972] Giant rabbits attack a small town in Arizona. Harebrained.

(3) *Jaws* [Steven Spielberg, 1975] Chief Brody (Roy Scheider) in his final confrontation with the monstrous great white shark in Spielberg's summer blockbuster.

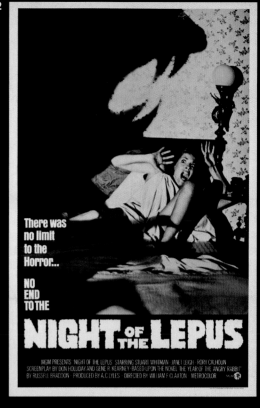

HUMANOIDS

"There are many strange legends in the Amazon. Even I, Lucas, have heard the legend of a man-fish."

Lucas (Nestor Paiva),
Creature from the Black Lagoon

▲ **Creature From the Black Lagoon** [Jack Arnold, 1954] Ben Chapman as the Gill-man on stage at Universal Studios. Ricou Browning played the Gill-man in all of the underwater sequences.

◄ **Humanoids From the Deep**
[Barbara Peeters, 1980]
A New World Pictures exploitation
creature-feature.

► **The Beach Girls
and the Monster**
[aka *Monster from the
Surf*, Jon Hall, 1965]
A mutated South
American "Fantigua Fish"
monster starts killing
surfers and their
girlfriends.

▲ **The Monster of Piedras Blancas**
[Irvin Berwick, 1959] A lighthouse keeper leaves food
for a sea creature. This turns out to be a mistake.

▲ **The Mole People** [Virgil W. Vogel, 1956] Archaeologists discover a race of Sumerian albinos that live underground and use humanoid Mole Men as slaves to harvest their primary food source—mushrooms!

▲ **Octaman** [Harry Essex, 1976] This photograph tells you everything you need to know about *Octaman*. Early Rick Baker.

▲ **SSSSSSS** [Bernard L. Kowalski, 1973] Mad ophiologist Dr. Stoner (Strother Martin) injects snake venom into his daughter's boyfriend, which transforms him into a malformed, half-man, half-snake.

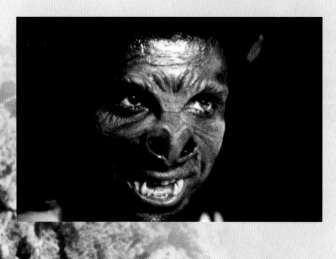

◄ **The Bat People** [Jerry Jameson, 1974] A doctor on vacation with his wife visits Carlsbad Caverns and is bitten by a bat. He soon finds himself transforming into a vampire bat man!

▲ **The Descent** [Neil Marshall, 2005] Six women go spelunking and encounter terrifying, subterranean, flesh-eating humanoids in this claustrophobic, scary movie.

▶ *Attack of the Giant Leeches* [Bernard L. Kowalski, 1959] Deep in the swamps of the Florida Everglades, a giant leech attacks another victim.

▲ *Mysterious Island* [Cy Endfield, 1961] The castaways fight a giant crab on Captain Nemo's island. Ray Harryhausen animated an actual crab shell purchased at Harrods Food Hall in London.

▶ *The Birds* [Alfred Hitchcock, 1963] Melanie Daniels (Tippi Hedren) runs from another unexplained bird attack. Based on the novella by Daphne du Maurier.

▲ *The Naked Jungle* [Byron Haskin, 1954] Charlton Heston struggles to save a Peruvian cocoa plantation from the "Marabunta"—millions of voracious army ants.

▲ *The Alligator People* [Roy Del Ruth, 1959] Strange goings-on in the bayou, as Beverly Garland locates her missing husband and discovers that he is metamorphosing into half-man, half-alligator!

Eight-Legged Terrors

TARANTULA!

JOHN AGAR
MARA CORDAY
LEO G. CARROLL

Regie-Jack Arnold

▲ *Tarantula!* [Jack Arnold, 1955] The tremendous tarantula in the movie never holds a woman as illustrated here in the ad art. It was not unusual for exploitation picture promotional art to exaggerate.

"In my hunt for food, I had become the hunted."

Scott Carey (Grant Williams), *The Incredible Shrinking Man*

▲ *The Incredible Shrinking Man* [Jack Arnold, 1957] Growing ever smaller, Scott Carey (Grant Williams) uses a nail as a spear to defend himself from a common household spider.

► *Kingdom of the Spiders* [John Cardos, 1977] Pesticides have killed off their normal insect diet, so the tarantulas of Verde Valley begin to attack in large numbers to bring down bigger prey.

▲ *Arachnid* [Jack Sholder, 2001] Bad enough their plane crashed, now they're being attacked by giant spiders!

► *Eight Legged Freaks* [Ellory Elkayem, 2002] Toxic waste creates giant spiders, yet again. The CG spiders look creepy, but the movie is not.

▶ *Grizzly*
[aka *Killer Grizzly*,
William Girdler, 1976]
Identical in plot to *Jaws*,
but with an 18-foot-tall
grizzly bear instead of a
great white shark.

▶ GRIZZLY
18 feet of gut-crunching, man-eating terror!

CHRISTOPHER GEORGE · ANDREW PRINE · RICHARD JAECKEL
in GRIZZLY
starring JOAN McCALL · JOE DORSEY

EDWARD L. MONTORO and FILM VENTURES INTERNATIONAL present Grizzly A WILLIAM GIRDLER FILM
Written by HARVEY FLAXMAN & DAVID SHELDON · Produced by DAVID SHELDON & HARVEY FLAXMAN · Directed by WILLIAM GIRDLER
Executive Producer EDWARD L. MONTORO · Music by ROBERT O. RAGLAND · Paperback Edition of GRIZZLY by PYRAMID BOOKS
Filmed in TODD-AO 35 · COLOR by MOVIE LAB   PG

◀ *Day of the Animals*
[William Girdler, 1977]
Depletion of the ozone layer
causes every animal above
5,000 feet to go crazy. Bad
news for hikers in a forest in
Northern California.

"My God,
look at
the rats!"

Mr. Martin (Ernest Borgnine), *Willard* [1971]

◀ *Willard* [Daniel Mann,
1971] A lonely young
man is unable to kill the
rats in the basement.
Soon, they do his bidding.
Based on the novel *The
Ratman's Notebooks* by
Stephen Gilbert.

▲ *Willard* [Glen Morgan, 2003] A remake of the
1971 film with Crispin Glover in the Bruce Davison role.
This has none of the pathos of the original and suffers
from the lack of Elsa Lanchester and Ernest Borgnine.

▲ The Savage Bees [Bruce Geller, 1976] A swarm of African killer bees comes ashore off a ship in New Orleans and just about ruins Mardi Gras!

▲ The Food of the Gods [Bert I. Gordon, 1976] Ralph Meeker is eaten by giant rats in this low-rent and very loose adaptation of H. G. Wells' novel *The Food of the Gods and How It Came to Earth* [1904].

Bee Stings

hives of horror!
Excited by the smell of fear they inflict their fatal stings!

PARAMOUNT PICTURES PRESENTS

THE DEADLY BEES

◄ The Deadly Bees
[Freddie Francis, 1967]
A British pop star takes a vacation on Seagull Island, where a beekeeper has specially bred bees to attack and kill.

◄ Empire of the Ants [Bert I. Gordon, 1977] A toxic spill turns ordinary ants into intelligent, rampaging monsters, bent on conquering mankind. Another Bert I. Gordon trashing of an H. G. Wells story.

"This is more than a movie. It's a prediction!"

Publicity tagline for *The Swarm*

the BEES

JOHN SAXON · ANGEL TOMPKINS · JOHN CARRADINE

► Mysterious Island [Cy Endfield,1961] Michael Callan and Beth Rogan are about to be sealed up in a honeycomb by a giant bee.

▲ The Bees
[Alfredo Zacharias, 1978]
Gigantic swarms of South American killer bees attack North America. Not only that, "They prey on HUMAN FLESH!"

◄ The Swarm [Irwin Allen, 1978] Olivia de Havilland wonders how her career ever came to this. Henry Fonda and Michael Caine are also in this ridiculous Irwin Allen movie.

▲ *Piranha* [Joe Dante, 1978] "Operation Razorteeth," a covert Vietnam War research project, ends up creating the menace for New World Pictures' jump onto the *Jaws* bandwagon.

◀ *Mysterious Island* [Lucien Hubbard, 1929] Undersea creatures crowd around the unconscious Lionel Barrymore, in the first movie version of Jules Verne's sequel to *20,000 Leagues Under the Sea.*

▲ *Deep Blue Sea* [Renny Harlin, 1999] Searching for a cure for Alzheimer's disease, scientists increase the brain capacity of three mako sharks, making them—in the words of the movie's tagline—"Bigger. Smarter. Faster. Meaner." Things go awry for the scientists.

▲ *Leviathan* [George Cosmatos, 1988] Deep water miners deal with an undersea monster that is determined to eat them.

▲ *Lake Placid* [Steve Miner, 1999] A huge crocodile causes trouble in a lake in Maine. This movie got a decidedly mixed reaction but still spawned two sequels.

Calamari!

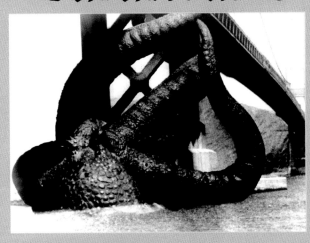

▲ It Came From Beneath the Sea
[Robert Gordon, 1955] A gigantic octopus destroys
the Golden Gate Bridge in this Ray Harryhausen thriller.

▲ 20,000 Leagues Under the Sea [Richard Fleischer, 1954] Ned Land (Kirk Douglas)
and Captain Nemo (James Mason, in white sweater) battle a giant squid in Walt Disney's
first major live-action picture.

**▶ Monster From the
Ocean Floor**
[Wyott Ordung, 1954]
A one-eyed sea monster
terrorizes Mexico. "Up from
the forbidden depths comes
a Tidal Wave of Terror!"

▶ Tentacles
[Ovidio G. Assonitis,
1997] A giant
octopus starts
eating tourists in
Ocean Beach,
much to John
Huston, Shelley
Winters, and Henry
Fonda's chagrin.

▶ Octopus [John Eyres, 2000]
A Soviet nuclear submarine sinks off of the
coast of Cuba during the Cuban Missile
Crisis. The subsequent radiation leak
creates a gigantic, mutant octopus,
which promptly sinks passing ships.

Snakes!

◄ *Raiders of the Lost Ark*
[Steven Spielberg, 1981]
Indiana Jones (Harrison Ford) has only
one phobia—he hates snakes!

▲ *Stanley* [William Grefe, 1972] A young
Seminole Indian uses rattlesnakes to get
revenge on those who have wronged him.

▲ *Jaws of Satan* [aka *King Cobra*, Bob
Claver, 1981] Satan takes the form of a giant
snake in this silly movie.

▲ *Snakes on a Plane* [David R. Ellis,
2006] The passengers and crew are not
happy about snakes on the plane.

▲ *Anaconda* [Luis Llosa, 1997] An insane hunter enlists a film crew to help him
find and trap the biggest snake in the Amazon.

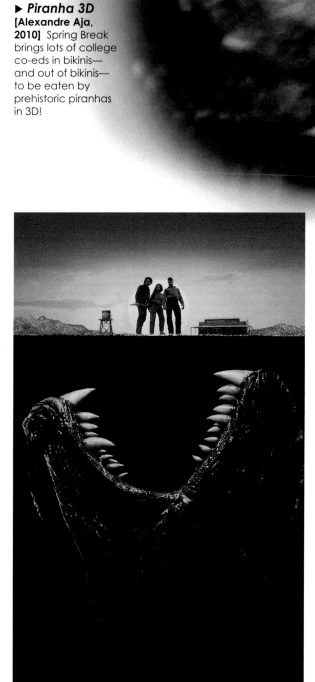

▶ *Piranha 3D*
[Alexandre Aja,
2010] Spring Break
brings lots of college
co-eds in bikinis—
and out of bikinis—
to be eaten by
prehistoric piranhas
in 3D!

▲ *Tremors* [Ron Underwood, 1990] A very entertaining
movie about two modern cowboys (Kevin Bacon and
Fred Ward) coping with big underground monsters in the
Nevada desert.

◀ *Squirm* [Jeff Lieberman, 1976] A storm knocks down high power lines, sending electricity into the ground. For some reason, this causes thousands of bloodworms to attack humans. This actor is actually covered in thousands of real bloodworms, which is not dangerous, but is pretty gross.

▶ *Cujo* [Lewis Teague, 1983] A rabid St. Bernard is enough to generate real chills in this suspenseful adaptation of the book by the prolific Stephen King.

▲ *Frankenfish* [Mark Dippé, 2004] "Genetic engineering" turns normal snakehead fish into enormous monsters, killing people in the bayou.

Atomic Mutations

Atomic Mutations

The threat of nuclear annihilation has been a Sword of Damocles over our planet for more than 65 years. But usually we just prefer not to think about it. The fear of destruction on an apocalyptic scale was very real in 1962, when the Cuban Missile Crisis brought the USA and the Soviet Union to the brink of nuclear conflict.

A movie that captures the sense of impending doom and paranoia of that time is Joe Dante's excellent *Matinee* [1993]. Although ostensibly about a William Castle-like schlock Hollywood producer (John Goodman), the movie also boasts a terrific parody of the then-popular Atomic Mutation pictures, which reflected audiences' atomic anxiety. *Mant!*, the film within the film, is perfectly done.

An atomic bomb test in the Arctic awakens *The Beast From 20,000 Fathoms* [Eugène Lourié, 1953], which swims down to New York City and, through the exquisite stop-motion animation of Ray Harryhausen, creates urban chaos. The giant dinosaur is finally destroyed while ravaging Coney Island.

The same studio, Warner Brothers, saw the box-office gold in radioactive monster pictures and began its next movie with a haunting sequence of two police officers discovering a little girl found wandering in the New Mexico desert. Terrified and in shock, she can only scream, "Them!" *Them!* [Gordon Douglas, 1954] tells the story of gigantic ants, mutated by exposure to the radiation from

▲ *Kiss Me Deadly* [Robert Aldrich, 1955] Gaby Rodgers opens "the great whatsit"—a Pandora's Box of nuclear detonations. Based on the novel by Mickey Spillane.

atomic tests. The giant ants leave havoc and death in their wake. The army finally tracks the ants and their queen to the famous concrete LA River in Los Angeles, and destroys them with machine guns and flamethrowers. The scientist in charge surveys the charred remains of the monsters and declares, "When Man entered the atomic age, he opened the door to a new world. What we may eventually find in that new world, nobody can predict."

That same year, Japan's Toho Studios released their version of *The Beast From 20,000 Fathoms*, titled *Godzilla* [Ishirô Honda, 1954]. This is a dark tale of yet another huge reptilian monster rising from the sea, but this time to destroy Tokyo. Also the result of a nuclear explosion, Godzilla is truly enormous and breathes radioactive fire as he flattens cities. A heavily edited version, incorporating new footage featuring Raymond Burr as reporter "Steve Martin," was released in the US in 1956 with the title *Godzilla, King of the Monsters!* (Note: yes, the character in Godzilla is named "Steve Martin." But also remember that the soulless killer wearing that blank mask in *Halloween* is named "Michael Myers!")

Exposure to a mysterious radioactive cloud somehow causes Grant Williams to grow smaller and smaller in *The Incredible Shrinking Man* [Jack Arnold, 1957]. Based on the novel and screenplay by the great Richard Matheson, *The Incredible Shrinking Man* is both serious and ultimately profound. Jack Arnold's exemplary direction of the intense battle in the basement between the tiny protagonist and a normal but now giant-seeming spider, clearly inspired the battle with the huge spider Shelob in Peter Jackson's *The Lord of the Rings: The Return of the King* [2003] and the

Previous pages: Them! **[Gordon Douglas, 1954]** Giant ants, the result of atomic mutation, in the first of the 1950s Big Bug movies.

Opposite page: Godzilla, King of the Monsters! **[Ishirô Honda, 1956]** The US poster for the 1956 American release of this Japanese response to being the only country so far that has been atomic-bombed. The tagline says it all: "Civilization crumbles as its death rays blast a city of 6 million from the face of the Earth!"

encounter with the massive spider Aragog in *Harry Potter and the Chamber of Secrets* [Chris Columbus, 2002]. And speaking of spiders…

A biologist (Leo G. Carroll) experimenting with "atomic nutrients" to further food production, first suffers disfigurement and then finds that he has unleashed upon the world a gargantuan *Tarantula!* [Jack Arnold, 1955]; a tarantula so large that only jets dropping napalm can eventually stop it. The jet pilot that saves the day is played by a young Clint Eastwood.

Another notable victim of the effects of radiation is poor Lt. Col. John Manning who, after being exposed to a plutonium bomb blast, grows into a 60-foot giant wearing what looks like a diaper in *The Amazing Colossal Man* [Bert I. Gordon, 1957]. Even though we think he is dead at the end of that movie, Lt. Col. Manning makes a spectacular comeback in *War of the Colossal Beast* [Bert I. Gordon, 1958], still 60-feet tall, still wearing a diaper. This time, however, his face is disfigured—which, I guess, is the reason his billing was changed from "Colossal Man" to "Colossal Beast."

Radiation from a meteorite is the cause of a family curse in *Die, Monster, Die!* [Daniel Haller, 1965], a very loose adaptation of H. P. Lovecraft's story "The Color Out of Space," starring Boris Karloff and Nick Adams.

Donald Pleasence's experiments with radiation result in *The Mutations* [1974], directed by Jack Cardiff, one of the cinema's greatest directors of photography. *The Mutations*, however, is a sleazy piece of work with scenes reminiscent of Tod Browning's masterwork *Freaks* [1932], using physically handicapped people to cruel effect.

Doomwatch [Peter Sasdy, 1972] was based on a BBC television series in which the population of a small island off the English coast becomes malformed and violent after eating fish made toxic with pollution. Pollution is also responsible for *The Toxic Avenger* [Lloyd Kaufman, Michael Herz, 1984] and the ridiculous mutant bear in *Prophecy* [John Frankenheimer, 1979]. However, my favorite result of exposure to toxic waste happens spectacularly to one of the bad guys in Paul Verhoeven's breathtaking *RoboCop* [1987].

Hell Comes to Frogtown [Donald G. Jackson, R. J. Kizer, 1988] concerns a group of mutant amphibians in a post-apocalyptic future that capture a group of non-mutant, fertile women to use as sex slaves!

No explanation is given for the hideous monsters in *The Mist* [Frank Darabont, 2007]. Based on a novella by Stephen King, people find themselves trapped in a supermarket surrounded by dense mist and lots of genuinely creepy monsters. I suggest that the monsters are not aliens, or some form of biblical retribution, but the result of a military atomic weaponry program gone wrong— that way I can put a cool photo of one of the gross creepy crawlies seen through a blood spattered windshield into this chapter!

All this mutating should warn us about the dangers of atomic energy, atomic weapons, basically all things atomic. Of course, in the real world, events like the Chernobyl disaster, or a tsunami hitting Fukushima, rarely happen. But listing the growing number of countries with nuclear weapons is hardly reassuring: The UK, Russia, the US, China, France, probably Israel, and perhaps India and Pakistan; both Iran and North Korea are working hard and will have them soon.

In the words of *Mad Magazine*'s immortal Alfred E. Newman, "What, me worry?"

▲ *The Incredible Shrinking Man* [Jack Arnold, 1957]
Grant Williams fights for his life against his former pet cat as he grows smaller and smaller. Based on the novel by Richard Matheson.

Opposite page: (1) *Day the World Ended* **[Roger Corman, 1955]** In a post-apocalyptic world, a scientist battles for survival against a three-eyed mutant monster designed and built by make-up artist Paul Blaisdell.

(2) *Attack of the Crab Monsters* **[Roger Corman, 1957]** An expedition testing for effects from the Bikini Atoll nuclear test discover giant mutated crabs that absorb the intelligence of the people they eat.

(3) *The Incredible Shrinking Man* **[Jack Arnold, 1957]** The poster's tagline is accurate: "A fascinating adventure into the unknown!"
(4) *Them!* **[Gordon Douglas, 1954]** launched a thousand oversized-insect movies.

1

The screen's new high in NAKED SHRIEKING TERROR!

DAY THE WORLD ENDED

ATTACKED... by a creature from hell!

SUPERSCOPE

Starring RICHARD DENNING
★
LORI NELSON
★
ADELE JERGENS
with TOUCH CONNORS
★
PAUL BIRCH

RAYMOND HATTON · PAUL DUBOV
JONATHAN HAZE · PAUL BLAISEDELL
Produced and Directed by ROGER CORMAN
A Golden State Production
Story and Screenplay by LOU RUSOFF
Presented by JAMES H. NICHOLSON
and SAMUEL Z. ARKOFF
Executive Producer ALEX GORDON

American RELEASING CORPORATION

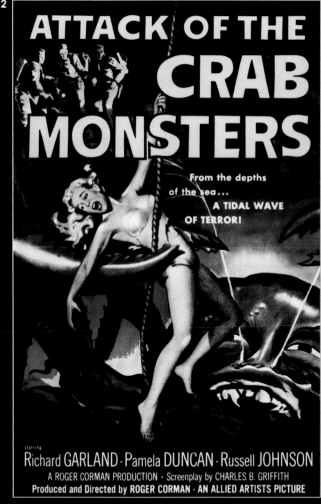

2

ATTACK OF THE CRAB MONSTERS

From the depths of the sea...
A TIDAL WAVE OF TERROR!

starring
Richard GARLAND · Pamela DUNCAN · Russell JOHNSON
A ROGER CORMAN PRODUCTION · Screenplay by CHARLES B. GRIFFITH
Produced and Directed by ROGER CORMAN · AN ALLIED ARTISTS PICTURE

4

A HORROR HORDE OF CRAWL-AND-CRUSH GIANTS
CLAWING OUT OF THE EARTH
FROM MILE-DEEP
CATACOMBS!

THEM

"This city is under martial law until we annihilate THEM!"

Kill one and two take its place!

THE AMAZING NEW WARNER BROS. SENSATION!

3

A FASCINATING ADVENTURE INTO THE UNKNOWN!

THE INCREDIBLE
SHRINKING MAN

A UNIVERSAL INTERNATIONAL PICTURE STARRING
GRANT WILLIAMS · RANDY STUART
with APRIL KENT · PAUL LANGTON · RAYMOND BAILEY
DIRECTED BY JACK ARNOLD · SCREENPLAY BY RICHARD MATHESON · PRODUCED BY ALBERT ZUGSMITH

▶ Creature With the Atom Brain
[Edward L. Cahn, 1955]
An American gangster deported to Europe forces an ex-Nazi scientist to reanimate cadavers with radiation to create zombie hit men. I am not making this up.

▲▼ Tarantula! [Jack Arnold, 1955] Scientist Leo G. Carroll's experiments not only cause him to be terribly deformed, but result in a colossal tarantula being unleashed upon the world. The military end up dropping napalm on the huge spider!

◀ Monster From Green Hell
[Kenneth G. Crane, 1958]
Wasps, sent into space in a rocket ship with other insects and animals, are exposed to "cosmic radiation." The rocket crashes in the African jungle and the creatures emerge as giant monsters. But don't worry, a volcano erupts and the lava destroys them.

▶ Them!
[Gordon Douglas, 1954]
Entomologist Joan Weldon encounters a mutant ant in the New Mexico desert.

▲ Matinee [Joe Dante, 1993] A scene from *Mant!*, the movie within the movie. A pitch-perfect parody of the many Big Bug films of the 1950s.

▲ *The Amazing Colossal Man* [Bert I. Gordon, 1957] Lt. Col. Glenn Manning (Glenn Langan) is exposed to plutonium radiation after a bomb test and grows 60-feet tall. And worse, he goes crazy.

"A colossal freak, Major, and he's my brother!"

Joyce Manning (Sally Fraser), *War of the Colossal Beast*

▲ *The Incredible Shrinking Man* [Jack Arnold, 1957] A publicity paste-up photo that clearly shows the title character's dilemma.

▲ *War of the Colossal Beast* [Bert I. Gordon, 1958] The sequel to *The Amazing Colossal Man*, although the character of Lt. Col. Glenn Manning is played by Dean Parkin. Luckily, Lt. Col. Manning's face is now horribly disfigured, so nobody notices he's a different actor.

▲ *The 30-Foot Bride of Candy Rock* [Sidney Miller, 1959] The "magic" (read radioactive) water of Dinosaur Springs turns Dorothy Provine into a giantess. The only movie Lou Costello made without longtime partner Bud Abbott.

207

GODZILLA

◀ *King Kong vs. Godzilla*
[Ishirô Honda, 1962] The first time that either King Kong or Godzilla were in a color (and TohoScope) film. A preposterous and extremely entertaining movie.

▲ *Godzilla* [Roland Emmerich, 1998] The big-budget Hollywood remake gets off on the wrong foot with an ill-conceived re-design of Godzilla, making him a sort of giant T.-Rex-Iguana.

◀ *Godzilla*
[Ishirô Honda, 1954] This image from a hand-tinted lobby card gives Godzilla the proper golden atomic glow.

▲ *Die, Monster, Die!* [aka *Monster of Terror*, Daniel Haller, 1965] Loosely based on H. P. Lovecraft's short story "The Color Out of Space," a radioactive meteorite causes trouble.

▲ *The Horror of Party Beach* [Del Tenney, 1964] This classic schlock, teenage-drive-in movie features rock'n'roll, bikinis and, as its poster proclaims, "Weird Atomic Beasts Who Live Off Human Blood!!!" The three exclamation marks are on the poster!!!

◀ *Godzilla vs. the Smog Monster* [aka *Godzilla vs. Hedorah*, Yoshimitsu Banno, 1971] In this, the 11th *Godzilla* movie, a microscopic alien lifeform feeds on the Earth's pollution and becomes a toxic monster. Godzilla defeats it and saves the world once more.

▲ *Brides of Blood* [Eddie Romero, 1968] Veteran Filipino exploitation director Eddie Romero brings us to a tropical island where radiation has mutated plants and animals into monsters. The native population begins virgin sacrifices to the monsters in an effort to placate them.

▲ *Atom Age Vampire* [aka *Seddok, l'erede di Santana*, Anton Giulio Majano, 1963] Dr. Levin is mutated into a "Seddok" while doing research into mysterious murders in post-Hiroshima Japan. A stylish and idiotic Italian movie.

"An ecological nightmare gone berserk!"

Doomwatch publicity tagline

◀ *From Hell It Came* [Dan Milner, 1957] A prince is executed and buried in a tree trunk. Nuclear radiation blends his spirit into the tree creating the dreaded Tobonga! The Tobonga is a walking tree and one of the dumbest-looking monsters in film.

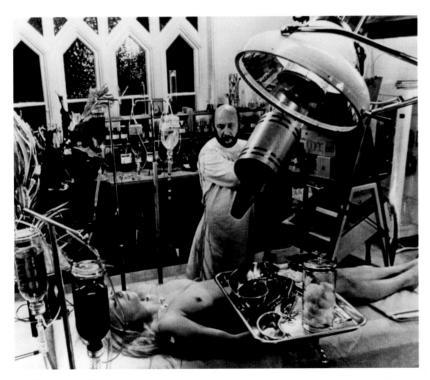

▲ *The Mutations* [aka *The Freakmaker*, Jack Cardiff, 1974] A trashy effort from the celebrated cinematographer Jack Cardiff. Donald Pleasence is a mad scientist, whose experiments create mutant monsters. Julie Ege (on the operating table) supplies the glamor.

▶ *Doomwatch* [Peter Sasdy, 1972] An island's population become deformed and violent from eating fish made toxic through chemical dumping. Based on the BBC-TV series.

▲ *Prophecy* [John Frankenheimer, 1979] A very good director makes a very bad movie featuring a mutant grizzly bear.

▲ *RoboCop* [Paul Verhoeven, 1987] This is what happens to a bad guy when a big vat of liquid clearly labeled TOXIC WASTE is dumped onto him.

◄ *Hell Comes to Frogtown* [Donald G. Jackson, 1988] Pictured is one of the mutant amphibians in a post-apocalyptic wasteland.

> "Puny human!"

The Hulk (Eric Bana), *The Hulk*

▶ *The Hulk* [Ang Lee, 2003] Another example of a good director making a bad movie. Another big-budget Hulk movie, *The Incredible Hulk* [Louis Leterrier, 2008] was produced just five years later to save the franchise.

▲ *Class of Nuke'Em High* [Richard W. Haines, 1986] From Lloyd Kaufman's Troma Entertainment, a typical story of what happens when a nuclear power plant is built next to a high school.

◄ *The Mist* [Frank Darabont, 2007] From a novella by Stephen King, Darabont's movie is filled with monsters like this creepy big spider-like thing. Not something you want to see through the windshield of your car.

▲ *The Toxic Avenger* [Lloyd Kaufman, Michael Herz, 1984] A nerd falls into a drum of toxic waste and is transformed into the hideous hero of the title. A comedy tribute to bad taste, there have been sequels, a cartoon series, and an off-Broadway musical based on Toxie.

▲ *Spider-Man 3* [Sam Raimi, 2007] Spider-Man Peter Parker developed his powers when bitten by a genetically engineered spider in *Spider-Man* [Sam Raimi, 2002]. In *Spider-Man 3*, criminal Flint Marko falls into a particle accelerator that fuses his body with the sand around him and he becomes the Sandman, pictured here confronting Spider-Man.

► *C.H.U.D.* [Douglas Cheek, 1984] Homeless people who live in the sewers are exposed to toxic nuclear waste and become "Cannibalistic Humanoid Underground Dwellers" in this nifty B picture.

The Devil's Work

The Devil's Work

"The Devil made me do it" is a marvelous excuse for all kinds of illicit behavior. This must be one of the reasons Satan remains such a popular subject in the cinema. Witches, warlocks, demons, and worse not only wage a constant battle with the forces of good, they also make very entertaining movies.

Actors love to play the Devil. Robert De Niro intriguingly underplays the role as the mysterious "Louis Cyphre" in *Angel Heart* [Alan Parker, 1987]. Cyphre hires seedy private eye Harry Angel (Mickey Rourke) for an investigation that involves Voodoo and ultimately, his soul.

Jack Nicholson in *The Witches of Eastwick* [George Miller, 1987] and Al Pacino in *The Devil's Advocate* [Taylor Hackford, 1997] both clearly enjoy themselves as Lucifer, giving grandstanding performances. Nicholson's devil has his hands full with three bored, beautiful women who dabble in a bit of black magic themselves.

In *The Devil's Advocate*, Keanu Reeves plays young, whiz-kid attorney Kevin Lomax, whose new job at a top law firm brings him under the spell of Al Pacino as Senior Partner "John Milton." *The Devil's Advocate* proves to both Kevin and to us that everything evil we ever thought about lawyers is true.

Ray Walston makes a weasly but potent Satan (although he calls himself "Applegate"), in an enjoyable musical comedy version of

▲ **The Golem: How He Came Into the World** **[Paul Wegener, Carl Boese, 1920]** The third movie starring Wegener as the Golem, made of clay by Rabbi Loew and brought to life to protect the Jews of the Prague Ghetto from persecution. The creature turns on its creator and runs amok. The five-pointed star on the Golem's chest gives it power.

Faust entitled *Damn Yankees* [George Abbott, Stanley Donen, 1958]. Applegate calls forth from Hell the witch Lola (Gwen Verdon) to assist him in his quest for the soul of baseball player Joe Hardy (Tab Hunter).

The great Walter Huston makes a canny Mr. Scratch in *All That Money Can Buy* [William Dieterle, 1941], the film version of Stephen Vincent Benét's short story "The Devil and Daniel Webster." Sexy Simone Simon as Belle helps Mr. Scratch get the soul of simple farmer Jabez Stone (James Craig) who enlists the great Daniel Webster (a terrific performance by Edward Arnold) to argue his case in front of a "jury of the damned." A wonderful morality story, told as a very thick slice of Americana. The film is also notable for Bernard Herrmann's lively score.

Christopher Lee plays a rare good-guy role in Hammer Films' *The Devil Rides Out* [aka *The Devil's Bride*, Terence Fisher, 1968], based on the occult thriller by Dennis Wheatley. A tale of devil worship in which Lee's Duc de Richleau uses his knowledge of the dark arts to protect his friends from suave, satanic cult leader Mocata (played by the urbane Charles Gray) and his plans to sacrifice them on the altar of Satan. At a devil-worshipper's orgy, we even get to see The Goat of Mendes himself!

Horror films based on bestselling books acquire a literary patina of respectability. And three bestsellers featuring Satan have given us three of the best devil movies. Ira Levin's novel *Rosemary's Baby* was brilliantly adapted for the screen by Roman Polanski in 1968. A weird story of devil-worshippers in modern Manhattan conspiring to help Satan rape a young woman in their

Previous pages: *The Exorcist* **[William Friedkin, 1973]** Regan (Linda Blair), a young girl possessed by Satan, has the upper hand during her exorcism by Father Merrin (Max von Sydow).
Opposite page: *Legend* **[Ridley Scott, 1985]** The magnificent Tim Curry as The Lord of Darkness, in an extraordinary make-up by Rob Bottin.

apartment building (the elegantly creepy Dakota on Central Park West in New York) and give him a son. The movie is full of wonderful performances from a great cast—Mia Farrow (as Rosemary Woodhouse), John Cassavetes (as her scheming actor husband), Ralph Bellamy, and Ruth Gordon all succeed in being funny and frightening in turns.

William Peter Blatty's novel *The Exorcist* was a publishing sensation. When the film, directed by William Friedken, was released on December 26, 1973, widespread reports of audiences fainting and screaming generated huge lines at the box office. I've always felt that the Vatican should make William Friedkin at least a saint, because no film has done so much for the Roman Catholic Church as *The Exorcist*. The concept of "suspension of disbelief" is essential to the enjoyment of a movie; as we watch, we have to be able to accept what transpires (no matter how outrageous or impossible) as reality. *The Exorcist* is a textbook example of a movie creating suspension of disbelief. I am an atheist but, for the running time of *The Exorcist*, I bought into all of it! "The power of Christ compels you!"—Max von Sydow's soulful Father Merrin and Jason Miller's troubled Father Karras are brought in to perform an exorcism in Georgetown, a wealthy neighborhood of Washington, D.C. A 12-year-old girl named Regan (Linda Blair) is possessed by a demon, maybe even the Devil himself. With superb make-up by Dick Smith (assisted by a young Rick Baker), the exorcism itself is as harrowing as any scene in movies and still has power to shock. *The Exorcist* is meant to be seen with a large audience and on a big screen.

▲ *The Exorcist* [William Friedkin,1973] Linda Blair as Regan in a make-up by Dick Smith. Friedkin's film is considered one of the scariest movies of all time.

David Seltzer wrote both the book and the screenplay for *The Omen* [Richard Donner, 1976], a film about the son of Satan. Gregory Peck brought gravitas to the project as the American Ambassador to the Court of St. James. Peck discovers that Damien, the little boy he and wife Lee Remick have taken in to raise is, in fact, the Antichrist! *The Omen* is a solid and well-made thriller that makes the supernatural seem real and present in our everyday world. The movie became another big hit at the box office for Satan.

A very funny retelling of Faust, *Bedazzled* [Stanley Donen, 1967] starred Dudley Moore as the hapless Stanley Moon, Peter Cook as George Spiggott, aka Lucifer, Lord of Darkness and, as two of the Seven Deadly Sins, Barry Humphries as Envy, and Raquel Welch as Lillian Lust—the Girl with the Bust!

Sam Raimi's *Drag Me to Hell* [2009] is essentially a fun house variation on *Night of the Demon* [Jacques Tourneur, 1957], which was based on a story by M. R. James called "Casting the Runes." In Raimi's movie, Christine Brown (Alison Lohman) is cursed by witch Sylvia Ganush (Lorna Raver) for not approving a bank loan. The object that brings forth the demon is a coat button. In *Night of the Demon*, the fantastic Niall MacGinnis plays the leader of a satanic cult (and children's party entertainer) who places the object, in this case a parchment with runic inscriptions, on the skeptical Dana Andrews. MacGinnis plays a character of equal parts charm and menace who asks Andrews' professor: "How can we differentiate between the powers of darkness and the powers of the mind?" Exactly.

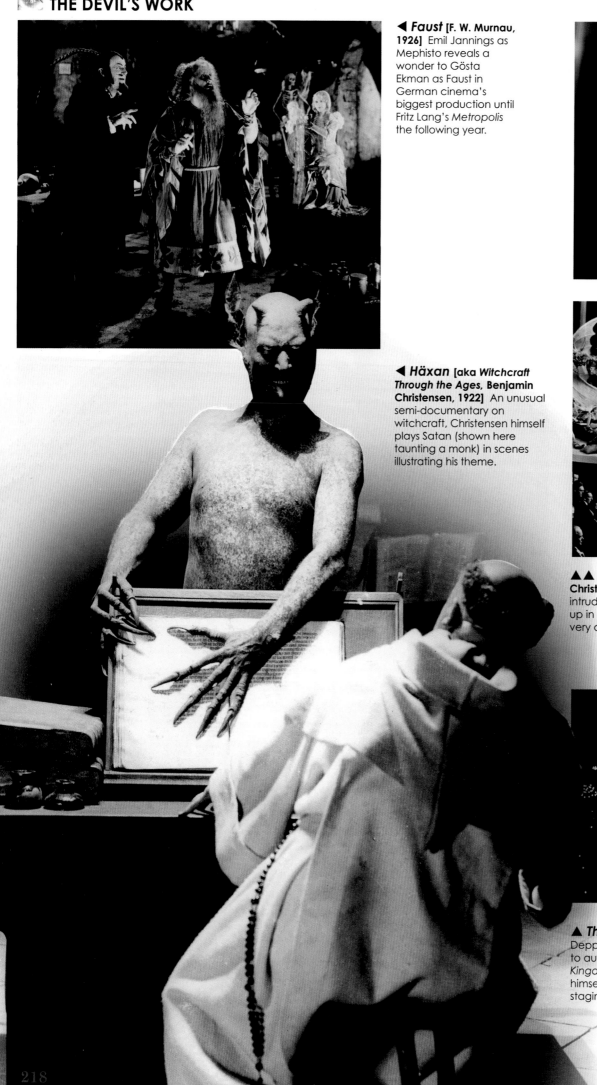

◀ *Faust* [F. W. Murnau, 1926] Emil Jannings as Mephisto reveals a wonder to Gösta Ekman as Faust in German cinema's biggest production until Fritz Lang's *Metropolis* the following year.

◀ *Häxan* [aka *Witchcraft Through the Ages*, Benjamin Christensen, 1922] An unusual semi-documentary on witchcraft, Christensen himself plays Satan (shown here taunting a monk) in scenes illustrating his theme.

▲▲ *Seven Footprints to Satan* [Benjamin Christensen, 1929] Thelma Todd feels her personal space intruded upon by an unsavory character. Newlyweds end up in a mansion full of upper-class devil-worshipers in this very dark comedy.

▲ *The Ninth Gate* [Roman Polanski, 1999] Johnny Depp plays a rare-book dealer hired by Frank Langella to authenticate a book titled *The Nine Gates of the Kingdom of Shadows*, supposedly written by the devil himself. Notice how similar the devil-worshippers' set and staging is to the one in *Seven Footprints to Satan* (above).

▲ *The Magician* [Rex Ingram, 1926] Paul Wegener in the
Aleister Crowley-like title role at a costume ball with Alice Terry,
a virgin whose blood Wegener wants for a black magic ritual.
Based on the novel by Somerset Maugham.

▶ *Hercules in the Haunted World*
[Mario Bava, 1961] Hercules (Reg Park) and his
friends Theseus and Telemachus must go to Hades to
recover The Stone of Forgetfulness. His rival King Lico
(Christopher Lee) is in league with the Underworld.
Director Mario Bava makes all this stylish and fun.

▶ *Night of the Demon*
[Jacques Tourneur, 1957]
Dana Andrews investigates
a Satanic cult led by Dr.
Julian Karswell (a terrific Niall
MacGinnis). This demon was
supposedly put into the film
by the studio over the
director's objections, but I
have to say that I agree
with the studio!

▲ *Black Sunday* [aka *The Mask of Satan*, Mario Bava,1960]
Barbara Steele plays a witch who has an iron mask lined with
spikes hammered into her face. Before being burned at the stake,
she puts a curse on her brother's descendants that is horribly
fulfilled. A beautifully composed and photographed black and
white horror classic from Mario Bava.

"It's in the trees!
It's coming!"

Professor Harrington (Maurice Denham),
Night of the Demon

▲ **The Masque of the Red Death** [Roger Corman, 1964] Based on two stories by Edgar Allan Poe ("Hop-Frog" is used as a subplot) and featuring Vincent Price as the decadent Prince Prospero. Pictured are the Red Death, the Black Death, and the other Deaths who discuss the fate of mankind at the conclusion of this, the most poetic of Corman's films.

▲ **Five Million Years to Earth** [aka *Quatermass and the Pit*, Roy Ward Baker, 1967] Based on the BBC-TV series by Nigel Kneale. During an excavation at the London Tube station Hobbs End, first early man fossils and then an alien space craft is discovered. Kneale's screenplay is a science-fiction explanation not only for mankind's progress, but also for the existence of the Devil. Pictured are James Donald and Andrew Keir (as Professor Quatermass) examining the corpse of an ancient horned Martian just before it crumbles to dust.

◄ **Curse of the Crimson Altar** [Vernon Sewell, 1968] Christopher Lee about to make a ritual sacrifice as the leader of a cult of witches at Craxted Lodge. Boris Karloff appears as an expert on the occult who helps to destroy the evil bastards.

◄ **Bedazzled** [Stanley Donen, 1967] Raquel Welch as one of the Seven Deadly Sins, "Lillian Lust—the girl with the bust," in Peter Cook and Dudley Moore's comic retelling of Faust. Barry Humphries makes a very funny appearance as Envy.

► **Rosemary's Baby** [Roman Polanski, 1968] From the bestselling novel by Ira Levin. With an exceptionally fine cast, Polanski does full justice to Ira Levin's sly commentary on actors, motherhood, and apartment dwelling.

▲ **The Devil Rides Out** [aka *The Devil's Bride*, **Terence Fisher, 1968**] Christopher Lee as the Duc de Richleau in the pentacle he has drawn to protect his friends from demons summoned by Mocata (Charles Gray), the leader of a cult of devil-worshippers in the English countryside. Based on Dennis Wheatley's novel, with a screenplay by Richard Matheson. This movie would have benefited from a bigger special-FX budget.

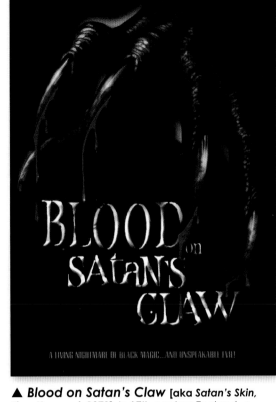

BLOOD on SATaN'S CLAW

A LIVING NIGHTMARE OF BLACK MAGIC...AND UNSPEAKABLE EVIL!

▲ **Blood on Satan's Claw** [aka *Satan's Skin*, **Piers Haggard, 1971**] In 17th-century England, a farmer's plow digs up a weird, one-eyed skull. Soon the children of the village are behaving unnaturally. A well photographed occult thriller, featuring a fine performance from Patrick Wymark as the Judge.

◀ **Jack the Giant Killer** [**Nathan H. Juran, 1962**] Pictured is a group of the wicked sorcerer Pendragon's demons in this copy by Juran of his own, superior, *The 7th Voyage of Sinbad* [1958].

▶ **Onibaba** [**Kaneto Shindō, 1964**] In feudal Japan, a mother and daughter murder passing samurai for their valuable armor and dispose of the bodies in a pit. The mother becomes jealous of her daughter's affair with their male partner in crime. To frighten her, the mother dons a demon mask, but then cannot remove it. A violent, brutal film, with Nobuko Otowa outstanding as the tormented mother.

"I'm not a demon! I'm a human being!"

The Mother (Nobuko Otowa), *Onibaba*

221

"Your mother sucks cocks in hell, Karras, you faithless slime!"

Regan (Linda Blair), *The Exorcist*

▶ *The Exorcist* [William Friedkin, 1973] Linda Blair as Regan in full satanic-possession mode, just before her head rotates 360 degrees! Based on the bestseller by William Peter Blatty, this is still the gold standard for scary movies.

▲ *The Legacy* [Richard Marquand, 1978] The director of *Return of the Jedi* [1983] made this confusing occult thriller, starring Katharine Ross and Sam Elliott as American interior decorators whose English clients want more than just new décor.

▶ *Abby* [William Girdler, 1974] A blatant rip-off of *The Exorcist*, this blaxploitation picture has a woman possessed by an African spirit, etc, etc. Not worth watching.

◀ *Beyond the Door* [aka *The Devil Within Her* and *Chi Sei?*, Ovidio G. Assonitis, Robert Barrett, 1974] This Italian *Exorcist* rip-off stars Juliet Mills as a pregnant woman carrying the Anti-Christ, which makes her extremely hard to be with.

▲ *The Wicker Man* [Robin Hardy, 1973] Christopher Lee as Lord Summerisle (his favorite role) praying to pagan gods before the Wicker Man is set aflame—with Edward Woodward's virginal policeman inside! From an original screenplay by Anthony Shaffer. Although tampered with by British and US distributors, *The Wicker Man* is one of the highpoints of British horror. To further the indignities, it was remade in 2006 by Neil LaBute in what has to be the worst remake of all time.

◄ *The Omen* [Richard Donner, 1976] Harvey Stephens is truly creepy as Damien, the Antichrist in Richard Donner's beautifully crafted film of David Seltzer's screenplay (from his own novel). Composer Jerry Goldsmith contributes a brilliant and often-imitated score.

▲ *Pumpkinhead* [Stan Winston, 1988] Stan Winston's directorial debut, a solid B creature-feature with a nifty creature. Lance Henriksen asks a witch to help him get revenge on the boys who killed his son. The witch agrees, but warns him it comes with a heavy price.

► *Carrie* [Brian De Palma, 1976] After being doused with pig's blood by school bullies, Carrie (Sissy Spacek) uses her telekinetic power to wreak havoc at her high-school prom. De Palma made a terrific supernatural thriller, featuring a sensitive, heartbreaking, and scary performance from Sissy Spacek in the title role. Based on the novel by Stephen King.

"The box.
You opened it.
We came."

Pinhead (Doug Bradley), *Hellraiser*

▶ *It* [Tommy Lee Wallace, 1991] The gifted Tim Curry as It, who can transform into his victim's worst fears. Pictured here as Pennywise, a children's clown. Based on the novel by Stephen King, this two-part television mini-series does a good job actualizing King's unnerving book.

▶ *Hellraiser*
[Clive Barker, 1987]
Clive Barker directs his own script in this sadomasochistic take on the legend of Pandora's Box. Here is Doug Bradley as Pinhead, leader of the Cenobites. The Cenobites are Barker's inspired demons: former humans who come to earth through the "Lament Configuration" to collect people's souls.

◀ *The Golden Child*
[Michael Ritchie, 1986]
Eddie Murphy plays a social worker asked to protect a child in Tibet, unaware that he is the Golden Child. The bad guy pursuing them (played by Charles Dance) is actually a demon, pictured here in his true form.

▲ *Hellbound: Hellraiser II* [Tony Randel, 1988]
The second in the series of movies based on Clive Barker's novella *The Hellbound Heart*. Doug Bradley returns (in a more featured role this time) as Pinhead.

◀ Harry Potter and the Order of the Phoenix
[David Yates, 2007] Ralph Fiennes as Lord Voldemort the satanic wizard who is the main villain in the *Harry Potter* movies. Fiennes also played a serial killer in *Red Dragon* [Brett Ratner, 2002], a mass-murdering Nazi in *Schindler's List* [Steven Spielberg, 1993], and Hades, god of the Underworld, in the remake of *Clash of the Titans* [Louis Leterrier, 2010]. What can I say?

▶ Necromancy
[Bert I. Gordon, 1972] Orson Welles as the sinister Mr. Cato, a necromancer who performs rituals designed to bring the dead back to life. Orson manages to keep a straight face throughout.

▲ Conan the Barbarian [John Milius, 1982] James Earl Jones as the evil Thulsa Doom in this tale of sorcery and steroids based on the fantasy stories of Robert E. Howard.

▲ The Lord of the Rings: The Fellowship of the Ring
[Peter Jackson, 2001] Christopher Lee as the commanding Dark Lord Sauron who also seeks the power of the Ring.

Evil Wizards

▲ To the Devil... A Daughter [Peter Sykes, 1976] Christopher Lee as Father Michael Rayner "protecting" young Nastassja Kinski. The priest is actually the head of a group of satanists who intend to sacrifice her, making her an "avatar of Astaroth"! Another Dennis Wheatley adaptation by Hammer.

▶ The Devil Rides Out
[Terence Fisher, 1968] Charles Gray as the ominous Mocata, the powerful high priest of a cult of devil-worshippers, gets to grips with Tanith (Nike Arrighi), the beautiful medium through whom he summons the Angel of Death. A typical Hammer publicity shot; not in the finished movie.

◀ Conan the Destroyer
[Richard Fleischer, 1984] Jeff Corey as the Grand Vizier, an evil wizard who kidnaps the Princess and is subsequently killed by Conan (Arnold Schwarzenegger).

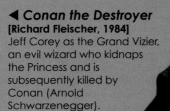

◀ The Manitou
[William Girdler, 1978]
Susan Strasberg has a tumor on her neck, which turns out to be a growing, demonic, 400-year-old Native American spirit called a Manitou. Pictured is the Manitou itself, moments after birth. A wacky and entertaining show, with a funny performance by Tony Curtis.

▲ The Gate [Tibor Takács, 1987] While removing a tree in a suburban backyard, workmen uncover a pit that turns out to lead to the Gates of Hell! This movie features some very good stop-motion animation work on the small, demonic creatures that climb out of the hole.

> "It's too late, Krueger. I know the secret now... You're not alive. This whole thing is just a dream!"
>
> Nancy (Heather Langenkamp), *A Nightmare on Elm Street*

◀▼ A Nightmare on Elm Street
[Wes Craven, 1984] Freddy Krueger (Robert Englund) can only harm you while you sleep, literally appearing in your dreams. Krueger, with razor sharp knives attached to his fingers, is an indelible image. A franchise is born.

▲ Friday the 13th Part III [Steve Miner, 1982] Jason, wearing a hockey mask, seeks revenge on the campers of Camp Crystal Lake. In the original movie [Sean S. Cunningham, 1980], the killer turns out to be Jason's mother! *Friday the 13th* was the other major horror franchise from the 1980s; so far there have been *eleven* sequels.

▲ Final Destination 2 [David R. Ellis, 2000] The second of several movies (there are four so far) that are essentially just a series of elaborate situations in which a member of the cast is killed. Here, a victim is having his head crushed in an elevator.

▲ Cemetery Man [aka *Dellamorte Dellamore*, Michele Soavi, 1994] Death himself visits Rupert Everett, the caretaker of a cemetery in Buffalora, a small town in Italy. Rupert's problem is that the dead keep returning as zombies, so he shoots them and puts them back into their graves.

Images of Death

Death makes an appearance in a number of movies. In *Death Takes a Holiday* [Mitchell Leisen, 1934], Death, in the person of handsome Fredric March, takes time off from his job to vacation on Earth, causing havoc with the natural order of things. Brad Pitt starred in the remake, which was inexplicably called *Meet Joe Black* [Martin Brest, 1998]. On this page are some other, less attractive, big-screen characterizations of Death.

▲ Bill & Ted's Bogus Journey [Peter Hewitt, 1991] William Sadler as the Grim Reaper challenges Bill and Ted to a series of games in which all they can lose is their lives. Sadler may not get their lives, but he does steal the picture.

▲ Tales From the Crypt [Freddie Francis, 1972] Death rides a motorcycle in one of the grisly stories the Crypt Keeper (Ralph Richardson) tells to a group of tourists. Loosely based on the classic EC comic books.

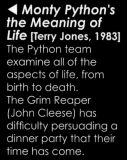

◄ Monty Python's the Meaning of Life [Terry Jones, 1983] The Python team examine all of the aspects of life, from birth to death. The Grim Reaper (John Cleese) has difficulty persuading a dinner party that their time has come.

▲ Love and Death [Woody Allen, 1975] Woody Allen as Boris Grushenko walks with Death in his delicious parody of the works of Tolstoy, Dostoyevsky, and other Russian novelists.

▲ Dr. Terror's House of Horrors [Freddie Francis, 1965] Peter Cushing, as the mysterious Dr. Schreck, reads the tarot cards of the five unfortunate passengers he shares a train journey with in this enjoyable anthology horror movie.

◄ *Highway to Hell* [Ate de Jong, 1992] The zombie Hell Cop (C. J. Graham) kidnaps Kristy Swanson, who was on her way to Las Vegas with Chad Lowe to get married. Chad has to go to Hell and back to rescue her. He has run-ins with various demons and eventually with Satan himself, who proposes a race with the Hell Cop for their mortal souls.

"If there's one thing worse than dying and going to Hell. It's not dying and going to Hell."

Publicity tagline for *Highway to Hell* [1992]

► *Hellboy* [Guillermo Del Toro, 2004] Based on the Hellboy graphic novels by Mike Mignola, the movie begins during World War II, when Nazi occultists open a portal into Hell. After Allied forces attack and close the portal, a small, bright-red, horned, demon boy, with one hand made of stone, is left behind. Hellboy (Ron Perlman) is raised by the BPRD (Bureau of Paranormal Research and Defense) and grows up to be our first line of defense against other supernatural foes.

▼ *Hellboy II: The Golden Army* [Guillermo Del Toro, 2008] Not only is Prince Nuada (son of Elf King Balor) building a new mechanical Golden Army, Hellboy is having romantic problems with his pyrokinetic girlfriend, and there is this huge monster thing loose in the city! Del Toro lets his imagination run wild in this sequel to his first film based on the Dark Horse comics.

▶ Ghost Rider
[Mark Steven Johnson, 2007] Computer-generated skull and flames over Nicolas Cage's face as he portrays motorcycle stunt driver Johnny Blaze in this mediocre movie adaptation of the Marvel comic book character.

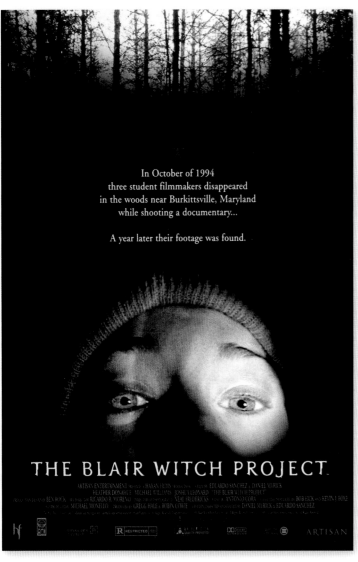

▲ The Blair Witch Project [Daniel Myrick, Eduardo Sánchez, **1999**] The first movie to be marketed on the internet, this recycles the premise of *Cannibal Holocaust* [Ruggero Deodato, 1980], claiming to be authentic "lost" footage shot by the characters. Many people thought this was the real thing. I felt that the movie only got scary when we see one of the cast facing the wall in the basement, but then it ends. The merits of this one escape me.

◀ Legion [Scott Stewart, 2010] One of the "possessed" in this lunatic story of God losing his faith in mankind and sending down an army of angels to destroy us. Only the Archangel Michael (Paul Bettany) will fight for us, but first he has to cut off his wings! Well crafted and truly blasphemous in the best sense of the word.

▲ Death Note [Shusuke Kaneko, 2006] Based on a bestselling manga and anime series by Tsugumi Ohba and Takeshi Obata. A student named Light finds a supernatural notebook that kills anyone who has their name written into it. With the help of Ryuk, a *shinigami* (death spirit), Light decides to rid the world of evil.

▲ Death Note: The Last Name [Shusuke Kaneko, 2006] Light's girlfriend finds another Death Note; she is shown here with Shinigami Rem, who becomes her ally in this continuation of the manga-based story.

The Devil

▲ The Devil & Daniel Webster [aka *All That Money Can Buy*, **William Dieterle, 1941**] The great Walter Huston plays the mischievous Scratch, who checks his notebook, looks directly into the camera and, smiling, makes a note to come and collect your soul later. Right after he finishes eating the apple pie he has just stolen from Jane Darwell's windowsill.

◄ The Devil's Rain **[Robert Fuest, 1975]** Ernest Borgnine is Corbis, the leader of a Satanic Cult who takes the evil into himself and becomes a horned devil. This is, of course, before he melts. Ida Lupino and a very young John Travolta melt, too.

▲ Damn Yankees [George Abbott, Stanley Donen, 1958] Ray Walston as Applegate and the fabulous Gwen Verdon as Lola in the film of the hit Broadway musical, a Faust story set in the world of baseball. Ray Walston's Devil sings "Those Were The Good Old Days," recalling with relish various wars and disasters. Gwen Verdon performs her show-stopper "Whatever Lola Wants" to seduce Tab Hunter. A lovely movie.

▲ Alias Nick Beal [John Farrow, 1949] Another retelling of the Faust story, with Ray Milland as Nick Beale, a suavely sinister Mephistopheles luring Thomas Mitchell to the dark side.

► The Devil Rides Out **[Terence Fisher, 1968]** The Goat of Mendes watches over his satanic followers at an outdoor orgy.

► Bedazzled **[Stanley Donen, 1967]** Peter Cook as George Spiggott, who has a wager with God as to who will be the first to gather 100 billion souls in this droll comedy.

◄ Faust [F. W. Murnau, 1926] Emil Jannings as Mephisto, looming over a village and about to unleash a plague.

▲ Something Wicked This Way Comes [Jack Clayton, 1983] Jonathan Pryce plays Mr. Dark, the owner of a malevolent carnival that visits a small American town. Based on the novel by Ray Bradbury.

▶ The Devil's Advocate
[Taylor Hackford, 1997]
Al Pacino plays lawyer John Milton in a none-too-subtle reference to *Paradise Lost*. As the Devil, Pacino is given free rein in a ferocious, enjoyably mad performance. Poor Keanu Reeves is blown off the screen whenever Al is present.

▶ Angel Heart
[Alan Parker, 1987]
Robert De Niro's character is called Louis Cyphre, but his claw-like fingernails and understated menace should have been a dead giveaway to private detective Mickey Rourke. Based on the novel *Falling Angel* by William Hjortsberg.

◀ South Park: Bigger, Longer & Uncut [aka *South Park: The Movie*, Trey Parker, 1999]
Based on the TV series, this features Satan as the abused lover of Saddam Hussein. In a genius parody of Disney's *The Little Mermaid* [Ron Clements, John Musker, 1989], Satan sings longingly about the world "up there." The best musical of the decade.

◀ End of Days [Peter Hyams, 1999]
Gabriel Byrne as Satan in this truly stupid Arnold Schwarzenegger movie. Schwarzenegger was reportedly paid $25 million for his performance as Jericho Cane. Obviously Satan was directly involved with this production.

▶ The Witches of Eastwick
[George Miller, 1987]
Jack Nicholson as Daryl Van Horne, the Devil in this adaptation of John Updike's novel.

◀ Legend [Ridley Scott, 1985] Tim Curry
as the Lord of Darkness, who wants the only two unicorn horns in the world in order to banish sunshine forever. Curry is awesome in this movie, which also features excellent visuals and Tom Cruise's worst-ever haircut.

▲ Little Nicky [Steven Brill, 2000] Harvey Keitel is Satan in this tacky Adam Sandler comedy. Sandler is one of Satan's three sons and his father's favorite. All hell breaks loose, but I doubt the audience will care.

▲ **Dante's Inferno** [Harry Lachman, 1935] Spencer Tracy opens a fairground attraction based on Dante's Inferno with tableaus of Hell (the entrance is pictured). Cutting corners causes a terrible fire and Tracy has a nightmare—a striking ten-minute sequence—in which Dante's poem comes to life.

◀ **Dante's Inferno** [Henry Otto, 1924] The poet Virgil (Howard Gaye) shows Dante (Lawson Butt) around Hell.

▼ **Faust** [F. W. Murnau, 1926] A vision of hell from the *Walpurgisnacht* celebration on Bald Mountain. The sequence later inspired the *Night on Bald Mountain* section of Walt Disney's animated feature *Fantasia* [1940].

Hell

▲ *Hellzapoppin'* [H. C. Potter, 1941]
Devils barbecue Hollywood chorus cuties—a vision of Hell from the main title sequence of this crazy adaptation of comedians Olsen and Johnson's hit Broadway show. How did they make a movie out of *Hellzapoppin'*? This truly postmodern film is the very funny answer.

▲ *The Sentinel* [Michael Winner, 1977]
John Carradine as Father Halloran, a blind priest who sits in the window of a Brooklyn brownstone that turns out to be the Gateway to Hell.

◄ *Bill & Ted's Bogus Journey* [Peter Hewitt, 1991] Originally titled *Bill & Ted Go To Hell* before the marketing people made them change it. Bill and Ted go to hell, mostly long hallways lined with doors. Behind every door is each person's own idea of hell.

▲ *Constantine* [Francis Lawrence, 2005]
Los Angeles as Hell, with a demonic thing in the foreground from this asinine movie based on the DC/Vertigo comic book *Hellblazer*. Keanu Reeves stars as supernatural detective John Constantine.

▲ *Harry Potter and the Order of the Phoenix* [David Yates, 2007] Helena Bonham Carter as the very nasty Bellatrix Lestrange, one of Lord Voldemort's scarier Death Eaters.

▲ **The Wizard of Oz** [Victor Fleming, 1939] Margaret Hamilton as the unforgettable Wicked Witch of the West. "I'll get you, my pretty. And your little dog, too!"

WICKED WITCHES

Witches have always been perfect characters for the movies, whether good, like Billie Burke as Glinda the Good Witch of the North, or bad, like Margaret Hamilton as the Wicked Witch of the West in *The Wizard of Oz*. Witches can be young, old, sexy, or hideous, depending on the story requirements. Here are some memorable movie witches.

◀ *Le Streghe* [aka *The Witches*, Franco Rossi, Luchino Visconti, Mauro Bolognini, Pier Pasolini, and Vittorio De Sica, 1967] Silvano Mangano makes a spectacular-looking witch in a portmanteau film that is less than the sum of its parts.

▼ *Something Wicked This Way Comes* [Jack Clayton, 1983] Pam Grier as the enigmatic Dust Witch, a member of Mr. Dark's sinister carnival.

▲ *Bell, Book and Candle* [Richard Quine, 1958] Kim Novak as the beautiful and sexy young witch who falls in love with Jimmy Stewart in this comedy based on the hit Broadway play by John Van Druten. Co-starring Jack Lemmon and Ernie Kovacs, with Hermione Gingold a standout as another witch named Bianca de Passe.

▲ **The Witches** [Nicolas Roeg, 1990]
Anjelica Huston, as Miss. Eva Ernst, reveals herself as the Grand High Witch in this excellent adaptation of Roald Dahl's children's book.

▲ **The Witches of Eastwick** [George Miller, 1987] Michelle Pfeiffer, Susan Sarandon, and Cher in the title roles. From John Updike's best-selling novel.

▲ **Clash of the Titans** [Desmond Davis, 1981]
Anna Manahan, Flora Robson, and Freda Jackson as the three blind Stygian witches, who tell Perseus (Harry Hamlin) how to defeat the Kraken.

▲ **Suspiria** [Dario Argento, 1997] Jessica Harper stabs the witch in Argento's delirious tale of an American ballet student who discovers the dance academy she has come to in Germany is run by a coven of witches. In vibrant Technicolor and with a throbbing score, *Suspiria* is a ghoulish treat.

▲ **Stardust** [Matthew Vaughn, 2007]
Michelle Pfeiffer as Lamia the witch queen, who wants to cut out Claire Danes' heart to regain her youth and achieve immortality.

▶ **Sleeping Beauty** [Les Clark, Eric Larson, Wolfgang Reitherman, 1959] The gloriously evil Maleficent who, insulted by not being invited to Princess Aurora's christening, curses the entire kingdom. She later transforms into a ferocious dragon, hoping to destroy handsome Prince Phillip and any chance for the Princess' happiness.

▲ **Drag Me to Hell** [Sam Raimi, 2009]
Lorna Raver as the gypsy witch Mrs. Ganush with the button, instrumental in the curse she puts on a young bank officer (Alison Lohman) who turns down her loan application.

KILLER DOLLS

Pygmalion carved a woman from ivory that he named Galatea. The statue was so beautiful that he fell in love with it and asked the gods to give her life. Geppetto carved Pinocchio out of wood and wished the puppet could be a real boy. Inanimate objects coming to life is inherently creepy—all of us have taken a second look at that doll or teddy bear that seemed to move in the moonlight.

▲ *Asylum* [Roy Ward Baker, 1972] Dr. Byron (Herbert Lom) regards the little automaton he's created in his own likeness, into which he intends to transfer his soul. He succeeds, with horrifying results. A good portmanteau (anthology) film from Amicus Productions.

◀ *From Beyond the Grave* [Kevin Connor, 1973] Peter Cushing as the owner of an antique shop whose customers have very unhappy endings. Here he is stroking a doll, which I wouldn't buy if I were you! Another portmanteau movie from Amicus.

> " Hi, I'm Chucky. Wanna play?"

Chucky the doll, *Child's Play*

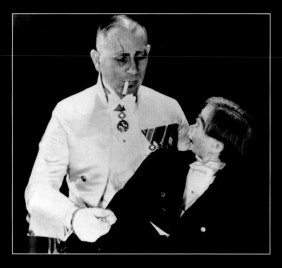

▲ *The Great Gabbo* [James Cruze, 1929] Erich von Stroheim plays The Great Gabbo, a ventriloquist who is going mad and uses his dummy Otto more and more to speak for him. Based on the short story *The Rival Dummy* by Ben Hecht.

▶ *Dead of Night* [Alberto Cavalcanti, 1945] The greatest portmanteau film of them all, with four different directors from Ealing Studios, and the best framing story ever. In this scene from "The Ventriloquist's Dummy," Michael Redgrave, as ventriloquist Maxwell Frere, is trying to keep his dummy quiet. The dummy bites him, and when Maxwell looks at his palm, there are teeth marks! *Dead of Night* is well worth seeking out.

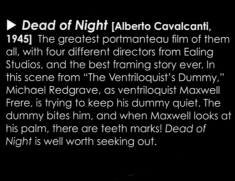

▲ *Magic* [Richard Attenborough, 1978] Anthony Hopkins is the insane ventriloquist this time; his dummy, Fats, gives him very bad advice. With excellent support from Ann-Margaret and Burgess Meredith and a great score by Jerry Goldsmith.

▲ Poltergeist [Tobe Hooper, 1982] Heather O'Rourke sees something "other." That clown doll is scary enough anyway. An exciting and scary movie.

▲ Child's Play
[Tom Holland, 1988]
Brad Dourif is psycho serial killer Charles Lee Ray who, when shot, takes refuge in a toy store. There he uses a voodoo ritual to transfer his soul into a Good Guy doll. The doll ends up being given to a young boy named Andy... *Child's Play* is a nasty horror picture, directed by Tom Holland (who also directed the fun *Fright Night* in 1985), certain to scare the shit out of little kids.

▲ Team America: World Police [Trey Parker, 2004] Trey Parker and Matt Stone's loving tribute to every Gerry and Sylvia Anderson puppet TV show and a scathing political satire to boot. Here is the Stalinist dictator of the Democratic People's Republic of Korea (aka North Korea) Kim Jong, who sings the lovely ballad "I'm Ronely" in this funny movie.

▲ Puppet Master [David Schmoeller, 1989] Puppets, under the influence of an ancient Egyptian spell, kill people. Producer Charles Band has spun this into a franchise, with nine sequels so far.

▲ Saw II [Darren Lynn Bousman, 2005] The second in this series of the new genre of "torture porn," in which the audience waits in glee for the next Rube Goldberg way of dismembering someone. The *Saw* movies are heavily influenced by David Fincher's *Seven* [1995]. Here is Billy, the puppet through which Jigsaw Killer John Kramer gives instructions to his victims.

◄ Dead Silence [aka *Shhhh*, James Wan, 2007] A couple receives a package with no return address that contains a ventriloquist's dummy named Billy. I kind of liked this over-complicated horror thriller, but apparently no one else did.

SCARY CHILDREN

Children are usually associated with innocence, so when movies use children as monsters, it can be especially disquieting. Is the child being manipulated by an evil outside force? Or is the child doing the manipulating? Is Peter Pan the wonderful, always-youthful, magic flying boy who takes children on a wonderful adventure into Neverland? Or is Peter Pan an evil fairy that kidnaps children from their parents and takes them to a place where they will never grow up? Well, it depends on the telling, doesn't it?

▲ **Bad Seed** [Mervyn LeRoy, 1956] Patty McCormack as Rhoda Penmark (here with Nancy Kelly as her unfortunate mother) is unforgettably evil in this film from the hit Broadway play by Maxwell Anderson, based on William March's novel. In the book, and onstage, the mother dies and the little-girl killer survives. The Hays Code (Hollywood's censor at the time) would not allow this, so, at the end, the mother is saved and the girl is struck by lightning!

▲ **Twilight Zone** [Joe Dante, segment three, 1983] Jeremy Licht as Anthony, a little boy with terrifying powers in *It's a Good Life*. Joe Dante masterfully directed this segment of the anthology movie, based on the Rod Serling TV show.

▲ **Pet Sematary** [aka *Stephen King's Pet Sematary*, Mary Lambert, 1989] Miko Hughes as Gage, the child returned from the grave to kill. Here is Miko, only three years old when he acted in the film, making his best scary face.

◀ **Village of the Damned** [Wolf Rilla, 1960] All human and animal life in the small English village of Midwich suddenly falls unconscious. Months later, every woman of childbearing age gives birth on the same day. The children are all blonde and identical in demeanor. Based on the novel *The Midwich Cuckoos* by John Wyndham, this eerie science-fiction film features a chilling performance from young Martin Stephens (pictured), who was equally creepy a year later in Jack Clayton's *The Innocents*.

▲ **It's Alive** [Larry Cohen, 1974] The monster baby in Cohen's unexpectedly moving, killer-mutant-baby movie. The baby was designed and built by Rick Baker.

▲ **The Omen** [John Moore, 2006] Seamus Davey-Fitzpatrick is Damien in this remake of Richard Donner's classic. Why they decided to give the Anti-Christ Moe Howard's haircut I do not know.

▲ **The Unborn** [David S. Goyer, 2009] Ethan Cutkosky as the Dybbuk of an unborn twin in this bastardization of Jewish folklore. A lousy movie with some effectively scary parts.

"I'll burn you up! I'll fry you!!"

Charlie McGee (Drew Barrymore), *Firestarter*

▲ **Firestarter** [Mark L. Lester, 1984] Drew Barrymore as the pyrokinetic little girl that George C. Scott's secret government agency wants to control. Based on Stephen King's novel.

◄ **Children of the Corn** [Fritz Kiersch, 1984] John Franklin as the strange boy preacher who leads the children in killing all of the adults to appease "He who walks behind the rows." More scary kids from the pen of the prolific Stephen King.

John Carpenter

John Carpenter with *The Fog* [1980] cast members Adrienne Barbeau, Jamie Lee Curtis, and Janet Leigh.

JL: You've created yourself as a brand, as a master of horror. How would you define a monster? What do you think a monster is?

JC: Primarily, it's us. It's parts of us, parts of the dark heart of humanity. But it's also the other: the other tribe, the other people, the people that look different, the ferocious demons out there.

JL: By the other, do you mean the Unknown?

JC: Well, there are two basic horror stories. Where does the evil come from? It comes from out there, or it comes from in here. That's it, there's nothing else. So if you have an Outer Space invasion, the evil is out there and they're coming to get us. That's the evil outside of us. The harder story to tell is the evil in here, in our own hearts. Each of us is capable of evil, under certain circumstances.

JL: The John Carpenter quote that I quote all the time, is: "Monsters don't scare me—people scare me."

JC: A fear of monsters is part of the basic nature of humanity. When we came out of the trees and started walking upright, we still had these fears of predators. We see something coming at us and we respond to it. It's self-preservation. All this stuff gets jumbled up in our myths, in our stories. And here it is: Here are monster movies.

JL: OK, so let's talk about Vampires—Dracula. There are more movies with Dracula in them than any other kind of monster.

JC: Vampires are all-purpose monsters for each new generation.

JL: The new abstinence vampire is now. The Mormon vampire!

JC: You had the Rudolph Valentino vampire originally, with Béla Lugosi and his slicked-back hair and this kind of come-hither look but, throughout the years, look at Christopher Lee and his Dracula—it's entirely different.

JL: About vampires: Is there anything you particularly like or dislike, or think is cool?

JC: Well the original myth works. It's a myth of decay. The European aristocracy is falling to ruin in Gothic castles, and who do the aristocrats live on? They live on the peasants. They suck their blood. Think about that. Where does that come from? It comes from European attitudes way back when. European attitudes about how things work. But then they slowly corrupt…

JL: Now, what about the Wolf Man?

JC: The Wolf Man is a take on Dr. Jekyll and Mr Hyde. This innocent man is bitten by something, and he can do nothing about it. He's good and evil, both.

JL: I think that the Jekyll and Hyde thing is not entirely right, because in Jekyll and Hyde, it is basically two sides of himself, whereas with the Wolf Man, it's more of a disease. He's a victim.

JC: He is a victim, yes. The Wolf Man is a victim of life's circumstance, of something that has just happened to him.

JL: OK, so what about the Mummy?

JC: The original [Karl Freund, 1932] Mummy movie with Boris Karloff is just Dracula. It's literally a remake.

JL: Yeah.

JC: He comes back, he's after the girl… but it's still a great movie.

JL: It's slow, but I love the opening when the Mummy walks out.

JC: Fabulous. But that's Dracula, and the legend is that he's a sort of fallen character. In the Christopher Lee version [*The Mummy*, Terence Fisher, 1959], he wanted to live with his love forever…

JL: In the first *Mummy*, Karloff's Mummy is the bad guy, but in other Mummy movies it's the priest, and the Mummy is just a kind of killing machine.

JC: That's why I like the Christopher Lee version.

JL: He's fabulous in both *The Curse of Frankenstein* [Terence Fisher, 1957] and *The Mummy*, and totally different.

JC: His eyes in *The Mummy*! He can be so sad and haunted by this ancient love for this girl, and yet he can become so cold. I mean, he's fabulous! *The Curse of Frankenstein* just transformed me when I was a little kid.

JL: What I love in that is, when they shoot him, Chris has clearly got blood in his hand and he goes (slaps face)…

JC Of course.

JL: It works totally.

JC: But it was like "Ooh!"

JL: The gore was amazing.

JC: I was eight years old when I saw that.

JL: Frankenstein's monster, the Creature. He's always very sympathetic to me.

JC: Yeah, it's sad because he had no choice in his existence.

JL: Doctor Frankenstein in the Hammer films—Peter Cushing—becomes the monster.

JC: That's what's so fabulous. He's great, and evil. But poor Christopher Lee in that movie is kind of just walking flesh.

JL: OK, so what about zombies? Zombies were Voodoo zombies; then, starting with George [George A. Romero] really, they were vampire zombies. George copied his zombies from an Italian movie, *The Last Man on Earth* [Ubaldo Ragona, 1964] with Vincent Price, based on the Richard Matheson novel. Did you ever see that?

JC: Yes, I did.

JL: Because I said to George: "You got your

zombies from that," and he said, "Absolutely!" But you know, the idea of zombies, they were Voodoo, and then they became caused by disease, accidents, radiation spills…

JC: There was a film in 1959 that no one mentions, a movie called *Invisible Invaders*. Invisible moon people come down here and take over dead bodies, and the dead bodies rise up. Edward L. Cahn, who also did *It! The Terror From Beyond Space* [1958] directed it. *Invisible Invaders* was the first rising dead movie that I can remember.

JL: So, do you know what a ghoul is?

JC: Tell me.

JL: Well, a ghoul is basically a re-animated corpse.

JC: That's a zombie.

JL: A zombie is also a re-animated corpse. See, I never understood it.

JC: It's the Walking Dead.

JL: The Walking Dead, exactly. But a ghoul knows what he's doing and has a purpose. Zombies are either eating or killing machines, and they just shamble around. Why do you think zombies are so popular now?

JC: Everybody's been re-making *Night of the Living Dead* since 1968. Over and over. I've never seen anything like it. Specifically the rules of *Night of the Living Dead*.

JL: Like shooting zombies in the head to kill them?

JC: Everything about it! George A. Romero transformed horror movies. He really did.

JL: Well, *Halloween* [John Carpenter, 1978] inspired many other films. Here's a question: In the first *Halloween*, Mike Myers (the killer) is clearly human.

JC: Sort of.

JL: No, he's human. The only thing that's supernatural about him is that he gets up and walks away after he's been shot.

JC: But he's everywhere. His behavior is of the other world. He's partially supernatural, but nothing is explained. It's an intentional overlay on this kind of banal story of a guy running around killing people.

JL: Now, what about giant monsters, like Godzilla?

JC: I love Godzilla. He's everything to every generation. He was friendly, he was evil, he works *for* Japan, he works *against* Japan, he fights other monsters…

JL: Now what is this big thing about dinosaurs? In movies, we always have people coexisting with dinosaurs. You know *One Million Years B.C.* [Don Chaffey, 1966] and all

that kind of stuff… I asked Ray Harryhausen why he thinks that is, and he said, "Because without people, it's boring!"

JC: Well, I think that's true. I've got a question for you, pal! What is the Golem?

JL: The Golem? It's made of clay, very much like Frankenstein. They say it's a legend, but it's not. I can't remember the name of the guy who wrote it (Berthold Auerbach for his 1837 novel *Spinoza*), but it's set in Prague and it's a story about the rabbi of a ghetto where the Jews are being killed, who makes this clay model, and he comes alive through Kaballah and prayer. The Golem is basically a monster, an avenger for the Jews. But then he falls in love with a Gentile. There are three movies where Paul Wegener wrote, directed, and starred as the Golem. But they're kind of anti-Semitic movies; they're weird!

But let's get back to zombies. Why are zombies so popular now?

JC: I don't know. They started as something actually frightening; when you saw *Night of the Living Dead* in 1968, it was actually scary. You started worrying what you were going to see. Are the filmmakers going to go too far here and show me something I don't want to see? When the girl goes after her mother…

"Monsters don't scare me—people scare me!"

JL: No, her father. You saw the zombies eat her mother, and then she goes after her father.

JC: Yeah, her father. And she chomps up the bones! But one of the things George [A. Romero, the director] said was, every time he did one of those zombie movies, critics would come and visit the set, and all they'd want is to be a zombie… that's all they'd want!

JL: Do you think the appeal of zombies has something to do with death? Or is it not even about that any more?

JC: No. It's us. As George says: "They're us."

JL: That's a good title: "Zombies Are Us."

JC: What do you think, John? Are you going to make it? You could do it as a comedy!

JL: Everyone's making them. Now, I have another one for you—monsters in the ocean. *Jaws* is a monster movie.

JC: But it's not based in any kind of fantasy world. It's not a monster created by science.

JL: Except Jaws, much like Moby Dick, really is out to get the hunters. The first half of that movie is a classic, by-the-numbers monster movie, and the second half becomes an adventure on the high seas! Even the music changes. It's two different movies!

JC: *Jaws*, I think, is probably a monster movie. The monster in it isn't like the Mummy or Dracula. It's more like Moby Dick, and Moby Dick is not a monster: he's somebody's obsession.

JL: Ahab is the monster.

JC: *Jaws* is a "Force of Nature" story.

JL: What about religious angles? What about *The Exorcist*, the Devil?

JC: What do you think?

JL: I think *The Exorcist* [William Friedkin, 1973] is the best horror film ever made.

JC: It's pretty good.

JL: The original version, not the remake. And the reason I say that is that I'm an atheist, and a Jew on top of that: I don't believe in Jesus, and I don't believe in the Devil. The reason I credit *The Exorcist* so much, is that I bought it. I bought into the church, I bought into the power of Christ, and I bought into the possession. I was so pleased when Father Karras showed up. Thank God, you know?!

JC: You see, I didn't buy into it at the time. Later I came to appreciate what he (director William Friedkin) did there. I remember I thought at the time that this movie requires a belief in the Devil to be believable.

JL: Now, what about ghosts? There are ghosts in your movies who kill people, who are out for revenge.

JC: That's true.

JL: And the two scariest ghost movies are…

JC: I bet you're going to say *The Haunting* [Robert Wise, 1963], aren't you?

JL: *The Haunting* and *The Innocents* [Jack Clayton, 1961].

JC: *The Haunting* is bullshit! It is so awful.

JL: I love it! What about *The Innocents*? They're both creepy and scary, and you never see anything.

JC: That's the bad and beautiful way of making horror movies.

JL: You think you have to see something?

JC: No, not at all. But I get pissed off when you don't. I pays my money, I want to see what the fuck it is!

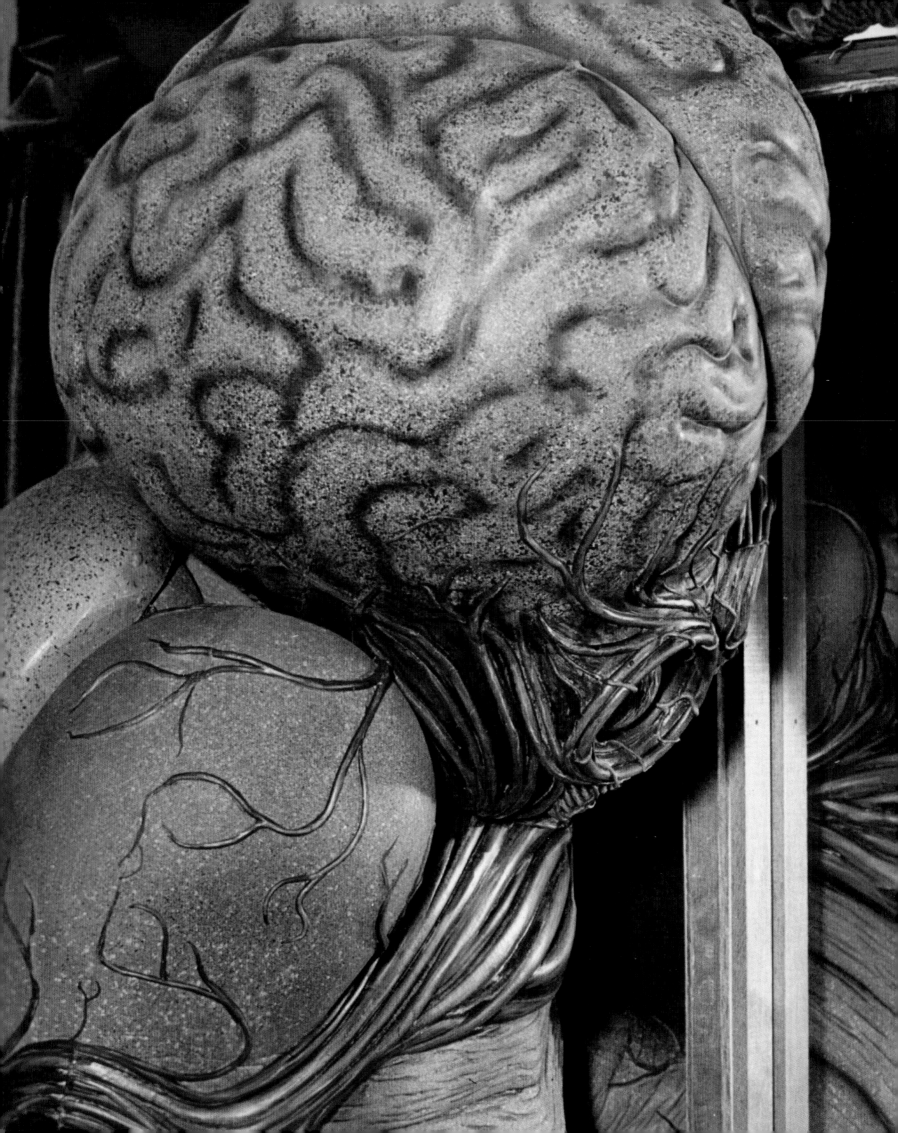

Space
Monsters

Space Monsters

There are monsters *from* outer space who come to the planet Earth to be in our movies [*Invaders From Mars*, William Cameron Menzies, 1953] and then there are monsters *in* outer space whom we send rocket ships to encounter [*The Green Slime*, Kinji Fukasaku, 1968]. There are aliens who come to Earth to *befriend* us [*Close Encounters of the Third Kind*, Steven Spielberg, 1977], there are aliens who come to Earth to *warn* us [*The Day the Earth Stood Still*, Robert Wise, 1951—I refuse to mention the remake!], and there are aliens who come to Earth to *destroy* us [*Mars Attacks!*, Tim Burton, 1996].

Most movie aliens want to destroy us. Howard Hawks produced one of the best scary alien-who-wants-us-dead movies, *The Thing from Another World* [Christian Nyby, 1951], a taut thriller based on the disturbing short story by John W. Campbell, Jr. *Who Goes There?*. When remade in 1982 as *John Carpenter's The Thing*, Bill Lancaster's screenplay stayed much closer to the Campbell story and Carpenter, with the aid of the extraordinary make-up effects of Rob Bottin, created a truly horrific and suspenseful classic. *The Thing* has one of my favorite lines in a monster movie: When one of the characters sees another character's decapitated head grow crab-like legs and skitter across the floor, he says, "You've got to be fucking kidding me!" Which, in context, is an extremely realistic reaction. Two years later *John*

▲ *Le Voyage dans la lune* [aka *A Trip to the Moon*, Georges Méliès, 1902] One of the first, if not *the* first, sci-fi movies, this image of the rocket ship stuck in the Moon's eye is unforgettable.

Carpenter's Starman [1984] landed on our planet with a sensitive performance by Jeff Bridges in the title role. Almost as if to make up for the ferocity of *The Thing*, *Starman*'s alien is so handsome, sweet, and charming, lovely Karen Allen falls in love with him.

Pioneering French special-effects filmmaker Georges Méliès probably made the first outer space movie with his silent version of Jules Verne's *A Trip to the Moon* in 1902. Méliès combined Verne's novel with H. G. Wells' novel *The First Men in the Moon* and brought us cinema's first aliens— the insectoid Selenites. This film is most famous for its iconic image of the Man in the Moon with a rocket ship stuck in his eye! Sixty-two years later, Ray Harryhausen gave us another version of H. G. Wells' *First Men in the Moon* [Nathan H. Juran, 1964] with remarkably similar-looking Selenites. The charming screenplay by Nigel Kneale adds an opening sequence in which modern-day astronauts discover a tattered Union Jack, left behind by the intrepid explorers who had set foot on the moon when Queen Victoria was still on the throne!

For every benign alien visitor, there are 50 hostile ones. And we Earthlings almost always greet our guests from space with suspicion and gunfire—like the Ymir in Ray Harryhausen's *20 Million Miles to Earth* [Nathan H. Juran, 1957], which is brought back from Venus as an egg. The rocket ship splashes down off the coast of Sicily, the egg hatches, and the alien creature is eventually gunned down atop Rome's Coliseum.

One of the greatest of all space monsters appears in *Forbidden Planet* [Fred M. Wilcox, 1956]. A lavish MGM production, with glorious Technicolor cinematography by George Folsey, and the first all-electronic score by avant-garde musicians Louis and Bebe Barron, this is one of the

Previous pages: *This Island Earth* [Joseph M. Newman, 1955] A Metaluna Mutant checks out his looks on a sound stage mirror before being filmed. Based on the novel by Raymond F. Jones, this is an exciting science-fiction film in glorious Technicolor.
Opposite page: *The Green Slime* [aka *Gamma 3: Operation Outer Space*, Kinji Fukasaku, 1968] Shot at Tokyo's Toei Studios with an entirely Caucasian cast. Luciana Paluzzi is pictured being harassed by one of the Green Slime. With a great title song!

most influential science-fiction films ever made. William Shakespeare's *The Tempest* inspired the screenplay by Cyril Hume and, although some of the costumes and dialog are dated, the ideas expressed are startlingly modern. Dr. Morbius (Walter Pidgeon) with his beautiful daughter Alta (Anne Francis) are the only survivors of a colony of settlers on the planet Altair. A rescue mission led by Commander John J. Adams (Leslie Nielsen) discovers that the two survivors are doing well, Dr. Morbius having learned much about the planet's former inhabitants the Krell and their amazing technology. But Alta's innocent sexual curiosity about the handsome men who have come to rescue them disturbs her father. A terrible, invisible monster kills several of the crew. It is an awesome sight, revealed only in outline by the crew's neutron-beam weaponry. Eventually, Dr. Morbius reveals the terrible secret of the Krell's disappearance... This splendid movie is clearly the template for the television series *Star Trek* and all of its sequels and prequels.

Two years after the release of *Forbidden Planet*, a meteor crashes down near the small town of Phoenixville, Pennsylvania. A red substance attacks an old man named Doc. Steve McQueen, in his first starring role, tries to convince the police of what he witnessed: "Something" was killing the Doc! The "something" turns out to be *The Blob* [Irvin Yeaworth, 1958], a gelatinous goo that grows larger as it consumes more and more victims. This quintessential 1950s sci-fi movie features a wonderfully loony cha-cha-cha title song by Burt Bacharach and Mack David.

Ridley Scott's seminal *Alien* [1979] revitalized the genre by placing a monster in an Old Dark House in outer space. Swiss artist H. R. Giger designed the creature, combining organic and

▲ *Le Voyage dans la lune* [aka *A Trip to the Moon*, Georges Méliès, 1902] One of the Selenites (the Moon's insectoid inhabitants) tries to prevent the humans' rocket ship from escaping.

mechanical elements in a truly original way. Dan O'Bannon's screenplay is rife with cliché, but Scott's stylish direction and a fine cast overcome the silliness and create a handsome, truly scary film. The wreckage of an alien spacecraft they find on another planet comes directly from Mario Bava's excellent *Planet of the Vampires* [1965], and once the alien is loose aboard the space ship *Nostromo*, *Alien* basically follows the storyline of *It! The Terror From Beyond Space* [Edward L. Cahn, 1958] a low-budget picture featuring Ray "Crash" Corrigan in a rubber monster suit.

Alien was a worldwide sensation and it was followed by James Cameron's *Aliens* in 1986, which brilliantly swapped horror for full-on action and made Sigourney Weaver's character Ripley into a feminist icon.

John McTiernan's *Predator* [1987] was a vehicle for Arnold Schwarzenegger, then at the height of his stardom. But the wonderfully designed Predator, an alien big-game hunter on Earth for sport, was far too interesting to disappear after just one movie. Sequels followed until, in 2004, *Alien vs. Predator* [Paul W. S. Anderson] attempted to become a contemporary *Frankenstein Meets the Wolf Man* [Roy William Neill, 1943]. I'm sure that if Abbott and Costello were still alive, they too would have eventually met the Predator and the Alien!

Roland Emmerich's *Independence Day* [1996] and 2011's *Battle: Los Angeles* [Jonathan Liebesman] clearly demonstrate that our planet is still not safe from alien invasion; however 2011 also brought us another gentle (if foulmouthed) alien in *Paul* [Greg Mottola]. So I think it's wise to remember the last words broadcast from that Arctic station at the end of *The Thing From Another World* [1951]: "Watch the Skies!"

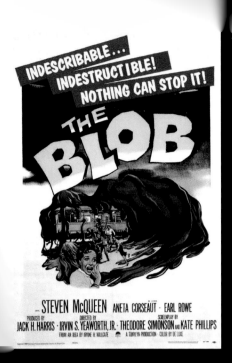

▲ *Flash Gordon* [Frederick Stephani, 1936] Charles B. Middleton as Ming the Merciless, ruler of the planet Mongo in the 13 exciting episodes of this popular serial. Buster Crabbe starred as Flash Gordon.

▲ *Flash Gordon* [Mike Hodges, 1980] Max von Sydow as Ming in Dino De Laurentiis' big-budget, campy remake. Sam J. Jones is Flash and the wonderful Ornella Muti is the insatiable Princess Aura. With a memorable score by Queen.

▶ *Invaders From Mars* [William Cameron Menzies, 1953] A tightly constructed, nightmarish scenario, in which all the authority figures— teachers, policemen, even your parents—are working for the Martians! The ending completely freaked me out when I was a child.

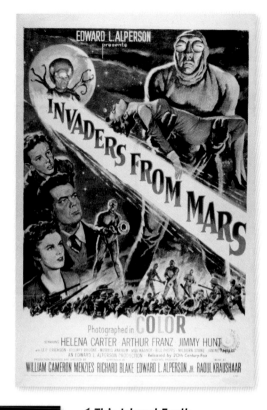

◀ *This Island Earth* [Joseph M. Newman, 1955] Alien scientists request help for their doomed world. Great special effects on the dying planet. And the Metaluna Mutant! (See pages 242-3.)

▼ *Monsters vs. Aliens* [Rob Letterman, Conrad Vernon, 2009] Benzoate Ostylezene Bicarbonate or B.O.B., is the result of a genetic experiment with a tomato gone wrong. However, he does look a lot like the alien in *It Came From Outer Space* (far left) but blue and with arms. Voiced by Seth Rogan.

▲▶ *It Came From Outer Space* [Jack Arnold, 1953] Richard Carlson stands in front of an alien craft that has crashed into the desert. In 3D! This frightening, one-eyed alien (right) turns out to be benign. From an original screen story by Ray Bradbury.

▲ **The Thing From Another World** [aka *The Thing*, Christian Nyby, 1951] Generally assumed to have been directed by producer Howard Hawks, this taut suspense thriller about a group of soldiers and scientists in the Arctic who find something in the ice is a bona fide classic.

▶ *I Married a Monster From Outer Space*
[Gene Fowler Jr., 1958] A young bride notices her new husband is acting strangely. A much better movie than the title would lead you to believe.

▲ **The Thing From Another World** [Christian Nyby, 1951] The indelible ad art for *The Thing*. George A. Romero once described this film as "a movie about doors," because you are never sure what is lurking behind each one.

▲ **The Thing** [aka *John Carpenter's The Thing*, 1982] Bill Lancaster's screenplay and Rob Bottin's astonishing make-up effects, coupled with Carpenter's dynamite direction, make this picture a modern classic.

"You gotta be fucking kidding me!"

Palmer (David Clennon), *The Thing* [1982]

Forbidden Planet

▶ **Forbidden Planet** [Fred M. Wilcox, 1956] Ad art showing Walter Pidgeon as Dr. Edward Morbius, Leslie Nielsen as Commander John J. Adams, Robby the Robot, and Anne Francis as Altaira, Morbius' beautiful daughter.

▲ **The War of the Worlds** [Byron Haskin, 1953] The Martian war machines attack (see page 309). The Martians even destroy Los Angeles City Hall! A George Pal Production, based on the classic novel by H. G. Wells. Inset: A close-up of a Martian, surprised in a barn by Gene Barry and Ann Robinson.

◀▼ **An original pencil drawing** on a CinemaScope-size paper cell of the Monster from the Id by animator Joshua Meador and how it looked in the movie (below). The Id Monster becomes visible when lasers are fired at it by the spaceship's crew. (From the collection of Bob Burns.)

"My evil self is outside that door, and I have no power to stop it!"

Dr. Morbius (Walter Pidgeon), *Forbidden Planet*

▼ **Dr. Morbius** realizes to his horror that the thing coming to kill them is in fact his own subconscious made real by the technology of the Krell. Anne Francis looks on in both love and fear. A great moment in a great movie.

▲ War of the Worlds [Steven Spielberg, 2002] The Martian war machines look more like the ones described in Wells' novel in Spielberg's remake, starring Tom Cruise.

▲ Invasion of the Saucer Men [Edward L. Cahn, 1957]
The police refuse to believe the teenagers who claim to see little green men in this drive-in movie. More preposterous monsters from make-up man Paul Blaisdell.

"YOU'RE NEXT!"

Dr. Miles J. Bennell (Kevin McCarthy), *Invasion of the Body Snatchers* [1956]

▲ Invasion of the Body Snatchers [Philip Kaufman, 1978]
Donald Sutherland is driving in San Francisco when Kevin McCarthy frantically pounds on his windshield trying to warn him—22 years after we last saw him on the highway at the end of the original film!

▲▶ Invasion of the Body Snatchers
[Don Siegel, 1956] Kevin McCarthy, Dana Wynter, and King Donovan regard the pod that is forming into a replica of Donovan in Don Siegel's outstanding film. An examination of conformity, paranoia, and loss of humanity, *Invasion of the Body Snatchers* is an important American film.

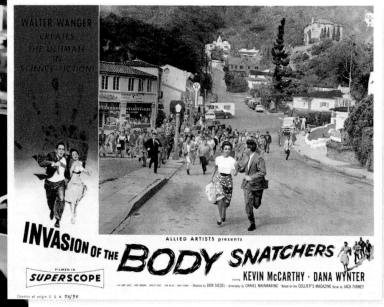

▲ *Little Shop of Horrors* [Roger Corman, 1960] A small potted plant demands human flesh and starts to grow. Famously shot in two days, this is a funny, genuinely offbeat comedy. Charles B. Griffith wrote the script, but it's hard to believe that the gifted Mel Welles did not ad-lib some of his lines. With Jonathan Haze, Jackie Joseph, Dick Miller, and a young Jack Nicholson as the perfect patient.

▲ *The Angry Red Planet* [Ib Melchior, 1959] In "Cinemagic"—which was essentially solarized black and white footage in this Eastmancolor movie. This movie frightened me when I saw it in a theater when I was nine years old. I watched it again recently. If you're older than nine, don't bother.

"FEED ME!"

Audrey Jr., the carnivorous plant,
Little Shop of Horrors [1960]

▶ *Little Shop of Horrors*
[Frank Oz, 1986]
A hit off-Broadway musical by Howard Ashman and Alan Menken, based on Roger Corman's film, made back into a movie by Frank Oz. With Ellen Greene in the role she originated on stage, Rick Moranis, Steve Martin, Bill Murray, and the wonderful Levi Stubbs as the voice of the hungry plant, Audrey 2.

▼ *The Quatermass Xperiment* [aka *The Creeping Unknown*, **Val Guest**, 1953] Based on the 1953 BBC television serial *The Quatermass Experiment* by Nigel Kneale. American movie star Brian Donlevy was imported by Hammer to play Professor Quatermass. Richard Wordsworth (great-great grandson of the poet William Wordsworth), gives a stunning and tragic performance as the astronaut infected while in Outer Space who slowly becomes an alien monster back in London.

▲ *Journey to the Seventh Planet* [Sidney W. Pink, 1962] On a trip to Uranus (the seventh planet in our solar system), the astronauts have strange dreams. Shot in Denmark, with the same crew that had just made *Reptilicus* [Poul Bang, Sidney W. Pink, 1961], one of the worst movies I ever paid to see in a cinema.

Space Babes

▲ **Cat Women on the Moon** [Arthur Hilton, 1953] Astronaut Sonny Tufts leads an expedition to the Moon where they find a race of beautiful women. Another movie with a marvelous title you can avoid. A young, "gray listed" Elmer Bernstein wrote the score.

▲ **It Conquered the World** [Roger Corman, 1956] Beverly Garland looks askance at another silly looking Paul Blaisdell creation. This monster from Venus is using scientist Lee Van Cleef to take over the world!

▲ **Devil Girl From Mars** [David MacDonald, 1954] Nyah (Patricia Laffan) comes to Earth looking for men to repopulate her planet. Mostly remembered for Nyah's black vinyl outfit.

▲ **Queen of Outer Space** [Edward Bernds, 1958] Eric Fleming and his crew land on Venus to find that mean Queen Ylana (Laurie Mitchell) has banished all men from her planet. Talleah (Zsa Zsa Gabor) and her friends plot to overthrow the Queen and get some men back into their lives. Just as good as it sounds.

▲ **The Day of the Triffids** [Steve Sekely, 1962] Broadway musical star Howard Keel stars in this movie based on John Wyndham's novel. After a spectacular meteor shower blinds everyone who witnesses it, alien plants that can uproot themselves and eat people are on the loose! I loved this movie when I saw it as a kid, but I am afraid to revisit it now for fear of being disappointed.

▶ **Barbarella** [Roger Vadim, 1968] Based on the sexy comic strip by Jean-Claude Forest, Vadim's pop art film stars his then wife Jane Fonda during her sex-kitten period. Her weightless striptease under the titles is a highlight. Typical title song lyric: "Barbarella-Psychedella..." A movie very much of its time.

253

▲ *Yog, Monster From Space* [aka *Space Amoeba*, Ishirô Honda, 1970]
A spaceship is boarded by a strange alien amoeba that takes control of animals on Earth. My favorite is the giant cuttlefish (called a "Gezora" in the movie). This is a paste-up publicity shot of Gezora and the cast.

▲ *Laserblast* [Michael Rae, 1978] A troubled teenager finds an alien weapon and goes on the rampage. The aliens return to take it back. Only notable for the skillful, stop-motion alien sequences by animator David W. Allen.

▲ *Escape From the Planet of the Apes* [Don Taylor, 1971]
The third of the *Planet of the Apes* movies. In this one, Roddy McDowall, Kim Hunter, and Sal Mineo are chimpanzees who, using Charlton Heston's spaceship from the first film, somehow go back in time to the present where they are perceived (correctly) as a threat to the future of mankind by the government. Kindly Ricardo Montalban hides them in his circus. Pictured are the chimp astronauts being escorted by Marines.

◀ *Horror Express* [Eugenio Martin, 1973] An alien intelligence is able to transfer into the bodies of others in this "who is it?" on the Trans-Siberian Express. Christopher Lee and Peter Cushing are stiff-upper-lipped British scientists and Telly Savalas a Cossack in this entertaining, period sci-fi thriller, made in Spain.

▲ *It! The Terror From Beyond Space*
[Edward L. Cahn, 1958] Ray "Crash" Corrigan as
It, a stowaway on the first spaceship to land on
Mars. An obvious influence on *Alien*, down to
the opening of a hatch to blow It from the ship.

▲ *Alien* [Ridley Scott, 1979] The Alien about to
be blown out of the open hatch of the escape pod
by the intrepid Ripley (Sigourney Weaver).

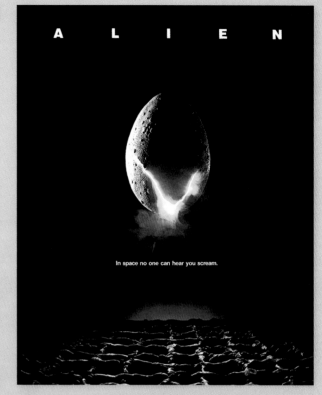

▲ *Alien* [Ridley Scott, 1979] Poster for *Alien* with
the fantastic tagline, "In space no one can hear
you scream."

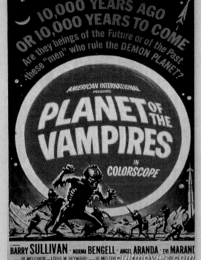

▲ *Planet of the Vampires*
[Mario Bava, 1965] *Alien*
screenwriter Dan O'Bannon and
director Scott say they have never
seen it, but it is hard to avoid this
film's influence on *Alien*. With little
budget and, literally, smoke and
mirrors, Bava created a marvelous,
other-worldly quality to the planet's
exteriors. When the astronauts
explore the ruins of another ship
containing the skeletal remains of its
giant alien pilot, it's hard to accept
Dan and Ridley's denials.
Regardless, *Alien* and *Planet of the
Vampires* are seminal sci-fi films.

▶▶ *Aliens* [James Cameron,
1986] "This time it's war"—
Cameron's brilliant sequel to *Alien*,
in which he changed the genre
from horror to action. A genuinely
exciting movie, with a wonderfully
anxious performance by Bill Paxton.

"This is Ripley, last
survivor of the *Nostromo*,
signing off."

Ripley (Sigourney Weaver), before putting herself
and the cat into a hibernation pod, *Alien*

▲ *Alien* [Ridley Scott, 1979] The Alien as it bursts from
the chest of Executive Officer Kane (John Hurt), in a truly
shocking sequence.

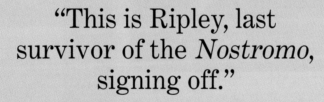

SPACE MONSTERS

◄ *Strange Invaders*
[Michael Laughlin, 1983]
Aliens invade smalltown America in this satirical sci-fi movie. Here, an alien reveals his true self by tearing off his human face.

▲ *Explorers* [Joe Dante, 1985] River Phoenix and Ethan Hawke (both in their first film) are two boys who build a spaceship that takes them to meet the aliens who sent them the instructions in their dreams. Their time on the alien spacecraft is one of my favorite Joe Dante extravaganzas. With Little Richard wailing on the soundtrack, all is going well until the Alien Dad (top) shows up!

▲ *Enemy Mine* [Wolfgang Petersen, 1985] Instead of Toshirô Mifune and Lee Marvin stranded on a desert island in the Pacific Ocean in World War II [*Hell in the Pacific*, John Boorman, 1968], it's Dennis Quaid and Lou Gosset, Jr. (as the Alien Drac) stranded on another planet. With elements of *Robinson Crusoe on Mars* [Byron Haskin, 1964] thrown in for good measure and skillful performances from the leads, this is an entertaining, retro sci-fi picture.

◄ *E.T. the Extra-Terrestrial*
[aka *E.T.*, Steven Spielberg, 1982] From an original screenplay by Melissa Mathison, an alien puppet built by Carlo Rambaldi, and product placement from Reece's Pieces candy, Spielberg fashioned an international blockbuster. With lovely performances from child actors Henry Thomas and Drew Barrymore, *E.T.* is a very well-crafted tearjerker.

▲ *Village of the Damned* [Wolf Rilla, 1960] An excellent adaptation of the novel *The Midwich Cuckoos* by John Wyndham. A superb use of children as objects of fear. Just keep thinking, "Brick wall. Brick Wall. Brick Wall."

SPACE BABIES

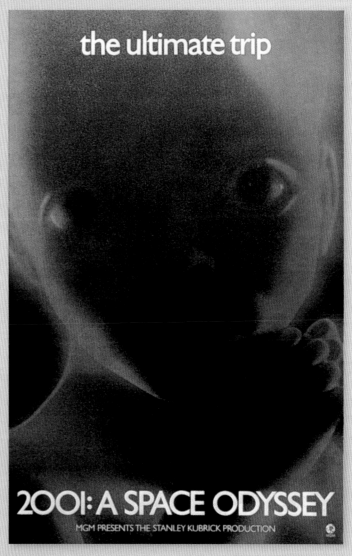

2001: A SPACE ODYSSEY

MGM PRESENTS THE STANLEY KUBRICK PRODUCTION

◀ *The Andromeda Strain* [Robert Wise, 1971] Wise's faithful version of Michael Crichton's novel is smart and suspenseful. Here, James Olson and Arthur Hill wonder why this baby has not succumbed to a deadly, extraterrestrial virus.

▲ *2001: A Space Odyssey* [Stanley Kubrick, 1968] This poster shows the "Star Child" we see at the conclusion of the movie. Is this the next step in mankind's evolution? The tagline, "the ultimate trip" was almost an invitation for the audience to use hallucinogenics while watching the film (and many of them did just that). One of the best movies ever.

▲ *Starman* [John Carpenter, 1984] Carpenter's *nice* alien movie (almost like an apology for his malevolent *The Thing*). This baby is Jeff Bridges' Starman! Karen Allen falls in love with him when he gets a little more mature.

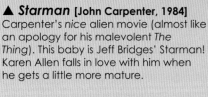

▶ *Men in Black* [Barry Sonnenfeld, 1997] Will Smith cradles the alien baby he has just helped to deliver in this hit sci-fi comedy. Rick Baker created all of the many different aliens.

▲ *Pro-Life* [John Carpenter, 2006] From Season Two of the Mick Garris-produced *Masters of Horror* series. An alien holds its half-human baby, created by Howard Berger and his special effects crew at KNB.

257

SPACE MONSTERS

▲ **Masters of the Universe** [Gary Goddard, 1987]
Frank Langella as Skeletor in this amusing movie based on
a line of toys. Dolph Lundgren is He-Man.

▲ **They Live** [John Carpenter, 1988] Carpenter's funny political rant is a deliberately
funky throwback in look and style. "OBEY!"

▶ **Killer Klowns From Outer
Space** [Stephen Chiodo, 1988]
A flying circus tent from outer
space lands in a small town.
Dangerous aliens emerge who
look like clowns, kill with custard
pies, and unleash attack balloon
animals! A nice piece of
craziness from gifted stop-motion
animators the Chiodo Brothers.

▼ **Starship Troopers**
[Paul Verhoeven, 1997]
Casper Van Dien as starship
trooper Johnny Rico leading the
troopers in their battle against
the alien "bugs." Adapted from
Robert A. Heinlein's novel, a
smart satire of a fascist military at
war, with spectacular special
effects by Phil Tippett. Verhoeven
has said, "The movie is about,
'Let's all go to war
and let's all die.'"
An underrated gem.

▲ **Mars Attacks!** [Tim Burton, 1996] Based on the infamous and
gruesome Topps bubblegum trading cards by *Mad Magazine* artist
Wallace Wood. The Martians kill indiscriminately and speak in a
language that consists entirely of the word "Ack." Burton fills the
film with homages to 50s and 60s sci-fi movies, specifically Ray
Harryhausen's *Earth vs. the Flying Saucers* [Fred F. Sears, 1956].

▲ **The Fifth Element** [Luc Besson, 1997] In a future inspired
equally by *Blade Runner* and *The Jetsons*, Bruce Willis' cab driver
searches for a legendary cosmic device to keep Gary Oldman's
Mr. Zorg from destroying the world. A lavish production with a
charming performance from Milla Jovovich as Leeloo, the
humanoid who is the key to saving mankind.

INDEPENDENCE DAY

DIGITALLY THX MASTERED
FOR SUPERIOR SOUND AND PICTURE QUALITY

▲ *Independence Day* [Roland Emmerich, 1996] One of Emmerich's movies of mass destruction, this time an all-out alien attack on Earth that is eventually thwarted by Will Smith's heroic jet pilot and Jeff Goldblum, using a laptop computer (in one of the all-time inane plot devices). A ridiculous, but very entertaining film. Emmerich destroyed the White House again in his *2012* [2009], this time with a tidal wave tossing an aircraft carrier onto it!

▲ *Return of the Jedi* [aka *Star Wars: Episode VI*, Richard Marquand, 1983] Luke Skywalker is thrown into a pit to be fed to a monster called the Rancor. Here you can see the bone Luke shoves into its mouth. Basically a hand puppet, and my favorite *Star Wars* monster.

STAR WARS MONSTERS

George Lucas filled his *Star Wars* movies with all kinds of creatures. Here are just a few of them.

▶ *Star Wars: Episode II—Attack of the Clones* [George Lucas, 2002] In the earlier movies, Yoda (voiced by the great Frank Oz) was originally a puppet. Here he is a CG character. I think that Yoda lost some of his charm when he ceased to be a puppet and became a bunch of pixels. But that's just me.

▼ *Star Wars: Episode I—The Phantom Menace* [George Lucas,1999] Two pleasing, old-school monsters. The loathsome Jabba the Hutt and his advisor, Bib Fortuna. The harem/slave-girl outfit Carrie Fisher wears as Jabba's prisoner is a fan favorite.

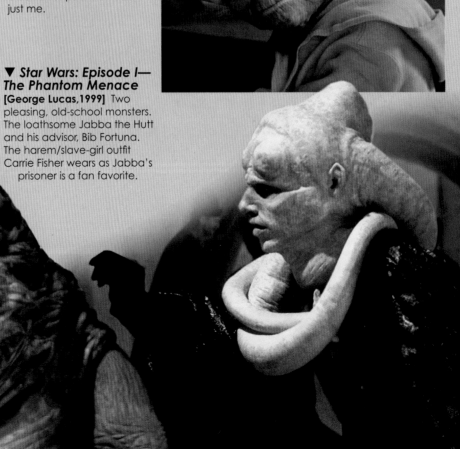

▶ Galaxy Quest
[Dean Parisot, 1999]
Tim Allen as the William Shatner-type actor in a storyline identical to *Three Amigos!* [John Landis, 1986]. This time, the actors mistaken for real heroes are the cast of a *Star Trek*-type TV series. With hilarious performances from Tony Shalhoub, Sam Rockwell, and Alan Rickman as the crew members, and terrific aliens by Stan Winston.

▲ Dark City [Alex Proyas, 1998] A sci-fi movie in *film noir* style, with aliens as tall, pale men in black trench coats and hats. A cool-looking, aliens-experiment-on-humans story. Jennifer Connelly looks like she's on to this guy.

▲ Transformers [Michael Bay, 2007] From the cartoon show. Cars turn into giant robots. Lots of CG, big box office success. Terrible.

▲ Slither [James Gunn, 2006] Grant Grant (Michael Rooker) is infected by an alien slug and mutates into this disgusting-looking guy. And worse, livestock and townsfolk are starting to go missing *and* there are zombies, too!

◀ Cloverfield [Matt Reeves, 2008] New York City is invaded by really huge monsters and we watch the whole thing through the video camera of one of the young people we do not care about who are trying to escape. The special effects are first-rate. Here, one of the aliens looks into the camera.

▶ District 9 [Neil Blomkamp, 2009] The US poster for this intelligent (if not subtle) sci-fi allegory, set in Johannesburg, South Africa. Very well made with a fine performance from Sharlto Copley.

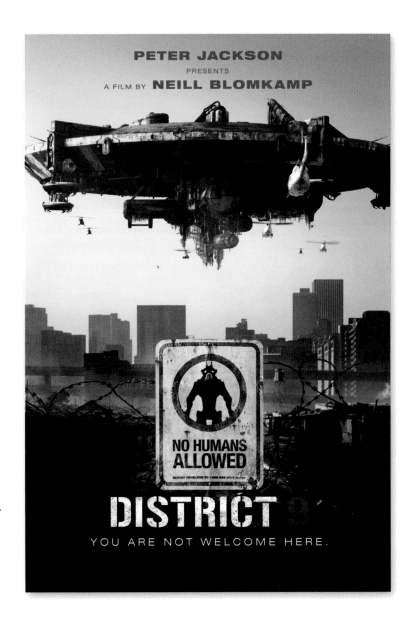

◀ *Avatar*
[James Cameron, 2009] A white man saves the blue man this time, instead of the red man. A mash-up of *Dances With Wolves* [Kevin Costner, 1990] and *FernGully: The Last Rainforest* [Bill Kroyer, 1992], but with spectacular visuals and flawless 3D. An international sensation at the box office. Pictured are Jake Sully (Sam Worthington) and Neytiri (Zoe Saldana) after their motion-capture performances have been fully animated.

"Everything is backwards now, like out there is the true world, and in here is the dream."

Jake Sully (Sam Worthington), *Avatar*

▼ *Predator* **[John McTiernan, 1987]** Another variation of *The Most Dangerous Game* [aka *The Hounds of Zaroff*, 1924] a short story by Richard Connell in which a big-game hunter hunts human prey. This time, it's an alien who travels the universe hunting the local species for sport. An elite unit of soldiers finds itself being hunted by the Predator in the jungles of Central America. Kevin Peter Hall plays the Predator in a creature suit by Stan Winston. An entertaining action picture that ends with Arnold Schwarzenegger surviving an atomic blast! Eventually, the Predator ended up fighting the Alien [*Alien vs. Predator*, Paul W. S. Anderson, 2004] just like *King Kong vs. Godzilla*. *Predators* [Nimrod Antal, 2010] (below) is the latest sequel.

▲ *Monsters* **[Gareth Edwards, 2010]** The ambiance of Mexico enduring an extraterrestrial infestation is brilliantly realized, as a photo journalist accompanies the boss' daughter to "safety" across the border in the USA. A love story in a standard outer-space-monsters-on-Earth story, but beautifully done. A textbook example of how good imaginative, low- budget filmmaking can be.

▲ **Soylent Green** [Richard Fleischer, 1973] Charlton Heston finds out what's in those green crackers—"It's people!" Based on the novel *Make Room! Make Room!* by Harry Harrison. Edward G. Robinson's last film.

▲ **A Clockwork Orange** [Stanley Kubrick, 1971] Based on the novel by Anthony Burgess, Kubrick's brilliant, bleak, and often funny vision of the near future. With a great performance from Malcolm McDowell as the Droogs' leader Alex DeLarge. Here the Droogs prepare for a bit of "the old ultra-violence."

▲ **Things to Come** [William Cameron Menzies, 1936] From H. G. Wells' screenplay, based on his 1933 novel *The Shape of Things to Come*. The movie tells a "future history" from 1940 to 2036, including this image of London, which was prophetic of the coming Blitz.

▶ **Metropolis**
[Fritz Lang, 1927]
A city of the future based on Lang's first sight of the New York skyline onboard the ship bringing him past the Statue of Liberty into Manhattan.

▲ **Logan's Run** [Michael Anderson, 1976] In the future, Michael York and Jenny Agutter stand in the ruins of the United States Senate.

▲ Fahrenheit 451 [François Truffaut, 1966] Based on the book by Ray Bradbury. Fahrenheit 451 is the temperature that paper burns. Here is Oskar Werner as Montag, a fireman. The firemen of this dystopian future burn books.

▲ The Time Machine [George Pal, 1960]
The dreaded Morlocks, mutants in the future that feed off of the human population. H. G. Wells' grandson, Simon Wells, directed an awful remake in 2002.

◀ 1984 [Michael Anderson, 1956] Edmond O'Brien runs by a billboard proclaiming "BIG BROTHER IS WATCHING YOU" in this, one of many adaptations of the disturbing George Orwell novel.

▲ Blade Runner [Ridley Scott, 1982] Scott's accomplished realization of the future skyline of Los Angeles.

▲ Minority Report [Steven Spielberg, 2002] Loosely based on the short story by Philip K. Dick, Spielberg and his designers brilliantly bring a futuristic version of our society to life. Here, police arrest a man *before* a crime is committed! The sequence where Tom Cruise enters a shopping mall is singularly probable. He is electronically recognized and bombarded with digital displays of items he might like to purchase.

▲ Brazil [Terry Gilliam, 1985] Gilliam's dark comedic look at the future is equal parts funny and horrific. The scenes satirizing cosmetic surgery are etched in my mind forever.

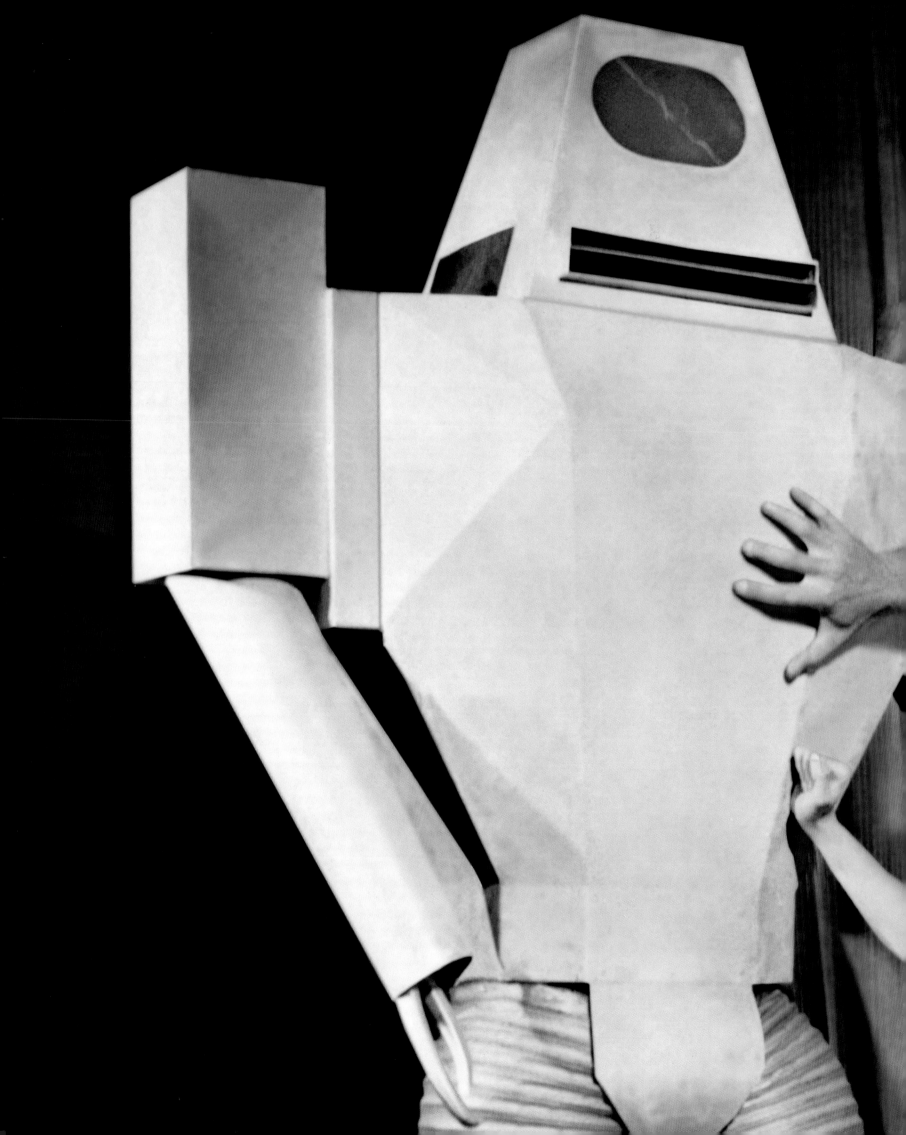

monstrous
machines

Monstrous Machines

Apart from the obvious advantages in manufacturing, transportation, agriculture, and communication it has given us, the Industrial Revolution has a lot to answer for: The clear and increasing damage that man-made pollution is doing to our planet, and all of the robots, automobiles, and computers that run amuck in the cinema! In the movies, machines turn on us with remarkable regularity. From malicious cars [*Christine*, John Carpenter, 1983] to malicious television sets [*The Twonky*, Arch Oboler, 1953], the movies have no doubts that our machines are untrustworthy.

Silent film's most famous robot would have to be the Machine Man disguised as the character Maria in Fritz Lang's iconic *Metropolis* [1927]. Another fabulous mechanical man, Robby the Robot, was introduced to us in *Forbidden Planet* [Fred M. Wilcox, 1956]. Robby was the first movie robot to speak with the robotic voice we now associate with all computers. His 1950s "space-age" design, with its revolving antennae, plastic dome, and many moving parts was such a hit that MGM immediately starred Robby in his own feature, *The Invisible Boy* [Herman Hoffman, 1957].

Another particularly memorable movie robot is Gort, which accompanies the alien Klaatu (Michael Rennie) on his mission to Earth in *The Day the Earth Stood Still* [Robert Wise, 1951]. In this elegant Cold War film, the populations of other worlds, concerned about the brutality of mankind, send Klaatu to warn Earthlings of the dangers of atomic power. If Earthlings attempt to expand their propensity for violence into outer space, Gort and his fellow robot enforcers will destroy us. So never forget the words, "Klaatu barada nikto." A good reason to see *The Day the Earth Stood Still* is to learn just what those words mean, so you will be prepared the next time a flying saucer from another world lands on the Mall in Washington, D.C.

Cold War paranoia also fuels *Gog* [Herbert L. Strock, 1954], where two robots, Gog and Magog, are being controlled by secret radio signals to sabotage an American space station. In *The Colossus of New York* [Eugène Lourié, 1958], a brilliant young scientist is killed in a car crash on the eve of winning the Nobel Peace Prize. His brain-surgeon father transplants the young scientist's brain into the skull of a large robot—a bad idea for all concerned.

Far eclipsing the brain power of a human mind, computers' processing capabilities have always made us nervous. This concern is reflected in a whole series of movies where computers attempt to take over the world. In Joseph Sargent's suspenseful *Colossus: The Forbin Project* [1970] and in Stanley Kubrick's seminal science-fiction epic *2001: A Space Odyssey* [1968], computers come to the logical conclusion that humans are incapable of making correct decisions and take steps to relieve them of that responsibility. In *The Forbin Project*, the supercomputers respectively placed in control of the American and Soviet nuclear arsenals join forces "for the betterment of mankind" with terrifying results. In *2001*, HAL, the onboard computer of the spacecraft Discovery One (given a calm but creepy monotone voice by actor Douglas Rain), comes to believe that the human crew will jeopardize the Jupiter Mission (to find the source of a mysterious black monolith discovered on the Moon), and begins to murder

▲ *The Wizard of Oz* [Victor Fleming, 1939]
The Tin Man (Jack Haley) with Dorothy (Judy Garland) and the Scarecrow (Ray Bolger).

Previous pages: Target Earth [Sherman A. Rose, 1954]
Richard Denning and Kathleen Crowley are threatened by an invasion of alien robots from Venus!

Opposite page: The Day the Earth Stood Still [Robert Wise, 1951]
Klaatu (Michael Rennie) and robot Gort (Lock Martin) emerge from their ship. A rare color still from this black and white classic.

them one by one. In a chilling sequence, HAL kills the astronauts who are in suspended animation, their deaths displayed in the flatlining of their life-support systems. HAL then tricks the two remaining astronauts (Keir Dullea and Gary Lockwood in brilliant, underrated performances) into going outside into space. HAL murders one of them and refuses entry to the other. The astronaut repeatedly orders: "Open the pod bay doors, HAL." HAL finally responds, "I'm afraid I can't do that, Dave." The astronaut literally blows his way back into the ship and gives HAL a lobotomy in an unsettling, starkly beautiful scene.

Another movie featuring machines running out of control is *Westworld*, written and directed by Michael Crichton [1973]. *Westworld* was inspired when Crichton took his kids to Disneyland. He wondered what would happen if the audio-animatronic pirates on the Pirates of the Caribbean ride began to kill the passengers. Notable for the perfect casting of Yul Brynner as a Western gun-slinging robot relentlessly pursuing hapless tourist Richard Benjamin, *Westworld* is the obvious model for James Cameron's low-budget classic *The Terminator* [1984], in which Arnold Schwarzenegger plays a relentless robot from the future. A smart and well-made action sci-fi movie, Cameron topped it with the dazzling *Terminator 2: Judgment Day* [aka *T2*, 1991]. With a bigger budget, terrific stunt work, revolutionary computer generated images, and Stan Winston's superb make-ups and puppetry, Cameron delivered a truly spectacular movie. This film not only made the bad guy Terminator from the first film into a good guy, it also introduced the awesome T-1000 robot, played by Robert Patrick with the help of some extraordinary special effects.

Isaac Asimov's classic and influential collection of short stories *I, Robot* was published in 1950. Asimov's "Three Laws of Robotics" (1. A robot may not injure a human being or, through inaction, allow a human being to come to harm. 2. A robot must obey any orders given it by human beings, except

where such orders would conflict with the First Law. 3. A robot must protect its own existence as long as such protection does not conflict with the First or Second Law) set the standards for practical artificial intelligence. *I, Robot* was made into an underwhelming, CG-laden, Will Smith vehicle in 2004 by Alex Proyas.

One robot that disregarded all of Asimov's Laws of Robotics was the Proteus IV in *Demon Seed* [Donald Cammell, 1977], in which an "artificially intelligent computer" ends up impregnating Julie Christie by force when it fails to charm her.

In *The Matrix* [Larry and Andy Wachowski, 1999], it is revealed that what most people experience is actually a simulation of reality created by intelligent machines to pacify the humans, whose bodies supply heat and energy to The Matrix. Neo (Keanu Reeves) becomes involved in a rebellion against the machines in a wonderful movie. I won't talk about the increasingly stupid sequels as I enjoyed the first one so much.

Be they robots, clones, androids, cyborgs, or replicants: when does enough artificial intelligence make a non-human human? This question is addressed in movies like *A.I. Artificial Intelligence* [Steven Spielberg, 2001] and Ridley Scott's visionary *Blade Runner* [1982]. The brilliantly realized and prophetic future of *Blade Runner* was done with traditional miniatures and an optical printer, before the existence of digital effects.

So what exactly does make us human? In the MGM classic, *The Wizard of Oz* [Victor Fleming, 1939], our four heroes are on a quest. The Cowardly Lion wants some courage. The Scarecrow wants something organic in his head, something other than straw; he (like many others in this book) wants brains. And Dorothy just wants to go home. But it is the Tin Man who understands exactly what he needs, and it is not just one of flesh he is singing about. The Tin Man sings that he's "presumin' " that he could be "kind-a-human, if I only had a heart."

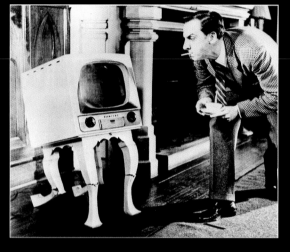

▲ **The Twonky** [Arch Oboler, 1953] Hans Conried is baffled by the actions of his new television set.

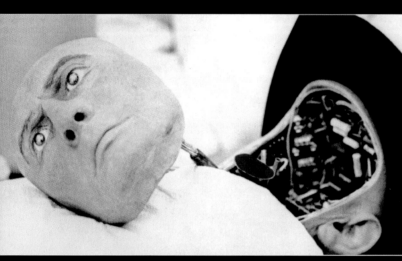

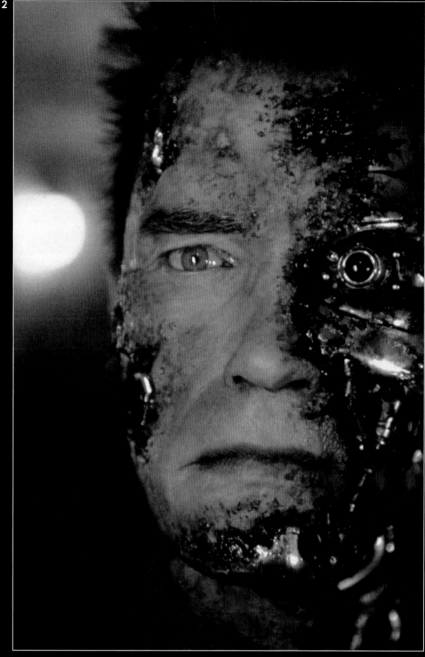

> "Remotely controlled. It could crush all opposition and make me the most powerful man in the world!"
>
> Dr. Zorka (Béla Lugosi),
> *The Phantom Creeps*

▶ *Metropolis* [Fritz Lang, 1927] Brigitte Helm as the "Maschinenmensch," the robotic version of her character Maria.

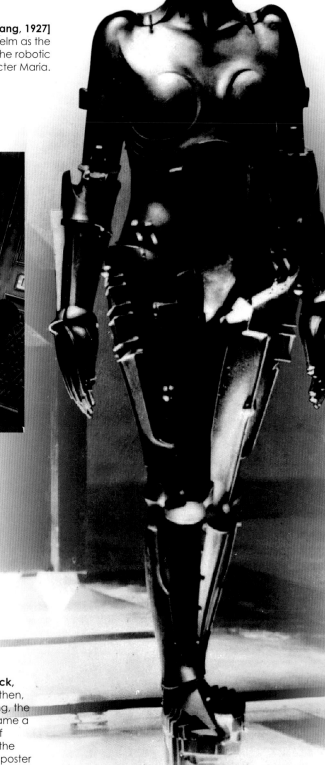

▲ *The Phantom Creeps* [Ford Beebe, Saul A. Goodkind, 1939] This 12-part Universal serial starred Béla Lugosi as the evil Dr. Zorka with yet another invention to try and take over the world. A completely looney looking Robot (played by Ed Wolff).

▶ *Old Mother Riley Meets The Vampire* [John Gilling, 1952] The last in a series of films starring British music hall comic Arthur Lucan in drag as Old Mother Riley. Béla Lugosi is in this one, too.

◀ *Gog* [Herbert L. Strock, 1954] "...and then, without warning, the machine became a Frankenstein of steel!!" So ran the tagline on the poster of this neat, low-budget sci-fi thriller.

◀▲ *The Invisible Boy* [Herman Hoffman. 1957] MGM recycled the Robby the Robot suit from the previous year's *Forbidden Planet* in this "boy and his robot" movie.

▶ *Tobor the Great* [Lee Sholem, 1954] Tobor the robot was designed by Robert Kinoshita, who later designed Robby the Robot for *Forbidden Planet*. Director Lee Sholem was a low-budget specialist who shot very quickly and was widely known as "Roll'em Sholem."

▲ *Zombies of the Stratosphere* [Fred C. Brannon, 1952] A serial from Republic Studios with special effects by the Lydecker Brothers. The third serial to use the rocket-powered flying suit first seen in *King of the Rocket Men* [Fred C. Brannon, 1949].

▲ *Robot Monster* [Phil Tucker, 1953] In 3D! The alien Ro-man is wearing George Barrows' gorilla suit, but not the head. Instead he wears a space helmet! The skull depicted inside the helmet on this poster never appears in the movie.

"I can't put my finger on it, but I sense something strange about him."

Dr. Frank Poole (Gary Lockwood), about the onboard computer HAL, *2001: A Space Odyssey*

▲ *2001: A Space Odyssey* [Stanley Kubrick, 1968] Astronauts Keir Dullea and Gary Lockwood suspect HAL, the spaceship's onboard computer, and lock themselves into a pod where HAL is unable to hear them. They are in for an unpleasant surprise. HAL, the red spot outside the window, can read lips!

◀ *The Colossus of New York* [Eugène Lourié, 1958] Another brain transplant movie! A Nobel Prize-winning young scientist is killed in a car accident and his surgeon father puts his brain into a giant robot, with predictably dire results. Here he is carrying off his widow, Marla Powers.

▲ *THX 1138* [George Lucas, 1971] Robert Duvall is taken away by robot police officers in Lucas' dark vision of a dystopian future.

▲ *The Stepford Wives* [Brian Forbes, 1975] Based on Ira Levin's satirical novel, a former male Disneyland employee creates perfect wife robots. Katharine Ross' unfinished robot has very big breasts, another sly detail in this twisted tale of domestic bliss.

MONSTERS
ON FOUR WHEELS

▲ Duel [Steven Spielberg, 1971] Dennis Weaver is menaced by a mysterious driver in an enormous truck in this intense and suspenseful television movie, directed by a young Steven Spielberg from an original teleplay by the great Richard Matheson.

In the year 2000 hit and run driving is no longer a crime. It's the NATIONAL SPORT!

DAVID CARRADINE

DEATH RACE 2000

DAVID CARRADINE ...DEATH RACE 2000... SIMONE GRIFFETH. SYLVESTER STALLONE
ROBERT THOM ... CHARLES B. GRIFFITH. IB MELCHIOR. ROGER CORMAN. PAUL BARTEL. focus film distributors

▲ Death Race 2000 [Paul Bartel, 1975] Roger Corman produced this vision of the future where vehicular manslaughter is the country's most popular entertainment. Silly and fun, courtesy of Paul Bartel.

▲ The Car [Elliot Silverstein, 1977] The poster read, "Is it a phantom, a demon, or the Devil Himself?". Actually, it's a big black car that forces people off of the road.

▲ King Kong Escapes [Ishirô Honda, 1967]
An evil scientist named Dr. Who builds a King Kong robot he names Mechani-Kong. Meanwhile, the real King Kong is on Mondo Island. I'm not making this up!

▲ Maximum Overdrive
[Stephen King, 1986] Emilio Estevez runs for his life from an angry truck. King's sole directing credit, which is probably a good thing.

▲ Christine [John Carpenter, 1983]
Another evil car movie, this one based on a Stephen King book. A witty opening sequence follows the manufacturing of the shiny red 1958 Plymouth Fury on its Detroit assembly line, as the song "Bad To The Bone" by George Thorogood & The Destroyers blares on the soundtrack.

▲ Logan's Run [Michael Anderson, 1976] Based on the novel by William F. Nolan and George Clayton Johnson, another movie where the future looks like a shopping mall. Jenny Agutter and Michael York listen to Box, a robot with the voice of Roscoe Lee Browne.

▶ The Cars That Ate Paris
[Peter Weir, 1974] Weir's first film is about Paris, a small town in Australia, whose inhabitants make money from traffic accidents.

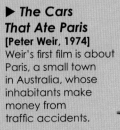

◀ *Demon Seed*
[Donald Cammell, 1977]
Based on a novel by
Dean Koontz, a computer
with artificial intelligence
named Proteus asks its
inventor: "When will
you let me out of this
box?". Proteus eventually
rapes Julie Christie who
gives birth to the silliest-
looking human/machine
hybrid in the movies.

▲ *Aliens* [James Cameron, 1986] Lance Henriksen as Bishop, an android who, despite being torn in half, heroically survives to help Sigourney Weaver defeat the Alien Queen.

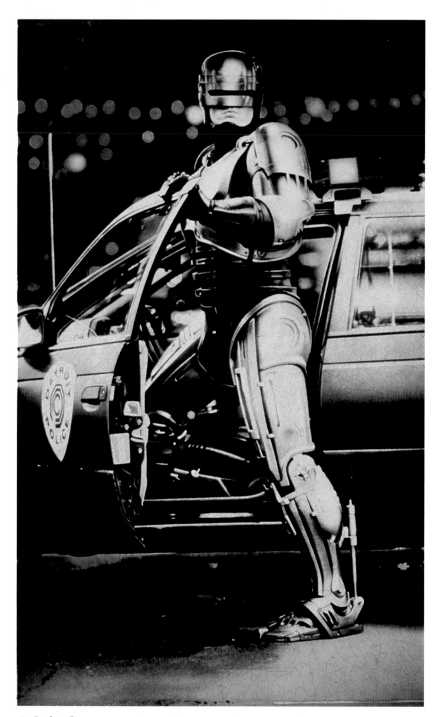

▲ *The Creation of the Humanoids* [Wesley E. Barry, 1962]
I saw this in a theater when I was eleven years old and loved it.
It is not as good if you are older than eleven. Forrest J Ackerman
has a cameo in a robot factory.

▲ *RoboCop* [Paul Verhoeven, 1987] Peter Weller as RoboCop in Paul Verhoeven's violent and action-packed satire. Verhoeven paces the film like a live-action comic book. A smart and very entertaining movie. RoboCop suit by Rob Bottin.

▲ *Blade Runner* [Ridley Scott, 1982] Rutger Hauer as a Replicant in the film based on the science-fiction novel *Do Androids Dream of Electric Sheep?* by Philip K. Dick.

▲ **The Iron Giant** [Brad Bird, 1999] An excellent animated movie based on the book *The Iron Man* by Ted Hughes. Brad Bird went on to direct wonderful movies for Pixar like *The Incredibles* [2004] and *Ratatouille* [2007].

◀ **Terminator 2: Judgment Day** [aka *T2*, James Cameron, 1991] Robert Patrick's incredible T-1000 model Terminator in mid-morph. Cameron raised the bar on special effects with this exciting movie.

▲ **Austin Powers: International Man of Mystery** [Jay Roach, 1997] "Oh, behave!"—Mike Myers as secret agent Austin Powers poses with Dr. Evil's seductive but deadly Fembots.

▶ **Surrogates** [Jonathan Mostow, 2009] A boring Bruce Willis vehicle, but I think this ad art is cool.

▲ **A.I. Artificial Intelligence** [Steven Spielberg, 2001] Haley Joel Osment and Jude Law star as androids in a film developed by Stanley Kubrick and with a screenplay credited to Steven Spielberg.

HUMAN
MONSTERS

HUMAN MONSTERS

The movies are populated with serial killers, psychopaths, sadists, perverts, men, women, and children who are a long way from what anyone could call "normal."

The most obvious human monsters are characters that are physically malformed, either by birth or accident. After the huge box office numbers of Universal's *Frankenstein* and *Dracula* [both 1931], MGM wanted a horror film of their own. But when they released Tod Browning's *Freaks* in 1932, critics and the public were so repulsed that the studio quickly withdrew it from theaters and sold it off to a grindhouse distributor. *Freaks* is a powerful, disturbing film, in which real sideshow freaks play themselves in a tragic love story. Although mostly presented in a sympathetic light, Browning betrays his sideshow stars by exploiting their handicaps in the grisly revenge sequence in the final reel. A more uplifting story is *The Elephant Man* [David Lynch, 1980], the true story of Joseph Merrick, a cruelly deformed man in 19th-century London and the kindly surgeon who befriends and protects him.

Lon Chaney, Sr. "The Man of a Thousand Faces," often portrayed physically grotesque characters in still-unmatched make-ups of his own design and execution. Chaney's touching portrayal of Quasimodo, the tragic *Hunchback of Notre Dame* [Wallace Worsley, 1923] clearly conveys the passion and sensitivity hidden inside of Quasimodo's ugly and misshapen exterior.

▲ *The Phantom of the Opera* [Rupert Julian, 1925] In this hand-tinted sequence, Lon Chaney as Erik the Phantom attends the Paris Opera's Gala Costume Ball dressed as Death.

Charles Laughton also gives an extraordinary performance as the Hunchback in William Dieterle's excellent 1939 remake.

Lon Chaney's most celebrated role is that of Erik, *The Phantom of the Opera* [Rupert Julian, 1925]. The Phantom, who wears a mask to cover his gruesome face, terrorizes the Paris Opera House from his hideout in the sewers. Chaney's unmasking by Mary Philbin remains one of the great moments of the horror film. Universal remade *The Phantom of the Opera* in 1943 [Arthur Lubin] with Claude Rains as the disfigured composer; and Hammer Films produced their own version [Terence Fisher, 1962] in which Herbert Lom was the Phantom. The lavish film adaptation of Andrew Lloyd Webber's *Phantom of the Opera* [Joel Schumacher, 2004] is best avoided, but Brian De Palma's rock'n'roll parody *The Phantom of the Paradise* [1974] is a lot of fun.

The Mystery of the Wax Museum [Michael Curtiz, 1933] shot in early two-color Technicolor, is the story of Ivan Igor (Lionel Atwill) a sculptor who makes life-like figures for a wax museum in London. When the museum's profits diminish, his partner burns it down for the insurance money. Trying to save his beloved wax figures from the flames, Ivan Igor is knocked out and left to die in the inferno. A dozen years later, Igor, now in a wheelchair, opens a new Wax Museum in New York. The beautiful wax exhibits are actually real people that the now-insane sculptor has murdered and dipped in wax! Half wisecracking newspaper story and half horror film, *Mystery of the Wax Museum* has another ghastly unmasking scene when Fay Wray hits Atwill's face and his wax mask cracks and breaks, revealing his hideously scarred countenance. The movie was remade by André de Toth in 1953 as *House of*

Wax, starring Vincent Price, in full Technicolor, and in 3D. Disfigured characters seeking revenge is a plot used over and over again in movies, from the silent version of Victor Hugo's *The Man Who Laughs* [Paul Leni, 1928], to Sam Raimi's delirious *Darkman* [1990].

Cannibalism is frowned upon in polite society, but it is the focal point of a lot of movies. The fictional, penny-dreadful character of the murderous barber Sweeney Todd, whose victims became ingredients in Mrs. Lovett's meat pies, was portrayed by the marvelous Tod Slaughter in *Sweeney Todd: The Demon Barber of Fleet Street* [George King, 1936], and again by Johnny Depp in Tim Burton's *Sweeney Todd* [2007]. *The Texas Chainsaw Massacre* [Tobe Hooper, 1974], the story of a group of friends who stumble across a deranged family of cannibals in the Texas badlands, is a truly nightmarish movie. It introduced us to one of modern cinema's most iconic human monsters in Leatherface (Gunnar Hansen), who wears a crude mask of somebody else's skin, a bloodstained leather butcher's apron, and carries a very loud chainsaw.

The graphic and gory Italian movie *Cannibal Holocaust* [Ruggero Deodato, 1980] is a *faux* documentary about a lost American expedition to the Amazon. The movie then shows us the "found footage" left by the missing film crew. This extremely unpleasant picture is one of the first "first-person camera" narrative movies.

The movies' most popular cannibal is brilliant serial killer Dr. Hannibal Lecter, from the crime novels of Thomas Harris. The first film to feature this repellent but fascinating character was Michael Mann's *Manhunter* [1986], where he was played by Brian Cox. Lecter next appeared in *The Silence of the Lambs* [Jonathan Demme, 1991], the only horror movie to win five Academy Awards, including Best Actor for

▲ *Monty Python's the Meaning of Life* **[Terry Jones, 1983]** Terry Jones as Mr. Creosote—"A wafer-thin mint?"

Anthony Hopkins' performance as Hannibal.

A person's lack of sanity is not necessarily obvious at first meeting. *The Old Dark House* [James Whale, 1932] opens on a dark and stormy night, in which stranded travelers take shelter in the old dark house of the title. This is the home of the eccentric Femm family and their brutish, alcoholic butler, Morgan (Boris Karloff). Rather than tell you the plot, I strongly suggest you watch this deliciously camp black comedy from James Whale. But be careful of Saul, and do not let Morgan anywhere near liquor!

James Cagney plays a gangster who not only has mother issues, but was genuinely psychotic in *White Heat* [Raoul Walsh, 1949], and Richard Widmark is unforgettable as Tommy Udo, the giggling killer who pushes an old lady in a wheelchair down the stairs in *Kiss of Death* [Henry Hathaway, 1947]. But nothing prepared the public for two films from 1960 that brought a new level of terror to the movies. *Psycho* [Alfred Hitchcock, 1960] and *Peeping Tom* [Michael Powell, 1960] are two films from master filmmakers; the first, an international sensation, the other ended the director's career. *Peeping Tom* is about a killer who murders women with a camera tripod that has a knife mounted on the end so that he can film his victims' last moments of fear and death. *Psycho* begins as the story of Marion Crane (Janet Leigh) and an illicit love affair, but becomes the story of Norman Bates (Anthony Perkins) an insane, murdering transvestite who, at the end of the film, has literally become his own mother! One shot in lurid color, the other in black and white, both movies are unsettling classics.

From Jack the Ripper to Charles Manson, Timothy McVeigh to that suspicious-looking guy sitting next to you, there are more than enough human monsters around to inspire filmmakers for generations to come.

The Phillips Film Co. Ltd. presents

"THE CABINET OF Dr CALIGARI"

THE MOST AMAZING STORY EVER SCREENED.

▲▶ Freaks [Tod Browning, 1932] Cleopatra (Olga Baclanova), the beautiful trapeze artist, flirts with Hercules the strongman (Henry Victor), humiliating her husband Hans, a midget (Harry Earles). Right: the performers in the circus sideshow gather round to see the Bearded Woman's (Olga Roderick) new baby. *Freaks* remains a powerful, and heartbreaking film.

▲ Arsenic and Old Lace [Frank Capra, 1944] Raymond Massey as Jonathan Brewster and Peter Lorre as Dr. Einstein toast the fate of Cary Grant with poisoned elderberry wine, in Capra's movie version of the hit play by Joseph Kesselring. Massey had Boris Karloff's part, as Karloff was contracted for the run of the Broadway show and could not leave New York.

◀ The Man Who Laughs [Paul Leni, 1928] Conrad Veidt as Gwynplaine, who King James II has had put in an iron maiden and permanently disfigured so that his face is always a hideous grin. An adaptation of the novel [1869] by Victor Hugo.

▲ **Shadow of a Doubt** [Alfred Hitchcock, 1943] Joseph Cotten as Uncle Charlie and Teresa Wright as his adoring niece, in this story of a smalltown girl slowly realizing that her beloved Uncle Charlie is a psychotic serial killer. Thornton Wilder was one of the screenwriters on this, Hitchcock's personal favorite of all his films.

▲ **House of Horrors** [Jean Yarbrough, 1946] Martin Kosleck is the mad sculptor who exploits Rondo Hatton as the Creeper, to do his evil work. Hatton suffered from acromegaly, a disorder of the pituitary gland. His increasing deformity gave him a strange career in movies playing heavies, and eventually a character called the Creeper in this and another film, *The Brute Man* [Jean Yarbrough, 1946].

▶ **The Black Cat** [Edgar G. Ulmer, 1934] Boris Karloff and Béla Lugosi play bitter enemies in this deeply bizarre and sadistic Ulmer film. It ends with Lugosi (the good guy) skinning Karloff alive!

QuAsImoDo

▲ **The Hunchback of Notre Dame** [Wallace Worsley, 1923] Lon Chaney as Quasimodo in an amazing make-up of his own design and execution. One of the few films that Irving Thalberg ever put his name on as a Producer (shared with boss Carl Laemmle). Patsy Ruth Miller is Esmeralda. From the novel [1831] by Victor Hugo.

▲ **The Hunchback of Notre Dame** [William Dieterle, 1939] Charles Laughton gives a magnificent performance as the hunchbacked bell ringer, conveying Quasimodo's humanity through the grotesque (and uncomfortable) make-up by Perc Westmore and George Bau. Maureen O'Hara is Esmeralda.

▼ **The Hunchback of Notre Dame** [Jean Delannoy, 1956] Anthony Quinn's Quasimodo is more like a punch-drunk fighter than monster in this French film. Gina Lollobrigida is Esmeralda.

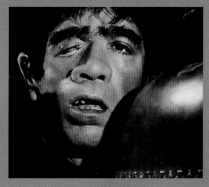

▲ **The Hunchback of Notre Dame** [Michael Tuchner, Alan Hume, 1982] Anthony Hopkins has a go at playing Quasimodo in this television movie. Lesley-Anne Down is Esmeralda.

THE PHANTOM

▲ *The Phantom of the Opera* [Terence Fisher, 1962]
Hammer had produced their own *Dracula* and *Frankenstein* and *Mummy* movies; some more rifling through Universal's vaults brought them to Gaston Leroux's *Phantom of the Opera*. Their version starred Herbert Lom as the Phantom and Heather Sears as Christine.

▲▶▼ *The Phantom of the Opera* [Rupert Julian, 1925] Lon Chaney's most famous role as Erik, the Phantom in this first movie adaptation of the novel [1910] by Gaston Leroux. Above: poster art showing how the Phantom holds the Paris Opera House in his thrall. Right and below: Erik reveals his true face to a terrified Christine (Mary Philbin).

▶ *The Phantom of the Paradise* [Brian De Palma, 1974] De Palma's satirical, rock'n'roll *Phantom* starred Paul Williams as Swan, a Mephistophelian figure to William Finley's Phantom.

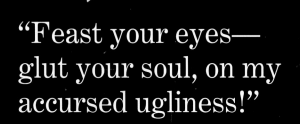

"Feast your eyes—glut your soul, on my accursed ugliness!"

Erik the Phantom (Lon Chaney), *The Phantom of the Opera* [1925]

▲ *The Phantom of the Opera* [Arthur Lubin, 1943]
Claude Rains as "Erique" instead of Erik (why character names are so often changed I do not know) and this time he is a violinist, not a composer. Universal's Technicolor remake of their own picture has more of Nelson Eddy singing than any real horror. But this film has the most spectacular falling chandelier sequence of all the *Phantom of the Opera* pictures. Susanna Foster is Christine.

▲ *The Phantom of the Opera* [Joel Schumacher, 2004] The film version of Andrew Lloyd Webber's musical. Gerard Butler is the Phantom and Emmy Rossum is Christine.

▲ **Horrors of the Black Museum** [Arthur Crabtree, 1959] Michael Gough is an author with his own private museum of torture devices. He hypnotizes his assistant to commit an escalating series of horrible crimes so that he can have something to write about!

▲ **Kiss of Death** [Henry Hathaway, 1947] A *film noir* that introduced Richard Widmark as psychotic killer Tommy Udo. Widmark plays Udo full tilt, complete with insane giggle as he ties an old lady to her wheelchair and then pushes her down the stairs.

▶▼ **The Mystery of the Wax Museum** [Michael Curtiz, 1933] Crazed sculptor Lionel Atwill has Fay Wray in his clutches. In a desperate attempt to escape, she beats on his face which cracks and breaks! His wax mask falls to reveal his disfigured face.

◀◀▲ **House of Wax** [André De Toth, 1953] Warner Brothers' 3D Technicolor remake of their own *Mystery of the Wax Museum* [1933]. Left: Vincent Price as Professor Henry Jarrod, watches in terror as his wax figures burn. Above: Jarrod's burned face is revealed after Phyllis Kirk (whom he intended to dip into bubbling, molten wax) has broken his wax mask.

▶ **White Heat** [Raoul Walsh, 1949] James Cagney as psychopathic, mother-fixated gangster Cody Jarrett. Edmond O'Brien's undercover cop corners Cody atop a gas storage tank; Cody shouts, "Made it Ma, top of the world!" and fires his gun into the tank, which explodes in a gigantic fireball.

▲ *House of Usher* [Roger Corman, 1960] Richard Matheson wrote the script based on the Edgar Allan Poe story, one of the Poe series of pictures from Corman. Here is Vincent Price as Roderick Usher being strangled by his now-insane wife, whom he knowingly buried alive.

▲ *Homicidal* [William Castle, 1961] A man who is a woman who is a man who might be a woman! William Castle was all about the marketing; in this case, he offered everyone who bought a ticket to *Homicidal* a one-thousand-dollar life insurance policy from Lloyd's of London!

"The more adventurous among you may remember our previous excursions into the macabre—our visits to haunted hills —to tinglers and to ghosts. This time we have even a stranger tale to unfold... The story of a lovable group of people who just happen to be homicidal."

William Castle in the trailer for *Homicidal*

▲ *The Pit and the Pendulum* [Roger Corman, 1961] Another Matheson script from a Poe story. Here, Vincent Price has John Kerr strapped to his pendulum torture machine. I saw this in the cinema when I was 10 years old and the ending when the chamber is sealed forever, with Barbara Steele inside the Iron Maiden still alive, scared the shit out of me.

▼ *Repulsion* [Roman Polanski, 1965] Catherine Deneuve plays Carole, a Belgian manicurist living with her sister in London who is slowly losing her mind. When her sister and her boyfriend go on holiday, Carole stays inside the flat with her paranoid sexual fantasies and we experience her madness with her. A very unsettling movie with some big jump scares as hands reach out from the walls to grab her. And that rabbit in the kitchen grows progressively more decayed...

Bluebeard

▲ **Witchfinder General** [Michael Reeves, 1968] Vincent Price as Matthew Hopkins, a witchfinder during the English Civil War. Hopkins and his assistant travel from village to village torturing confessions out of women they accuse of being witches. Price is convincing as a sadistic "soldier for God."

▲ **Death Line** [aka *Raw Meat*, Gary Sherman, 1972] Donald Pleasence is outstanding as a working-class detective investigating murders on the London Underground. His clash with Christopher Lee's upper-class MI5 agent is a delight. Pictured is Hugh Armstrong as the survivor of a cave-in who lives with his dying family in the tunnels. Armstrong gives a poignant, almost mute performance. His only words: "Mind the doors."

▶ **Bluebeard** [Edgar G. Ulmer, 1944] John Carradine as Gaston Morrell, a man who murders his wives. Based on *La Barbe bleue*, a French folktale by Charles Perrault, this serial killer is a popular villain for theater and film. The role fits Carradine like a glove.

▲ **Bluebeard's Ten Honeymoons** [W. Lee Wilder, 1960] A droll George Sanders plays Henri Landru in this serial-killer comedy. Although they use the more famous name of Bluebeard in the title, Henri Landru was a real French serial killer convicted of 11 counts of murder and guillotined in 1922. Landru was the inspiration for Charlie Chaplin's *Monsieur Verdoux* [1947].

▲ **Barbe-Bleue** [aka *Bluebeard*, Georges Méliès, 1901] Méliès version of the grisly tale. Here Bluebeard's wife discovers what he has done with his former wives!

▲ **Bluebeard** [Catherine Breillat, 2009] A new ending for this feminist retelling of Perrault's story. Lola Créton as Marie-Catherine with the head of Bluebeard (Dominique Thomas) on a platter.

▲ **Bluebeard** [Edward Dmytryk, 1972] Richard Burton is Bluebeard with a string of beautiful wives to kill, including Raquel Welch, Virna Lisi, Joey Heatherton, Nathalie Delon, and Sybil Danning.

287

▶ *Don't Look Now*
[Nicolas Roeg, 1973]
Adelina Poerio as the dwarf who murders Donald Sutherland at the end of the film. Gorgeously shot in a wintry Venice, this is a creepy and wonderful movie about second sight and perhaps fate. Roeg's masterwork. (Sorry for revealing the ending.)

▲ *Theater of Blood* [Douglas Hickox, 1973] Vincent Price as actor Edward Lionheart, here as Shylock about to take his pound of flesh from critic Harry Andrews, in a scene from *The Merchant of Venice*. In this superb black comedy, an actor, believed dead, takes bloody revenge on the critics who trashed his season of Shakespeare by murdering them in some of the bloodiest scenes from the Bard's plays. The incredible supporting cast includes Diana Rigg, Michael Hordern, Arthur Lowe, Robert Morley, Milo O'Shea, Dennis Price, Jack Hawkins, Ian Hendry, and Diana Dors!

◀ *Eaten Alive* [aka *Death Trap, Horror Hotel Massacre*, Tobe Hooper, 1977] Neville Brand, insane and armed with a scythe in Tobe's death-in-the-bayou movie. Brand feeds people to a huge alligator in the swamp out back. The 'gator eventually eats Neville, too. Texas serial killer Joe Ball, who allegedly fed 20 of his victims to alligators to dispose of the evidence, supposedly inspired this movie.

▲ *Marathon Man* [John Schlesinger, 1976] "Is it safe?"—Laurence Olivier as the Nazi dentist torturing Dustin Hoffman, in Schlesinger's great thriller, with a screenplay by William Goldman, based on his book.

▲ Eraserhead [David Lynch, 1977] Lynch's film is one of a kind. A surreal nightmare, this image is from Henry Spencer's (Jack Nance) dream, when his head falls off and the hideous baby's head comes out from his collar. Brilliant and still unique.

▲ The Elephant Man [David Lynch, 1980] John Hurt as John Merrick (whose real name was actually Joseph Merrick), in a lovely film that plays fast and loose with the true story. With Anthony Hopkins as the doctor who becomes Merrick's friend. Make-up artist Chris Tucker created Hurt's effective make-up from casts of Merrick's body, still held by the Royal London Hospital.

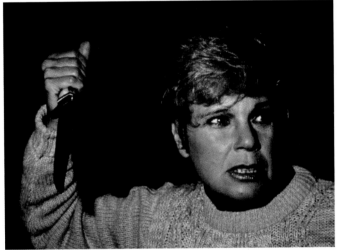

◄ Fatal Attraction [Adrian Lyne, 1987] Glenn Close as the psycho bitch from hell, trying to kill adulterous lover Michael Douglas. After a bad preview, the ending was reshot with a blatant steal from the French thriller *Les Diaboliques* [Henri-Georges Clouzot, 1955]. The ridiculous new ending allowed Douglas' wife (Anne Archer) to kill Glenn Close. A massive box-office success.

▲ Friday the 13th [Sean S. Cunningham, 1980] In the first of this endless franchise, the monster turns out not to be the dead Jason Voorhees, but his mother, Betsy Palmer! Since then the indestructible hockey-mask-wearing ghost has slashed his way through 11 movies.

"You see, Jason was my son, and today is his birthday..."

Pamela Vorhees (Betsy Palmer), *Friday the 13th*

▶ Basket Case 2 [Frank Henenlotter, 1990] A sequel that begins right at the end of Henenlotter's *Basket Case* [1982] when Duane Bradley (Kevin Van Hentenryck) and his monstrous, malformed twin Belial, fell from their hotel room window. They are taken to the hospital where even more weirdness follows. Henenlotter has also given us *Basket Case 3: The Progeny* [1991].

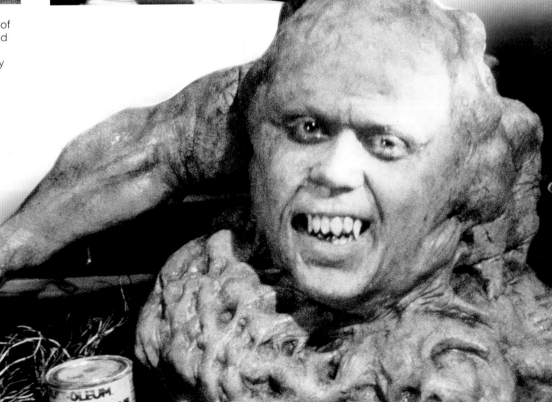

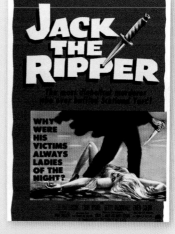

JACK THE RIPPER

▲ **The Lodger** [Alfred Hitchcock, 1926] Matinée idol Ivor Novello is Jack the Ripper in this early Hitchcock. A highlight of this silent movie is the famous glass ceiling/floor that shows us the lodger pacing upstairs.

▲ **The Lodger** [John Brahm, 1944] A remake of the British silent film [Alfred Hitchcock,1926]. Jack the Ripper (here called Mr. Slade and played by the incredible Laird Cregar) takes a room in the same house as lovely actress Merle Oberon. The sequence when detective George Sanders and his men trap Slade in the theater is memorable for Cregar's animal sounds and insane look as he is cornered.

▶ **Jack the Ripper** [Robert S. Baker, Monty Berman, 1959] A straightforward account of Britain's most infamous serial killer. Considered very brutal when it was released, its violence is rather tame for today's jaded audience.

▲ **Hands of the Ripper** [Peter Sasdy, 1971] Hammer had to get around to Jack the Ripper eventually, and when they did, they had the Ripper's daughter (Angharad Rees) go to a psychiatrist (Eric Porter) to deal with her murderous impulses.

▲ **The Ruling Class** [Peter Medak, 1972] Peter O'Toole as the 13th Earl of Gurney is completely bonkers in Medak's fabulous movie. Believing himself to be God, he is cured by The Electric Messiah (Nigel Green) and becomes Jack the Ripper! Another English film about class, this one ends with zombies in the House of Lords. Written by the great Peter Barnes, based on his own play.

▲ **Time After Time** [Nicholas Meyer, 1979] David Warner as Jack the Ripper in contemporary San Francisco, threatens Mary Steenburgen. Jack used H. G. Wells' (Malcolm McDowell) Time Machine! Wells himself goes to the future to stop the maniac.

▲ **Murder by Decree** [Bob Clark, 1979] James Mason as Dr. Watson, Frank Finlay as Inspector Lestrade, and Christopher Plummer as Sherlock Holmes in this terrific movie about the great detective in pursuit of Jack the Ripper. The royal connection comes from the book *Jack the Ripper: The Final Solution* by Stephen Knight.

▲ **From Hell** [Albert & Allen Hughes, 2001] Johnny Depp as a police inspector on the trail of Jack the Ripper in this disappointing adaptation of the graphic novel by Alan Moore and Eddie Campbell. The notion that the Ripper was a member of the Royal Family had already been explored by Bob Clark in *Murder by Decree* [1979].

▲ Misery [Rob Reiner, 1990]
Kathy Bates won the Best Actress Oscar for her role as Annie Wilkes, author Paul Sheldon's (James Caan) biggest fan. Here she is showing him some love. William Goldman wrote the script, based on the Stephen King novel.

"I thought you were good, Paul. But you're not good. You're just another lying ol' dirty birdy."

Annie Wilkes (Kathy Bates), *Misery*

▲ The Stepfather [Joseph Ruben, 1987] Terry O'Quinn in the title role is unforgettably chilling in this bloodcurdling family film. From a story by Donald E. Westlake who also contributed to the screenplay. Followed by two sequels and a remake.

▲ The Hitcher [Robert Harmon, 1986] Jennifer Jason Leigh and C. Thomas Howell pick up a hitchhiker named John Ryder (Rutger Hauer) and quickly regret it. A suspenseful thriller that teeters into horror. Rutger Hauer is terrifying as the hitcher from hell. Remade by producer Michael Bay in 2007 [Dave Meyers]. The remake was unpleasant, but it lacks the impact of the original.

▶ Naked Lunch [David Cronenberg, 1991]
Based on William Burroughs' novel, Cronenberg wrote the screenplay with Burroughs to create this semi-autobiographical, junkie's nightmare of a film. Here is Peter Weller at the bar with a friend in the Interzone.

▶ *Darkman* [Sam Raimi, 1990]
From an original story by Sam, this is his own twisted version of a comic book superhero movie. Liam Neeson plays Peyton Westlake, disfigured by the bad guys when they blow up his lab. Darkman is shown here with Frances McDormand as Julie Hastings.

▼ *Scream* [Wes Craven, 1996]
Craven's much-parodied slasher movie that was already a parody of slasher movies! This opening sequence with Drew Barrymore is still the high point of what is now another seemingly endless franchise.

▲ *Natural Born Killers* [Oliver Stone, 1994] Woody Harrelson as Mickey and Juliette Lewis as his wife Mallory go on a killing-spree. Stone throws everything and the kitchen sink into this psycho-killer movie. I did like the very weird flashback shot like a sitcom, with Rodney Dangerfield as Mallory's abusive father.

▼ *Seven* [aka *Se7en*, David Fincher, 1995] Fincher's extremely stylized thriller is anchored by great performances by Morgan Freeman's weary detective and Kevin Spacey's sensational psycho John Doe. Brad Pitt is shouting, "What's in the box?". Trust me, Brad, you don't want to know.

"What's in the box?"

Det. David Mills (Brad Pitt), *Seven*

Cannibals

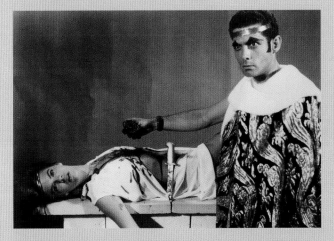

▲ **Blood Feast** [aka *Feast of Flesh*, Herschell Gordon Lewis, 1963] Produced by prolific schlockmeister David F. Friedman, this story about an Egyptian caterer who kills people to make meals and to sacrifice to the goddess Ishtar, was a low-budget grindhouse game-changer in its gleeful over the top blood and guts. Mal Arnold as Fuad Ramses redefines "bad acting."

▲ **The Hills Have Eyes** [Wes Craven, 1977] Craven's take on the "city folk versus country folk" plot, only these country folk are a clan of inbred, deformed cannibals. There were two sequels and a remake by Alexandre Aja in 2006.

▲ **The Texas Chainsaw Massacre** [Tobe Hooper, 1974] A relentless and brilliant movie about some college students who encounter a family of cannibals. Here Leatherface (Gunnar Hansen) is swinging his chainsaw in anger and frustration at the end of the movie. For such a brutal film, there is hardly any blood or violence onscreen. With an intricate and crazy-making soundtrack. Tobe then directed a comedy sequel, *The Texas Chainsaw Massacre 2* [1986], starring Dennis Hopper as Lefty, a Texas Ranger.

▲ **Cannibal Holocaust** [Ruggero Deodato, 1980]
Shot in the rainforests of the Amazon using indigenous people as the cannibals, this is about a documentary crew who are captured and eaten. Using "found footage" that shows us what happened in explicit detail, this is a pretty disgusting film. Over 30 years later it remains controversial.

▲ **Motel Hell** [Kevin Connor, 1980]
Rory Calhoun is the man wearing a pig's head and wielding a chainsaw. A motel is laden with booby traps to catch victims to grind up for sausage in this horror comedy. With Wolfman Jack as Reverend Billy.

▲ **Eating Raoul** [Paul Bartel, 1982]
Paul Bartel and Mary Woronov star as Paul and Mary Bland who solve the problem of their noisy neighbors, all "swingers," by murdering and eating them. Robert Beltran plays Raoul. Paul Bartel makes all of this charming and funny.

▶ **Manhunter** [Michael Mann, 1986] Brian Cox as Dr. Hannibal Lecter in Mann's adaptation of the Thomas Harris novel *Red Dragon* [1981]. The screen debut of "Hannibal the Cannibal."

◀ **The Silence of the Lambs,** [Jonathan Demme, 1991] Anthony Hopkins as Dr. Hannibal Lecter in this multi-Oscar winning film based on the Thomas Harris novel. The only horror film to ever win an Academy Award for Best Picture. Hopkins played Lecter twice more in uninteresting sequels.

▲ **Ravenous** [Antonia Bird, 1999] Robert Carlyle is hungry! Loosely based on the true stories of cannibal Alfred Packer and the Donner Party. A grim movie set in old California, although some of it is pretty funny.

▲ *Frailty* [Bill Paxton, 2001] Paxton directs and stars in screenwriter Brent Hanley's alarming and original tale of religious fanaticism. A father forces his two young sons to assist him in doing god's work.

◀ *The Demon Barber of Fleet Street* [aka *Sweeney Todd*, George King, 1936] Tod Slaughter relishes the role of Sweeney Todd, literally smacking his lips with glee when he slits his victims' throats and, with his specially rigged, trapdoor barber chair, dumps them into the cellar for Mrs. Lovett to bake into meat pies.

▲ *American Psycho* [Mary Harron, 2000] Christian Bale as Patrick Bateman in this excellent movie from the novel by Bret Easton Ellis. One of the rare cases of a film being superior to the book it is based on. In its depiction of yuppie consumerism literally going berserk, it manages to be both funny and hair-raising. An underrated gem. Not for the faint of heart.

"Don't cry for her son, she wasn't human."

Dad Meiks (Bill Paxton), *Frailty*

▲ *Sweeney Todd: The Demon Barber of Fleet Street* [Tim Burton, 2007] Burton's film of Stephen Sondheim's musical telling of the tale. With Johnny Depp as Sweeney Todd and Helena Bonham Carter as Mrs. Lovett.

◀ *The Dark Knight* [Christopher Nolan, 2008] Heath Ledger in an incredible performance as the Joker, raises this *Batman* movie above the others. From a screenplay by director Christopher Nolan and his brother Jonathan Nolan, based on the DC Comics characters.

▲ The Boston Strangler [Richard Fleischer, 1968]
Tony Curtis gives an unexpectedly realistic performance as real serial killer Albert DeSalvo, the Boston Strangler. Told from the point of view of the investigators tracking him down. With Henry Fonda as John S. Bottomly, the detective who caught DeSalvo and to whom DeSalvo made his confession.

▶ 10 Rillington Place
[Richard Fleischer, 1971]
Richard Attenborough as British killer John Christie. The third and last true-crime movie from director Richard Fleischer [*Compulsion*, 1959 (the Leopold-Loeb case), and *The Boston Strangler*, 1968]. From the book by Ludovic Kennedy.

TRUE CRIME

"But what can you expect from a society that itself spends 44% of its tax dollars on killing?"

Det. John S. Bottomly (Henry Fonda),
The Boston Strangler

◀ The Honeymoon Killers
[Leonard Kastle,1970] Shirley Stoler and Tony Lo Bianco as Martha Beck and Raymond Fernandez, who murdered at least 12 women in the 1940s and were known as the Lonely Hearts Killers. Believe it or not, Martin Scorsese was fired as director of this movie for working too slowly! His few completed scenes remain in this strangely fascinating film.

▼ Ed Gein [Chuck Parello, 2000]
A straightforward biopic of the notorious criminal who directly inspired *Psycho*, *The Texas Chainsaw Massacre*, and many other movies. Steve Railsback as Gein.

▲ Helter Skelter [Tom Gries, 1976]
A harrowing film of the book by Charles Manson's prosecutors Vincent Bugliosi and Curt Gentry. Steve Railsback makes Manson spookily real.

295

▲ **Ilsa, She Wolf of the SS** [Don Edmonds, 1974]
Dyanne Thorne as Ilsa, commandant of a POW camp, in his notorious "Naziploitation" sex film produced by David F. Friedman. This sordid piece of crap was shot on the prison camp sets of the television series *Hogan's Heroes!*

▲ **She Demons** [Richard E. Cunha, 1958] A Nazi mad scientist turns kidnapped beauty contest winners into monsters on a tropical island. A terrible movie starring the statuesque Irish McCalla.

Nazi Monsters

Nazi Germany (the Third Reich) was ruled by the psychotic dictatorship of Adolf Hitler and the Nazi Party from 1933 to 1945. The Nazis committed atrocities on such a large scale that the word "Nazi" is synonymous with evil. So who better to turn to when making a horror film? Here are some of the movies' most memorable Nazi monsters.

▲ **Shock Waves** [aka *Almost Human* and *Death Corps*, Ken Wiederhorn, 1977] During World War II, Nazi scientists create a troop of indestructible soldiers that are submerged in a shipwreck off an island near Florida, whose only inhabitant is ex-Nazi commander Peter Cushing.

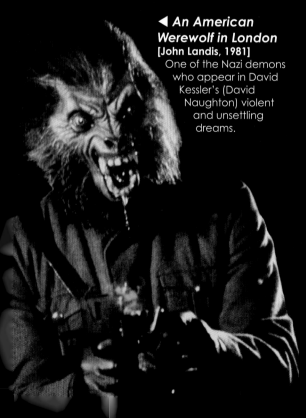

◀ **An American Werewolf in London** [John Landis, 1981]
One of the Nazi demons who appear in David Kessler's (David Naughton) violent and unsettling dreams.

▲ **The Frozen Dead** [Herbert J. Leder, 1967] Dana Andrews with a German accent is Dr. Norberg with some of the frozen Nazi officers he intends to revive. Sometimes this low-budget picture is called *Nazis on Ice!*

▲ **The Boys From Brazil** [Franklin J. Schaffner, 1978]
Gregory Peck as ex-concentration camp Dr. Josef Mengele in the movie based on Ira Levin's best-selling novel. An elderly Nazi hunter, played by Laurence Olivier, is on the trail of the Nazi mad doctor who, hidden in the Brazilian jungle, is cloning future Führer's from Hitler's DNA!

▲ **Marathon Man** [John Schlesinger, 1976] Laurence Olivier as Nazi Dr. Christian Szell, who comes out of hiding to collect stolen diamonds, gives one of the screen's greatest portrayals of pure evil. Recognized by concentration-camp survivors in Manhattan, the elderly Nazi coldly and efficiently murders one of them and then calls for help. A great movie from William Goldman's best-selling novel.

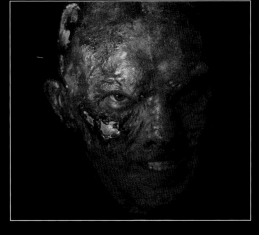

▲ **Bunker** [Rob Green, 2001] German soldiers take cover in a bunker and discover there is something else in there with them.

▲ **The Keep** [Michael Mann, 1983] During the war, German troops occupy a citadel in Romania in which a malevolent demon dwells. Based on the novel of the same name by F. Paul Wilson.

> "History has shown how one man's dream can turn the world into a nightmare. Can history repeat itself?"
>
> *The Boys From Brazil trailer narrator*

▶ **Dead Snow** [Tommy Wirkola, 2009] Seven Norwegian students rent a cabin in the mountains and discover stolen Nazi loot from the war. Nazi zombies attack them and want their treasure back.

▲ **Hellboy** [Guillermo Del Toro, 2004] Ladislav Beran as Karl Ruprecht Kroenen, a Nazi scientist and assassin born in 1897 and kept alive in his clockwork Nazi uniform.

SCARY OLDER WOMEN

The surprise success of Robert Aldrich's *What Ever Happened to Baby Jane?* [1962] unleashed a torrent of imitations. Esteemed actresses like Barbara Stanwyck, Olivia de Havilland, and Joan Fontaine rushed to join the new wave of pictures referred to as "Grande Dame Guignol" or even,"Hagsploitation." Kids all over America began to look at their grandmothers in a new light.

▲ *Straight-Jacket* [William Castle, 1964] Legendary Hollywood star Joan Crawford in a William Castle movie that shouted on its poster, "Warning! 'Straight-Jacket' vividly depicts ax murders!"

▲ *Whoever Slew Auntie Roo?* [Curtis Harrington, 1972] Shelley Winters as the crazy old lady in this companion to Harrington's *What's the Matter with Helen?* [1971]. The publicity tagline was "The hand that rocks the cradle has no flesh on it!"

▲ *What Ever Happened to Baby Jane?*
[Robert Aldrich, 1962] Bette Davis gives a fearless performance as a insane former child star Baby Jane Hudson, who lives with her crippled sister Blanche (Joan Crawford) in Hollywood. Based on the novel by Henry Farrell.

▲ *Die! Die! My Darling!* [aka *Fanatic*, Silvio Narizzano, 1965] Tallulah Bankhead is a homicidal religious maniac in this, her last film.

◀ **Arsenic and Old Lace** [Frank Capra, 1944]
Josephine Hull and Jean Adair as the two sweet little old ladies who poison "lonely men" and have their lunatic brother bury the bodies in the basement. Here, they hope that Edward Everett Horton will be another victim.

▲ **Rosemary's Baby** [Roman Polanski, 1968]
Ruth Gordon as neighbor Minnie Castevet, hands Rosemary (Mia Farrow) a drugged glass of milk. Gordon is very funny as the helpful little old lady whose intentions are satanic in nature.

▲ **Young Frankenstein** [Mel Brooks, 1974]
Cloris Leachman as Frau Blücher, whose very name frightens the horses! This wonderful actress also played the psychotic Nurse Diesel in Brook's *High Anxiety* [1977].

▲ **Sunset Boulevard** [Billy Wilder, 1950] Gloria Swanson as silent film star Norma Desmond after she's gunned down her young lover, Joe Gillis (William Holden). Shot and scored like the horror film it is, Wilder's cynical, dark Hollywood story is a masterpiece.

◀ **Psycho** [Alfred Hitchcock, 1960]
The real Mrs. Bates, as discovered in the basement by Lila Crane (Vera Miles)— just before Norman, wearing his mother's dress and wig, bursts in with his knife!

▲ **Rabid Grannies** [aka *Les Mémés Cannibales*, Emmanuel Kervyn, 1988] The gifts of a devil-worshipping nephew cause two grandmothers to behave very, very badly in this gory Belgian horror comedy.

BURKE & HARE

Many films have been based on the grisly true stories of grave-robbing and murder in Scotland in the 19th century. Edinburgh was the center of medical research in the 1800s, but cadavers were in short supply. Doctors were willing to "look the other way" and pay cash for dead bodies. William Burke and William Hare, two Irish laborers, began a lucrative career murdering and selling victims to the distinguished Doctor Knox of the Royal College of Surgeons. When exposed for their crimes, only Burke was hanged. His skeleton is on display at the University of Edinburgh Anatomy School Museum.

◄ **The Body Snatcher**
[Robert Wise, 1945]
Great performances from a sinister Boris Karloff and an elegant Henry Daniell, combined with wonderful direction from Robert Wise, to make this a chilling treat. Look for Béla Lugosi as a victim of "Burking." Based on the short story by Robert Louis Stevenson.

▲ **Burke & Hare** [Vernon Sewell, 1972] An atmospheric shot from a truly awful film, which spends most of its running time in a whorehouse to showcase the topless girls. The unbearable title song should be enough to warn you away.

"Up the close and down the stair,
No one's safe from Burke and Hare.
Burke's the butcher; Hare's the thief,
And Knox the one who buys
the beef!"

Scottish Nursery Rhyme

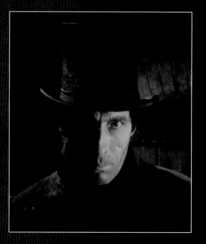

▲ **Corridors of Blood** [Robert Day, 1958] Christopher Lee as Resurrection Joe, a cool killer who is Burke & Hare combined into one character. Boris Karloff plays Dr. Bolton, a kindly version of Dr. Knox, who is unaware of the malignant source of his research subjects.

▲ **The Doctor and the Devils** [Freddie Francis, 1985] Based on a screenplay by Dylan Thomas and Thomas Harwood (poorly revised by Freddie Francis), Jonathan Pryce and Stephen Rea are Fallon & Bloom instead of Burke & Hare. Timothy Dalton plays the character based on Dr. Knox, inexplicably called Dr. Rock.

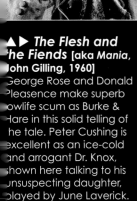

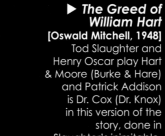

The Body Snatcher [Robert Wise, 1945]
Producer Val Lewton's RKO B Horror Picture Unit consistently turned out literate and haunting movies. Sometimes given ludicrous titles by the marketing department (eg. *I Walked With a Zombie*), Lewton always managed to create a quality product.

▲▶ The Flesh and the Fiends [aka *Mania*, John Gilling, 1960]
George Rose and Donald Pleasence make superb lowlife scum as Burke & Hare in this solid telling of the tale. Peter Cushing is excellent as an ice-cold and arrogant Dr. Knox, shown here talking to his unsuspecting daughter, played by June Laverick.

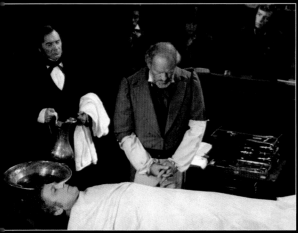

◀ Burke & Hare
[Vernon Sewell, 1972]
Harry Andrews as Dr. Knox maintains his dignity and gives a credible performance in a lousy movie.

▶ The Greed of William Hart
[Oswald Mitchell, 1948]
Tod Slaughter and Henry Oscar play Hart & Moore (Burke & Hare) and Patrick Addison is Dr. Cox (Dr. Knox) in this version of the story, done in Slaughter's inimitable, melodramatic style.

▼ Burke & Hare [John Landis, 2010] Simon Pegg and Andy Serkis as Burke & Hare attempting to rob a grave in this unorthodox romantic comedy. Also starring Isla Fisher, Tim Curry, Ronnie Corbett, Christopher Lee, Hugh Bonneville, Paul Whitehouse, Bill Bailey, and Reece Shearsmith.

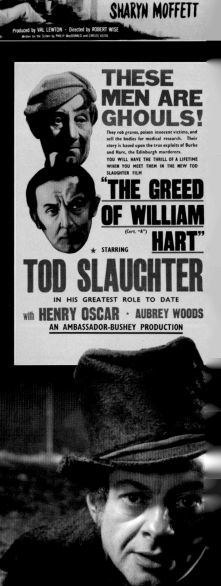

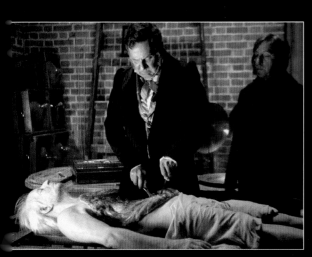

▲ Burke & Hare [John Landis, 2010]
Tom Wilkinson, as Dr. Knox, performs an autopsy on a cadaver supplied by Burke & Hare. Michael Smiley plays his loyal assistant Patterson.

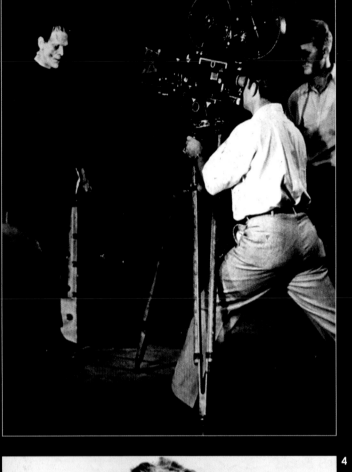

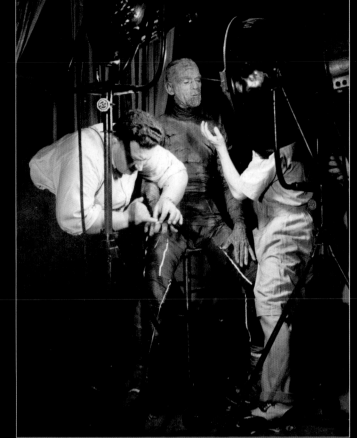

From the earliest days of the Nickelodeons, filmmakers have consistently invented new techniques to help us "suspend our disbelief."

The French filmmaking pioneer Georges Méliès was one of the first to use the camera to create visual effects. By pausing in turning the hand crank on his camera for a moment, Méliès was able to make people and objects appear and disappear as if by magic.

Linwood G. Dunn's work in the 1920s perfected the optical printer, revolutionizing optical effects. Literally a camera set up to re-photograph already exposed film, creating multiple layers of images onto a negative, the optical printer enabled the movies to present astonishing compositions on screen. One of the greatest creators of "optical effects" was John P. Fulton, whose innovative and stunning work on *The Invisible Man* [James Whale, 1933] still dazzles the eye. My favorite of Fulton's effects are the homunculi Dr. Pretorius so proudly displays (see page 69) in *The Bride of Frankenstein* [James Whale, 1935].

Building sets and vehicles to a much smaller scale allowed scenes of breathtaking destruction to be shot with minimal cost and danger. "Miniature" car crashes, airplanes, explosions, volcanoes, rocket ships, and more, have all been constructed on a stage or back lot to help visualize story elements that would have been impractical to recreate full size. Master miniature makers include the legendary Lydecker Brothers, Howard and Theodore. The Lydecker Brothers were on staff at Republic Pictures and worked on such classic serials as *Adventures of Captain Marvel* [1941], and *Commander Cody: Sky Marshal of the Universe* [aka *Radar Men From The Moon*, 1952-3]. Japanese master Eiji Tsuburaya was the resident special FX go-to guy for Toho Studios. Tsuburaya's work is seen in almost every *Godzilla* film.

▲ *Two giants of the fantasy film:* Georges Méliès and Carl Laemmle meet in Paris. Méliès is the father of special effects; Laemmle was one of the founders of Universal Pictures, the studio that produced most of the classic monster movies.

Derek Meddings started work on the Gerry and Sylvia Anderson puppet TV shows like *Fireball XL5* [1962] and *Thunderbirds* [1965-66] Derek went on to do the miniatures on *Superman* [Richard Donner, 1978] and for the James Bond pictures *The Man with the Golden Gun* [Guy Hamilton, 1974] and *The Spy Who Loved Me* [Lewis Gilbert, 1977].

Greg Jein built the iconic miniature of the Death Star for *Star Wars* [George Lucas, 1977], and the aliens' mother ship for *Close Encounters of the Third Kind* [Steven Spielberg, 1977].

Matte painters like Albert Whitlock, Harrison Ellenshaw, Peter Ellenshaw, Norman Dawn, and Matthew Yuricich created remarkable illusions for movies with a paint brush and a pane of glass (see the illustrations on page 309).

The producer and director George Lucas and his crew at Industrial Light & Magic have brought movies into the digital age. Special effects in the movies will continue to evolve, but never forget that every movie you see, has been literally handmade.

(1) Shooting a close-up of Boris Karloff as the Monster in *Frankenstein* [James Whale, 1931]. **(2) Putting finishing touches** on Boris Karloff's costume and make-up for *The Mummy* [Karl Freund, 1932]. **(3) Creature From the Black Lagoon [Jack Arnold, 1954]** Bob Dawn (white shirt), Robert Hickman (kneeling), and Jack Kevan (black suit) adjust the Gill-Man costume on Ben Chapman (Ricou Browning did the underwater swimming in Florida). Universal's head of make-up Bud Westmore got sole screen credit, but Jack Kevan did most of the work. **(4) Willis O'Brien** poses with the full-size head used for close-ups in *King Kong* [Cooper, Schoedsack, 1933].

Monster Directors

James Whale, Tod Browning, George A. Romero, William Castle, and Jack Arnold are five directors whose monster movies have had lasting impact and influence. Between them, they have brought us *Dracula*, *Frankenstein*, *Night of the Living Dead*, *The Tingler*, *Creature From the Black Lagoon*, *The Mummy*, *The Incredible Shrinking Man*, and many more classic movie monsters!

▲ **Boris Karloff** as the Monster is scrutinized by well-dressed director James Whale and cameraman John J. Mescall on the set of *The Bride of Frankenstein* [1935]. The elegant Whale never failed to inject an element of camp into all of his horror films.

▲ **Tod Browning** on set with Olga Baclanova, who played the beautiful, cruel trapeze artist in *Freaks* [1932]. Baclanova is in costume and make-up as the pathetic sideshow freak her character becomes in the film's gruesome climax.

◀ **George A. Romero** points to where some new zombie atrocity will take place on the set of *Land of the Dead* [2005]. Romero has single-handedly made the zombie *the* monster of the 21st Century.

▶ **William Castle** in a gag photo at the sound stage door of one of his many thrillers. Castle often used carny-style gimmicks to sell his movies to the public.

▲ **Jack Arnold** (white jacket) with actor Grant Williams on the set of *The Incredible Shrinking Man* [1957]. Both director and star are dwarfed by the giant set and props used to create the illusion of the lead character's tiny size.

A group of Ray Harryhausen's most illustrious fans gathered together to honor him on his 90th birthday at the British Film Institute's South Bank Theater on June 30th, 2010. Left to right:

Randall (Randy) Cook, gifted stop-motion animator who early on understood the potential of computer-generated effects. Cook won three Academy Awards as the Visual Effects Supervisor on Peter Jackson's *Lord of the Rings* trilogy [2001-2003].

Dennis Muren, the Senior Visual Effects Supervisor at Industrial Light & Magic and winner of nine Academy Awards. His work can be seen in all of the *Star Wars* movies, *Raiders of the Lost Ark* [1981], *Jurassic Park* [1993], *Terminator 2: Judgment Day* [1991], and many others.

Peter Jackson, the acclaimed director of *Heavenly Creatures* [1994], the *Lord of the Rings* trilogy [2001-2003], *King Kong* [2005] and, in production, *The Hobbit*.

John Landis, holding a bronze statuette of Ray Harryhausen.

Rick Baker, winner of seven Academy Awards for Make-up. His first was for *An American Werewolf in London* [1981].

Phil Tippett, a gifted stop-motion animator and the winner of two Academy Awards for Visual Effects. Phil has also moved into CG animation, creating the fantastic alien monsters and spacecraft in *Starship Troopers* [1997].

Ken Ralston, winner of four Academy Awards. With Dennis Muren and Phil Tippett, Ken was one of the founding special effects artists of George Lucas' famed Industrial Light & Magic company. He is now the Senior Visual Effects Supervisor at Sony Pictures Imageworks.

Photo by Mark Mawston

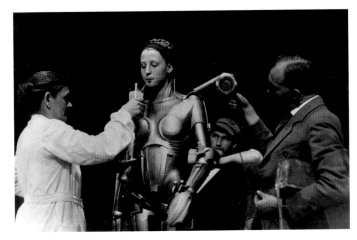

▲ **On the set of Metropolis,** [Fritz Lang, 1927], make-up and costume personnel attend to Brigitte Helm in most of her costume as the robot Maria.

▲ **Lon Chaney,** pictured with his make-up kit, checks out a set of false teeth in his mirror on the set of *A Blind Bargain* [Wallace Worsley, 1922]. Chaney was known as "The Man of a Thousand Faces" for his remarkable ability to turn himself into dozens of grotesque characters. Erik, *The Phantom of the Opera* [Rupert Julian, 1925] and Quasimodo, *The Hunchback of Notre Dame* [Wallace Worsley, 1923] are his two most famous roles.

▲ **William Tuttle** supervised the make-up on *The Wizard of Oz* [1939] eventually replacing Jack Dawn as Head of Make-up at MGM. In this photo can be seen a Morlock mask from *The Time Machine* [1960] and a head used in *The Picture of Dorian Gray* [1945], as well as life masks of MGM stars. Tuttle received an honorary Academy Award for *7 Faces of Dr. Lao* [1964].

Make-up Artists

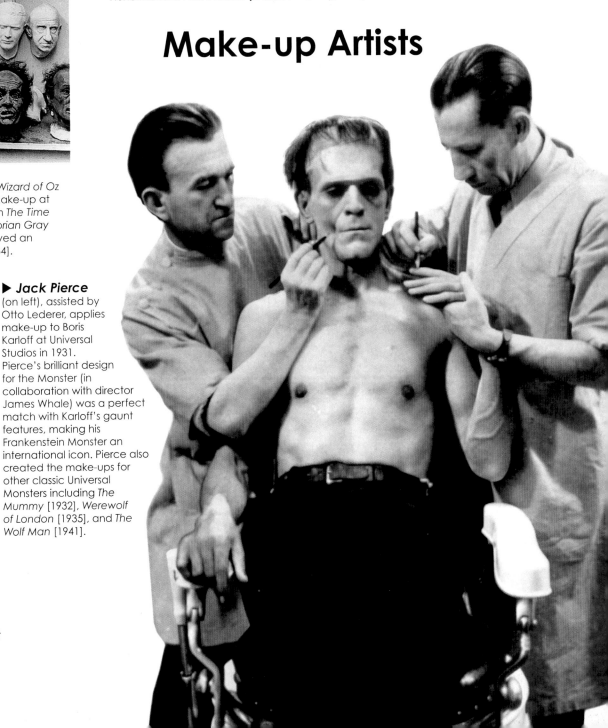

▶ **Jack Pierce** (on left), assisted by Otto Lederer, applies make-up to Boris Karloff at Universal Studios in 1931. Pierce's brilliant design for the Monster (in collaboration with director James Whale) was a perfect match with Karloff's gaunt features, making his Frankenstein Monster an international icon. Pierce also created the make-ups for other classic Universal Monsters including *The Mummy* [1932], *Werewolf of London* [1935], and *The Wolf Man* [1941].

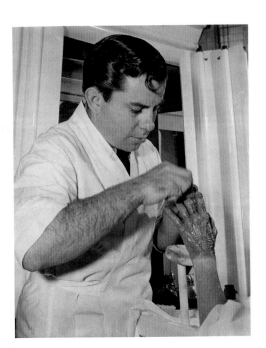

▲ **Bud Westmore,** of the Westmore dynasty of Hollywood make-up artists, was Head of Make-up at Universal and is credited on more than 450 movies and TV shows. His credits include the Lon Chaney biopic starring James Cagney, *Man of a Thousand Faces* [1957] and *The Andromeda Strain* [1971].

Monster Designers

◀ **Millicent Patrick** designing the Gill-Man for *Creature From the Black Lagoon* [Jack Arnold,1954]. Ms. Patrick was not given a screen credit for what many consider one of the greatest monster designs.

▶ **Chris Mueller** in the Universal Make-up lab, sculpting the original mask for *Creature From the Black Lagoon*.

▲ **H. R. Giger** is a Swedish artist known for his surreal and bizarre paintings. Ridley Scott hired him to design the title creature in *Alien* [1979]. Giger is pictured here with one of his friends.

Make-up Artists (continued)

▲ **Rob Bottin** (wearing scary contact lenses) poses with one of his creations for John Carpenter's *The Thing* [1982], a movie that really showcases his amazing work. Rob made the grotesque murder victim tableaus in David Fincher's *Seven* [1995], the werewolves in Joe Dante's *The Howling* [1981], and the mythical creatures in Ridley Scott's *Legend* [1985] including Tim Curry's remarkable Lord of Darkness.

▶ **Dick Smith,** pictured turning David Bowie into an ancient vampire in Tony Scott's *The Hunger* [1983], is called the godfather of special effects make-up. Dick's legendary make-ups include: *The Exorcist* [William Friedkin, 1973], *The Godfather* [Francis Ford Coppola, 1972], *Taxi Driver* [Martin Scorsese, 1976]; he received an Academy Award for *Amadeus* [Milos Forman, 1984].

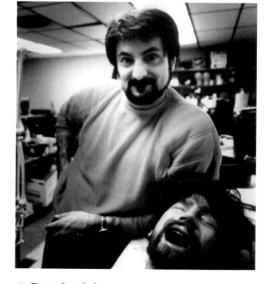

▲ **Tom Savini** is noted for his gory make-ups in *Maniac* [William Lustig, 1980] and *Friday the 13th* [Sean S. Cunningham, 1980], and his many collaborations with George A. Romero. Now active as an actor, he played Sex Machine in *From Dusk Till Dawn* [Robert Rodriguez, 1996]. Tom also runs a successful make-up academy.

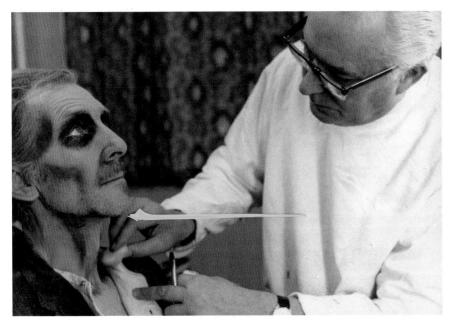

▲ **Roy Ashton** was Hammer Studios' main make-up artist, shown here making-up Peter Cushing as the living dead Arthur Grimsdyke for *Tales from the Crypt* [Freddie Francis, 1972].

▲ **Stuart Freeborn** made the apes for Stanley Kubrick's *2001: A Space Odyssey* [1968]. He is shown here working on Chewbacca's head for George Lucas' *Star Wars* [1977].

◄ **Stan Winston,** pictured with Michael Jackson in make-up for the short film *Ghosts* [Stan Winston, 1997]. Stan won three Academy Awards; one for Make-up and one for Special Effects for *Terminator 2: Judgment Day* [James Cameron, 1991], and one for Special Effects for his lifelike, full-size animatronic dinosaurs in *Jurassic Park* [Steven Spielberg, 1993].

▶ **Gregory Nicotero** is the N in famed special effects make-up company KNB. Greg often collaborates with Quentin Tarantino, Robert Rodriguez, Frank Darabont, and George A. Romero. Here's Greg working on the hit TV zombie series *The Walking Dead* [2010-].

◄ **Howard Berger** is the B in KNB. Howard won an Academy Award for his work on *The Chronicles of Narnia: The Lion, the Witch and the Wardrobe* [Andrew Adamson, 2005].

▲ **John Chambers** won an honorary Academy Award for his groundbreaking work on *Planet of the Apes* [Franklin J. Schaffner, 1968]. John's foam-rubber, prosthetic appliances allowed facial mobility and could be mass-produced to equip large numbers of actors. Chambers also did clandestine disguise work for the FBI and CIA and played the National Guard Captain in *Schlock* [1971].

▲ **Rick Baker** working on an appliance for Tim Burton's remake of *Planet of the Apes* [2001]. Rick and I first met on my first feature film *Schlock* [1971]. He was 20, I was 21. Since then, Rick has gone on to win seven Academy Awards, his first for *An American Werewolf in London* [1981], when the Academy established the category.

◀ *Ray Harryhausen* animating *Mighty Joe Young* [Ernest B. Schoedsack, 1949]. Ray's big break came when Willis O'Brien hired him as an assistant on this movie. Ray Harryhausen's tremendous body of work has had enormous influence on generations of filmmakers.

▼ *Willis O'Brien,* the pioneering stop-motion animator and innovator, whose crowning achievement is *King Kong* [Merian C. Cooper, Ernest B. Schoedsack, 1933]. O'Brien is pictured here with the triceratops the ship's crew discover on Skull Island. In his hand he holds a crew member puppet. O'Brien's film work goes back to 1915 with *The Dinosaur and the Missing Link: A Prehistoric Tragedy* for the Edison Co. His last film was Stanley Kramer's *It's a Mad, Mad, Mad, Mad World* [1963].

Stop-motion Animation

Stop-motion animation is an art that is still practiced by filmmakers like Henry Selick in *The Nightmare Before Christmas* [1993], *James and the Giant Peach* [1996], and *Coraline* [2009] and Nick Park. Park is the creator of Wallace and Gromit and has won four Academy Awards, for *Creature Comforts* [1989], *The Wrong Trousers* [1993], *A Close Shave* [1995], and *Wallace & Gromit: The Curse of the Were-Rabbit* [2005]. Pictured are three of the greatest stop-motion animators in movie history.

▲ *Randall Cook* is shown animating a demon from *Ghostbusters* [Ivan Reitman, 1984].

Matte Painting

Matte painting is now done digitally on computer, but it used to be done by hand-painting on glass. An example of traditional matte painting is shown on the right, in a scene from *The Age of Innocence* [Martin Scorsese, 1993].

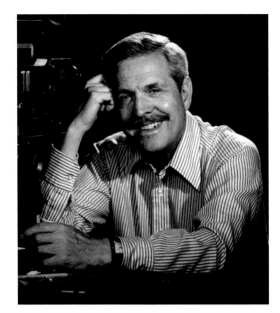

◄ ***Albert Whitlock*** won Academy Awards for his work on *Earthquake* [Mark Robson, 1974] and *The Hindenburg* [1975]. In *The Hindenburg*, his painting on glass of the huge zeppelin was so detailed that the illusion of flight was done by merely moving his glass painting past the camera! Albert's work can be seen in films as varied as *The Andromeda Strain* [Robert Wise, 1971], *Slaughterhouse Five* [George Roy Hill, 1972], *The Man Who Would Be King* [John Huston, 1975], and *The Blues Brothers* [John Landis, 1980].

▲ ***A painting on glass*** by Syd Dutton and Robert Stromberg, showing the interior of a grand train station.

▲ ***A live-action scene*** shot on a set with actor Daniel Day-Lewis.

► ***Bill Taylor and Syd Dutton*** An exceptional special-effects cameraman and a superb matte artist respectively, Bill Taylor (on left) and Syd Dutton worked with Albert Whitlock for many years. They formed Illusion Arts when Whitlock retired. They are pictured with in-house producer Catherine Sudolcan.

▲ ***The finished shot*** with the live-action seamlessly inserted into the painting on an optical printer.

Miniatures

◄ ***The War of the Worlds*** [Byron Haskin, 1953] Special-effects technicians on the miniature set on stage at Paramount Studios prepare the Martian war machines for another attack.

► ***The Land Unknown*** [Virgil W. Vogel, 1957] Technicians prepare a shot of a dinosaur in the water tank on stage. Notice the painted backdrop and prop trees made to scale to give the illusion of depth. In the finished film, this dinosaur is gigantic and dwarfs the superimposed actors.

PICTURE CREDITS

Unless otherwise stated, all the images in this book are from the archives of **The Kobal Collection** which owes its existence to the vision, courage, talent, and energy of the men and women who created the movie industry and whose legacies live on through the films they made, the studios they built, and the publicity photographs they took. Kobal collects, preserves, organizes, and makes these images available to enhance our understanding and enjoyment of this cinematic art.

The publisher wishes to thank all of the photographers (known and unknown) and the film distribution and production companies whose images appear in this book. We apologize in advance for any omissions, or neglect and will be pleased to make any corrections in future editions.

All images from **The Kobal Collection** except: **The Art Archive** 23, 48B, 67; **The Art Archive/Marc Charmet** 49; **The Art Archive/Kharbine-Tapador/S.Kakou** 112; **The Art Archive/Musee Saint Denis Reims/Gianni Dagli Orti** 113; **The Art Archive/Garrick Club/Eileen Tweedy** 153; **Bill Taylor** 309tl, tr, tc, bc, cl; **Bob Burns Collection** 1, 2, 6, 50, 53bl, rc, 68, 71tl, 81bl, 87t, 104l, 127tl, 156tr, b, 174tl, c, cr, 175bl, 176rcb, 190t, bl, 191tr, 192bl, 206tl, 250b, br, 251, 269tl, 270c, 271tr, 285cr, c, 308t, br, 309br; **Corbis** 89; **Everett Collection** 98tl; **Greg Nicotero** 36br, 105b, 211tl, 257br, 261br; **Howard Berger** 257br, 307c; **John Landis** 11, 12bl, 32tr, 48tl, 55cb, 56tl, tc, tr, 57tr, 58tl, br, 74tl, 78tr, 80br, 86tc, 93, 100cl, 102c, 104, 118bl, 120bl, 140bl, 148, 149, 160c, 162cl,163tr, 167, 168, 170tl, 172r, 174br, 176rct, 177 cl, 178bl, 182, 183B, 193br, 206bl, 223bl, 250c, 255 tc, cr, br, 256t, 260bl, 292tl, 294bl, 301cr, 302tl, bl, 306tl, cl,bl, 307c,bl; Photos 12 24, 38tl, 40tr, br, 41tl, 58bl, 79tr, 87lc (x2), 97br, 99tl, 100tr, 103cr, 105 (23) 129tr, 172tl, 191br, 211br, 226tl, 231bl, 260, 283cl, 289tl, 292c, 293cl, 296cl, 307cl.

FILM COMPANY CREDITS

10 Rillington Place, Columbia 295; *1984*, Columbia 263; *20,000 Leagues Under the Sea*, Walt Disney Pictures 197; *2001: A Space Odyssey*, MGM 173, 257, 269, 272; *28 Weeks Later*, Fox Atomic/DNA Films/UK Film Council 105; *30 Days of Night*, Ghost House/Columbia/Dark Horse 25, 39; *Abbott & Costello Meet Dr. Jekyll and Mr. Hyde*, Universal 2, 79, 87; *Abbott & Costello Meet Frankenstein*, Universal 1, 53; *Abbott & Costello Meet the Mummy*, Universal 127; *Abby*, AIP 222; *Abominable Doctor Phibes, The*, AIP 78; *Abominable Snowman, The*, Hammer Films 178; *Age of Innocence, The*, Columbia 309; *AI: Artificial Intelligence*, Amblin/Dreamworks/WB 275; *Alias Nick Beal*, Paramount 230; *Alice In Wonderland* (1933) Paramount 138; *Alice In Wonderland* (2010), Walt Disney Pictures163; *Alien*, 20th Century-Fox 255, 306; *Aliens*, 20th Century-Fox 255, 274; *Alligator People, The*, 20th Century-Fox 192; *Alraune*, Styria-Carlton 172; *Altered States*,Warner Bros 80; *Amazing Colossal Man, The*, AIP 207; *Amazon Women on the Moon*, Universal 160; *American Psycho*, Lions Gate 294; *American Werewolf in London, An*, Polygram/Universal 48, 56, 100, 183, 296; *Amityville Horror, The*, AIP 119; *Anaconda*, Columbia 198; *Andromeda Strain, The*, Universal 257; *Angel Heart*, Union-Carolco Int/Tri Star 231; *Angry Red Planet, The*, Sino 252; *Ape Man, The*, Monogram 171; *Arachnid*, Fantastic Factory/TVC 193; *Army of Darkness*, Dino De Laurentiis 102; *Arsenic and Old Lace*, Warner Bros 282, 299; *Asylum*, Amicus 236; *At the Circus*, MGM 174; *Atom Age Vampire*, Leone 29, 75, 209; *Atragon*, AIP/Toho 159; *Attack of the Crab Monsters*, Allied Artists 205; *Attack of the Fifty-Foot Woman*, Allied Artists 19; *Attack of the Giant Leeches*, AIP 192; *Attack of the Puppet People*, Alta Vista 72; *Austin Powers, International Man of Mystery*, New Line 275; *Avatar*, 20th Century-Fox 163, 261; *Bad Seed, The*, Warner Bros 238; *Barbarella*, Paramount 253; *Barbe-Bleue*, Méliès 287; *Basket Case 2*, Shapiro-Glickenhaus 289; *Bat People, The*, AIP 191; *Battle for the Planet of the Apes*, 20th Century-Fox 177; *Beach Girls and the Monster, The*, American Academy Prod 105, 190; *Beast From 20,000 Fathoms, The*, Warner Bros 152; *Beast of Hollow Mountain*, United Artists 157; *Beauty and the Beast*, Walt Disney Pictures 138; *Bedazzled*, 20th Century-Fox 220, 230; *Bees, The*, New World Pictures 195; *Beetlejuice*, Geffen/Warner Bros, 118; *Behemoth, the Sea Monster*, Artistes Alliance/Diamond Pictures 161; *Bell, Book and Candle*, Columbia 234; *Belle et la Bête, La*, Films Andre Paulve 132-3, 138; *Beneath the Planet of the Apes*, 20th Century-Fox/Apjac 177; *Beowulf*, Paramount/Shangri-La 147; *Bigfoot and the Hendersons*, Amblin/Universal 179; *Bill and Ted's Bogus Journey*, Nelson Entertainment/Orion 227, 233; *Birds, The*, Universal 192; *Black Cat, The*, Universal 283; *Black Sabbath*, AIP 31; *Black Sunday*, Galatea/Jolly 219; *Blade II*, New Line 37; *Blade Runner*, Ladd Company/Warner Bros 263, 274; *Blair Witch Project, The*, Artisan Pics 229; *Blind Bargain, A*, Goldwyn 305; *Blob, The* (1958), Allied Pictures 247; *Blob, The* (1988), Tri-Star 247; *Blonde Venus*, Paramount 169; *Blood and Roses*, Film Ege/Documento 29; *Blood Feast*, Friedman-Lewis 293; *Blood for Dracula* 41; *Blood From the Mummy's Tomb*, Hammer 128; *Blood of Dracula*, AIP 29; *Blood of the Vampire*, Artistes Alliance 73; *Blood on Satan's Claw*, Tigon/Chilton Films 221; *Blood: The Last Vampire*, Edko Film 38; *Blue Beard* (2009), Flach Film 287; *Bluebeard* (1944), Pathé 287; *Bluebeard* (1972), Barnabe/Gloria/Vulcano 287; *Bluebeard's Ten Honeymoons*, Anglo-Allied 287; *Body Snatcher, The*, RKO 300, 301; *Boston Strangler, The*, 20th Century-Fox 295; *Bowery Boys Meet the Monsters, The*, Allied Artists 172; *Boy Who Cried Werewolf, The*, Universal 57; *Boys From Brazil, The*, 20th Century-Fox 296; *Brain That Wouldn't Die, The*, AIP 73, 105; *Braindead/Dead Alive*, Wingnut Films 102; *Bram Stoker's Dracula*, Zoetrope/Columbia Tri-Star 31, 37, 41, 57; *Brazil*, Universal/Embassy 263; *Bride of Frankenstein*, Universal 69, 304; *Bride of the Gorilla*, Jack Broder Prods 175; *Brides of Blood*, Hemisphere 209; *Brides of Dracula*, Hammer/Universal 31; *Bridge to Terabithia*, Walt Disney Pictures/Walden Media 142; *Brothers Grimm, The*, Dimension/Miramax 141; *Bubba Ho-Tep*,Silver Sphere Corp. 128; *Buffy the Vampire Slayer*, 20th Century-Fox 36 ; *Bunker: Die Letzten Tage*, Twenty-Twenty Vision 297; *Burke & Hare* (1971), United Artists 300, 301; *Burke & Hare* (2010), Ealing Studios/Fragile Films 301; *C.H.U.D*, New World Pictures 211; *Cabinet of Dr. Caligari, The*, Decla-Bioscop 281; *Cannibal Holocaust*, FD Cinematografica 293; *Canterville Ghost, The*, MGM 117; *Captive Wild Woman*, Universal 171; *Car, The*, Universal 273; *Carrie*, United Artists 223; *Carry On Screaming*, Peter Rogers Prods 76; *Cars That Ate Paris, The*, Saltpaan/AFDC/Royce Smeal 273; *Cat People* (1942), RKO 51, 55; *Cat People* (1982), Universal 55; *Cat Women of the Moon*, Astor Prod. 253; *Cemetery Man*, Audio Film/Canal+, 102, 227; *Changeling, The*, Chessman Park/Tiberius 120; *Children of the Corn*, New World/Angeles/Cinema Group 239; *Child's Play*, United Artists 237; *Christine*, Columbia 273; *Christmas Carol, A*, MGM 117; *Chronicles of Narnia, The: The Lion, the Witch and the Wardrobe*, Walt Disney Pictures/Walden Media 140, 145, 146, 307; *Chronicles of Narnia, The: Prince Caspian*, Walt Disney Pictures/Walden Media 58; *Cinderella*, Méliès, 135; *Clash of the Titans* (1980), MGM 139, 144, 235; *Clash of the Titans* (2010), Warner Bros 139, 144; *Class of Nuke 'Em High*, Troma 210; *Clockwork Orange, A*, Warner Bros 262; *Cloverfield*, Paramount 260; *Colossus of New York, The*, Paramount 272; *Company of Wolves, The*, Palace/NFFC/ITC(ITV Global) 55; *Conan the Barbarian*, De Laurentiis 225; *Conan the Destroyer*, Universal 225; *Constantine*, Warner Bros 233; *Corridors of Blood*, MGM 300; *Count Dracula*, BBC Worldwide 40; *Count Yorga*, Vampire, AIP 40; *Countess Dracula*, Hammer 32; *Creation of the Humanoids, The*, Genie Prods 274; *Creature From the Black Lagoon*, Universal 104, 186, 190, 302, 306; *Creature With the Atom Brain*, Clover Prods 206; *Creeping Flesh, The*, Tigon 79; *Cronos*, Iguana/Ventana/Imcine 36; *Cujo*, Taft Entertainment 199; *Curse Of Frankenstein*, Hammer 69, 85; *Curse of the Crimson Altar*, Tigon/AIP 220; *Curse of the Faceless Man*, UA/Vogue Pictures 104, 126; *Curse of the Mummy's Tomb, The*, Hammer 127; *Curse of the Undead*, Universal 104; *Curse of the Werewolf, The*, Hammer 54; *Damn Yankees*, Warner Bros 230; *Dante's Inferno* (1924), Fox 232; *Dante's Inferno* (1935) Fox, 232; *Darby O'Gill and the Little People*, Walt Disney Pictures 145; *Dark City*, New Line 260; *Dark Knight, The*, Warner Bros/DC Comics 294; *Darkman*, Universal 292; *Dawn of the Dead* (1978), United Film 90-1; *Dawn of the Dead* (2004), Strike Entertainment/New Amsterdam 103; *Day of the Animals*, Warner Bros 194; *Day of the Dead*, Laurel Entertainment 100, 306; *Day of the Triffids, The*, Allied Artists 253; *Day the Earth Stood Still, The*, 20th Century-Fox 266; *Day the World Ended, The*, Golden State 205; *Daybreakers*, Pictures In Paradise 38; *Dead of Night*, Ealing Studios 236; *Dead One, The / Blood of the Zombie*, Mardi Gras Prods 97; *Dead Silence*, Universal 237; *Dead Snow*, Euforia Film 297; *Deadly Bees, The*, Amicus/Paramount 195; *Deadly Friend*, Warner Bros 101; *Death Becomes Her*, Universal 102; *Death Line*, K-L Prods 287; *Death Note 2: The Last Name*, Death Note Film Partners 229; *Death Note*, Death Note Film Partners 229; *Death Race 2000*, New World 273; *Deep Blue Sea*, Warner Bros/Village Roadshow 196; *Demon Seed*, MGM 274; *Descent, The*, Celador/Pathe 191; *Devil and Daniel Webster, The*, RKO 230; *Devil Girl From Mars*, Danziger Prods 253; *Devil Rides Out, The*, Hammer 221, 225, 230; *Devil Within Her*, Cinematografica 222; *Devil's Advocate, The*, Warner Bros/Monarchy 231; *Devil's Backbone, The*, Canal+Espana 110-11; *Devil's Rain, The*, Sandy Howard Prods 230; *Die! Die! My Darling/Fanatic*, Hammer 298; *Die, Monster, Die!*, Alta Vista 76, 208; *Dinosaurus!* Fairview Prods 158; *District 9*, Key Creatives 260; *Doctor and the Devils, The*, Brooksfilms 300; *Doctor Cyclops*, Paramount 72; *Dr. Heckyl and Mr. Hype*, Cannon 87; *Dr. Jekyll and Mr. Hyde* (1920), Famous Players/Lasky 86; *Dr. Jekyll and Mr. Hyde* (1932), Paramount 68, 86; *Dr. Jekyll and Mr. Hyde* (1941), MGM 86; *Dr. Jekyll and Ms. Hyde*, Rastar/Leider-Shapiro 87; *Dr. Jekyll and Sister Hyde*, Hammer 87; *Dr. Terror's House of Horrors*, Amicus/RF 42, 227; *Dog Soldiers*, Kismet Entertainment Group 58; *Don't Look Now*, Casey Prods-Eldorado Films 288; *Doomwatch*, Tigon 209; *Dracula* (1931), Universal 20-21, 27, 31, 40 ; *Dracula* (1958), Hammer 28, 40, 42; *Dracula* (1974), Warner Bros 41; *Dracula* (1979), Universal 105; *Dracula* (Spanish: 1931), Universal 25; *Dracula Has Risen From the Grave*, Hammer 22, 43; *Dracula: Dead and Loving It*, Castle Rock Entertainment 31, 41; *Dracula's Daughter*, Universal 25, 26; *Drag Me to Hell*, Mandate/Universal 108, 235; *Dragon War*, ShowBox/Younggu-Art Movies 163; *Dragonheart*, Universal 162; *Dragonslayer*, Paramount/Disney 161; *Drums of Fu Manchu*, Republic 74; *Dr. Strangelove*, Hawk Films/Columbia 82; *Duel*, Universal 273; *Eaten Alive/Death Trap*, Mars Prods 288; *Eating Raoul*, Bartel/Mercury 293; *Ed Gein*, Kunert/Manes Entertainment 295; *Edward Scissorhands*, 20th Century-Fox 78; *Eight-Legged Freaks*, Village Roadshow/Electric Entertainment 193; *Elephant Man, The*, Brooksfilm/Paramount 289; *Empire of the Ants*, Cinema 77 195; *End of Days*, Beacon Communications 231; *Enemy Mine*, 20th Century-Fox 256; *Eragon*, 20th Century-Fox 162; *Eraserhead*, AFI/Libra 289; *Erik the Viking*, Prominent Features 145 *Escape From the Planet of the Apes*, 20th Century-Fox 254; *E.T.: The Extra-Terrestrial*, Universal 256; *Evil Dead II*, Rosebud/Renaissance 100; *Evil Dead, The*, Renaissance Pictures 100; *Evolution*, Montecito Picture Co. 162; *Exorcist, The*, Warner Bros 212-13, 216, 222; *Explorers*, Paramount 256; *Exquisite Sinner, The*, MGM 145; *Eyes Without a Face*, Champs-Elysées/Lux 74; *Fabulous World of Jules Verne, The*, Csf/Filmove 184-5; *Face of Fu Manchu*, Hammer 74; *Fahrenheit 451*, Anglo Enterprise/Vineyard 263; *Fantasia*, Walt Disney Pictures 156; *Fatal Attraction*, Paramount 289; *Faust* (1926), UFA 230, 232; *Faust* (1929), Vitaphone 218; *Fearless Vampire Killers, The*, MGM 30, 38, 43; *Fido*, Lions Gate 104; *Fiendish Plot of Dr. Fu Manchu, The*, Orion/Playboy 74; *Fifth Element, The*, Columbia/Tri-Star 258; *Final Destination 2*, New Line 227, *Firestarter*, De Laurentiis/Paramount 239; *Flash Gordon* (1936), Universal 248; *Flash Gordon* (1980), Universal 248; *Flesh and the Fiends*, Triad Prods 301; *Flight of the Living Dead*, Imageworks Ent. International 104; *Fly, The* (1958), 20th Century-Fox 81; *Fly, The* (1986), 20th Century-Fox 81, 89; *Fog, The*, Debra Hill Prods 119, 240; *Food of the Gods, The,* AIP 195, *Fool There Was, A*, Fox 15; *Forbidden Planet*, MGM 69, 105, 250, 269; *Frailty*, David Kirschner Prods/American Ent. 294; *Frankenfish*, Bayou Film/Silver Nitrate Pictures 199; *Frankenstein* (1910), Edison 84; *Frankenstein* (1931), Universal 8-9, 64-5, 84, 302, 305; *Frankenstein and the Monster From Hell*, Hammer 85; *Frankenstein Created Woman*, Hammer 77; *Freaks*, MGM 282, 304; *Friday the 13th*, Paramount 289; *Friday the 13th Part 3 In 3D*, Paramount 105, 226; *Fright Night*, Columbia 33; *From Beyond*, Empire 80; *From Beyond the Grave*, Amicus 117, 236; *From Dusk Till Dawn*, Los Hooligans/A Band Apart 36; *From Hell*, 20th Century-Fox 290; *From Hell It Came*, Milner Bros 209; *Frozen Dead, The*, Warner 7 Arts 296; *Galaxy Quest*, Dreamworks 260; *Gamera vs. Barugon*, Daiei Studios 159; *Gate, The*, Gate Film Prods 226; *Gay Zombie*, Passion Fruit 104; *Gertie the Dinosaur*, Mccay 155; *Ghost*, Paramount 120; *Ghost and Mrs Muir, The*, 20th Century-Fox 116; *Ghost Breakers, The*, Paramount 96; *Ghost of Frankenstein, The*, Universal 61; *Ghost of Slumber Mountain, The*, World Pictures 155; *Ghost Rider*, Columbia/Marvel Enterprises 229; *Ghostbusters*, Columbia 308; *Ghostbusters 2*, Columbia 118; *Ghosts*, Heliopolis/MJJ Prods 307; *Ghoul, The*, Gaumont-British 96; *Ginger Snaps*, Lions Gate/TMN/Telefilm Canada 53; *Godzilla*, Toho 202, 208; *Godzilla* (1998), Centropolis/Tristar/ Toho 163, 208; *Godzilla vs. the Smog Monster*, Toho 208; *Gog the Killer*, United Artists 270; *Golden Child, The*, Paramount 224, *Golden Voyage of Sinbad, The*, Columbia 138, 143; *Golem, Wie Er in die Welt Kam, Der*, Ufa 215; *Goliath and the Dragon*, CFFP/Achille Piazzi/Gianni Fuchs 155; *Goliath and the Vampires*, Ambrosiana 30; *Gorgo*, King Brothers 159; *Gorgon, The*, Hammer 139; *Gorilla at Large*, 20th Century-Fox 170, 175; *Gorilla, The*, First National 105, 170; *Great Gabbo, The*, Sono Art 236; *Greed of William Hart, The*, Bushey Films 301; *Green Slime, The*, Southern Cross/Toei 244; *Gremlins*, Warner Bros 62, 143; *Gremlins 2*, Warner Bros 82; *Greystoke*, Warner Bros 169; *Grinch, The*, Imagine Ent. 147; *Grindhouse*, Dimension Films/A Band Apart 105; *Gritos en la Noche*, Hispamer Films/Eurocine 104; *Grizzly*, Film Ventures Int. 194; *Grudge 2, The*, Columbia/Sony 121; *Half Human*, Toho 173; *Halloween*, Falcon International 118; *Hands of the Ripper*, Hammer 290; *Harry Potter and the Order of the Phoenix*, Warner Bros/Heyday/Cool Music/Harry Potter Publishing Rights 225, 234; *Harry Potter and the Prisoner of Azkaban*, Warner Bros/Heyday/1492/ Pof A Prods 143; *Haunting, The*, MGM 118; *Haxan*, Svensk Filmindustri 218; *Hell Comes to Frogtown*, New World 210; *Hellbound: Hellraiser 2*, Filmfutures/New World 224; *Hellboy*, Revolution/Columbia/Tri Star 228, 297; *Hellboy 2: The Golden Army*, Universal Pictures 130, 228; *Hellraiser*, Cinemarque-Film Futures/New World 224; *Hellzapoppin!*, Universal 233; *Helter Skelter*, Lorimar 295; *Hercules in the Haunted World*, SpA 219; *Hexe Lilli, Der Drache und das Magische Buch*, Blue Eyes Film & TV 235; *Highway To Hell*, Goodman-Rosen/Josa/High Street 228; *Hills Have Eyes, The*, Blood Relations 293; *History of Violence, A*, New Line 88; *Hitcher, The*, Silver Screen/HBO/Tri Star 291; *Hollow Man, The*, Columbia 76; *Homicidal*, Columbia 286; *Honeymoon Killers, The*, Roxanne Prods 295; *Hook*, Hook Prods/Amblin 137; *Horde, La*, Capture the Flag/Le Pacte/Coficup/Canal+/Cinecinema 38; *Horror Express*, Granada/Benmar 254; *Horror Hospital*, Noteworthy Films 79; *Horror of Party Beach, The*, Iselin-Tenney Prods 208; *Horrors of the Black Museum, The*, Anglo Amalgamated 285; *House of Dracula*, Universal 28, 42; *House of Frankenstein*, Universal 42, 52; *House of Horrors*, Universal 283; *House of Wax*, Warner Bros 285; *House of Usher, The*, AIP 286; *House on Haunted Hill* (1958), Allied Artists 116; *House on Haunted Hill* (1999), Warner Bros 103; *How to*

311

INDEX OF NAMES

ACKNOWLEDGMENTS

▲ *The Monster and the Girl* [1941]

The Author would like to thank the following people for their invaluable assistance in the creation of this book. First and foremost Lauretta Dives of The Kobal Collection for suggesting we do a book together.

And then my editor Alastair Dougall and designer Guy Harvey for their hard work and good humor. And everyone else on this list (in alphabetical order):

Sarah Bailey
Rick Baker
Howard Berger
The Beverly Hills Public Library
Kathy and Bob Burns
Kevin Burns
John Carpenter
David Cronenberg
Tony Dalton
Giluia D'Agnolo-Vallan
Joe Dante
Paul Davis
Guillermo Del Toro
Scott Essman
Alberto Farina
Mick Garris
Ray Harryhausen
The Ray and Diana Harryhausen Foundation
Sara Karloff
Deborah Nadoolman Landis
Max Landis
Rachel Landis
Sir Christopher Lee
The Los Angeles Public Library
Mark Mawston
Tim Nicholson
Greg Nicotero
Simon Pegg
Sam Raimi
George A. Romero
Jared Rosen
Natasha Rubin
Tom Savini
Reece Shearsmith
Bill Taylor
Bill Warren

Special thanks to those at The Kobal Collection:
Paul Faherty
Dave Kent
Phil Moad
Darren Thomas
Jamie Vuignier (in NY)

Special thanks to those at DK:
Alex Allan
Simon Beecroft
Jo Casey
Lisa Lanzarini for jacket design

Dorling Kindersley would like to thank the following: Lauretta Dives, Dave Kent, Phil Moad, Darren Thomas, Jamie Vuignier, Paul Faherty at The Kobal Collection for their patience and help; DMB Photography for the jacket photography; Paul Davis; Charles Harvey for helping to sort through the images.

▶ *Bob Burns and the Creature*
A special thank you to Bob Burns for his generosity in allowing us to use so many unique photos from his collection. Kathy and Bob's Burbank home is a National Treasure.

▲ *John Landis, Forrest J Ackerman, Rick Baker, 1972.*

KEY TO PAGES 106–107

THE MONSTER CARRY

1. *Curse of the Faceless Man* [1958]
2. *Young Frankenstein* [1974]
3. *This Island Earth* [1955]
4. *I Was a Teenage Frankenstein* [1957]
5. *Curse of the Undead* [1959]
6. *Creature From the Black Lagoon* [1954]
7. *Monster on the Campus* [1958]
8. *Invasion of the Saucer Men* [1957]
9. *Robot Monster* [1953]
10. *Invaders From Mars* [1953]
11. *Gritos en la Noche* [1962]
12. *I Married a Monster From Outer Space* [1958]
13. *The Monster of Piedras Blancas* [1958]
14. *Susan's Plan* [1998]
15. *The Brain That Wouldn't Die* [1962]
16. *Dracula* [1979]
17. *Murders in the Rue Morgue* [1932]
18. *Friday the 13th, Part III in 3D* [1982]
19. *I Walked With a Zombie* [1943]
20. *The Mummy's Tomb* [1942]
21. *Satan's Satellites* [1958]
22. *It!* [1967]
23. *Forbidden Planet* [1956]
24. *Phantom From Space* [1953]
25. *The Time Machine* [1960]
26. *The Return of Swamp Thing* [1989]
27. *The Beach Girls and the Monster* [1965]
28. *The Gorilla* [1927]